Looking at *Antigone*

Also Available From Bloomsbury

Looking at Bacchae, edited by David Stuttard
Looking at Medea, edited by David Stuttard
Looking at Lysistrata, edited by David Stuttard
Sophocles: Antigone, Douglas Cairns
Sophocles: Oedipus at Colonus, Adrian Kelly
The Plays of Sophocles, A. F. Garvie

Looking at *Antigone*

Edited by

David Stuttard

BLOOMSBURY ACADEMIC
LONDON • NEW YORK • OXFORD • NEW DELHI • SYDNEY

BLOOMSBURY ACADEMIC
Bloomsbury Publishing Plc
50 Bedford Square, London, WC1B 3DP, UK
1385 Broadway, New York, NY 10018, USA

BLOOMSBURY, BLOOMSBURY ACADEMIC and the Diana logo are
trademarks of Bloomsbury Publishing Plc

First published in Great Britain 2018
Paperback edition published 2019

Cover design: Terry Woodley
Cover image: Nestoris, Lucanian (Greek), Lucania, Basilicat. Attributed to Dolon Painter.
© The Trustees of the British Museum

A catalogue record for this book is available from the British Library.

ISBN: HB: 978-1-3500-1711-5
PB: 978-1-3501-1276-6
ePDF: 978-1-3500-1713-9
epub: 978-1-3500-1712-2

Names: Stuttard, David, editor. | Sophocles. Antigone. English. 2017.
Title: Looking at Antigone / edited by David Stuttard.
Description: London : Bloomsbury Academic, 2017. | Includes bibliographical
references and index.
Identifiers: LCCN 2017024382| ISBN 9781350017115 (hardback) |
ISBN 9781350017122 (epub)
Subjects: LCSH: Sophocles. Antigone.
Classification: LCC PA4413.A7 L66 2017 | DDC 882/.01—dc23
LC record available at https://lccn.loc.gov/2017024382

Typeset by RefineCatch Limited, Bungay, Suffolk

In memory of Sophie Laws

Contents

List of Contributors

Stephen Esposito is Associate Professor of Classical Studies at Boston University, USA.

Helene Foley is Professor of Classical Studies at Barnard College, Columbia University, New York, USA.

Robert Garland is Roy D. and Margaret B. Wooster Professor of the Classics at Colgate University, New York, USA.

Alex Garvie is Honorary Professorial Research Fellow at the University of Glasgow, UK.

Ioanna Karamanou is Assistant Professor of Greek Drama at the University of the Peloponnese, Greece.

Brad Levett is Associate Professor of Classics at Memorial University, St. John's, Newfoundland, Canada.

Sophie Mills is Professor of Classics at the University of North Carolina at Asheville, USA.

Rush Rehm is Professor of Theater and Classics at Stanford University, California, USA.

Hanna M. Roisman is Professor of Classics, Arnold Bernhard Professor in Arts and Humanities at Colby College, Maine, USA.

Ruth Scodel is D.R. Shackleton Bailey Collegiate Professor of Greek and Latin at the University of Michigan, USA.

Alan H. Sommerstein is Emeritus Professor of Greek at the University of Nottingham, UK.

David Stuttard is a freelance writer, classical historian, dramatist and founder of the theatre company, Actors of Dionysus.

Betine van Zyl Smit is Associate Professor of Classics at the University of Nottingham, UK.

Preface and Acknowledgements

Antigone is arguably the most popular of all Greek tragedies. It explores what happens when a young girl defies the state, buries her traitorous brother, and willingly embraces death. Yet I know from personal experience that it is not an easy play either fully to appreciate or to stage. Part of the problem in presenting it for modern audiences can be the characterization of the two leading characters. It is all too easy for Antigone to come across as a strident activist and Creon as an unsympathetic dictator. Yet, for the tragedy to work, for audiences to experience not only fear but pity, directors must allow the two protagonists to be more rounded. This is especially true of Creon, the 'tragic hero' of the play.

Occasionally circumstances intervene, which can have a profound effect on the audience's appreciation. During a performance that I attended at Epidaurus Theatre in 2001, an audience member was taken ill during the first scene between Creon and Antigone. The performance was suspended while medics entered the auditorium. The house lights went up. The performers stood, frozen in position. Only George Kimoulis, who both directed and played Creon, climbed into the auditorium to help the patient onto the stretcher, which would carry him away to the awaiting ambulance. Then Kimoulis returned onto the stage to warm applause. And from that moment onwards, every member of the audience of 15,000 people felt such admiration for Kimoulis/Creon's compassion that his downfall in the final scene was devastating.

Later that year, when (with Actors of Dionysus) I staged my own adaptation (as opposed to the translation published here), with its references to 'the pulse of nature smothered in a concrete shell', 'night choking in the breathless air', and messages proclaiming that 'I love you' sent out into the darkness, we had no way of knowing in advance the impact that images like that would have on its first audience on the opening night – September 11th 2001.

My relationship with the play, then, whether as student, teacher, translator, adaptor, audience member or director, has been long and varied. The issues that it raises are constantly absorbing. So I am delighted and privileged to have been able to assemble this collection of chapters by twelve international experts, which not only sets *Antigone* in its historical context but explores many of the issues that it raises, while tracing its influence both as a work of literature and as a play-script from classical Greece right up to 2016.

As with other volumes in this series, I have allowed authors great freedom to choose those aspects of the play on which they wished to write, and most were relatively unaware of the content of each others' chapters. Inevitably, there is the occasional small overlap between some chapters, with which I have not interfered, and, while I suggested that authors use the forms 'BC' and 'AD', I respected the wishes of those for whom it was important to use 'BCE' and 'CE'.

Many of the quotations from *Antigone* are taken from my own translation (a heavily revised version of my 1994 version), which is printed after the chapters. Readers wishing to use it for productions of their own can contact me through my website, www.davidstuttard.com, where applications for performance should be made before the commencement of any rehearsals.

Finally, I would like to thank all those who have been involved in the production of this book, especially the twelve contributors, who have so generously given of their time, and with whom it has been such a pleasure to work. At Bloomsbury, my thanks go to Alice Wright, who commissioned the book, her editorial assistants, Lucy Carroll and Clara Herberg, Mark Fisher, and Terry Woodley, who designed the splendid cover. A very big thank you, too, is due to my wife Emily Jane, whose support and love both sustain me and enable me to indulge in the quixotic pursuits of writing and directing, and to the home team, our cats Stanley and Oliver, who help make each day a drama, but happily not a tragedy.

David Stuttard
Brighton, 2017

Introduction: *Antigone*, A Play for Today?

David Stuttard

Sophocles' *Antigone* holds the record for being the most frequently performed Greek tragedy. It is the story of the clash of opposites: male *versus* female, age *versus* youth, religion *versus* secularism, to list but a few. With its feisty heroine prepared not just to stand up to an autocratic leader but to die for her beliefs, it seems to resonate with us today as much as it did with its first audiences, seated in Athens' Theatre of Dionysus more than twenty-four centuries ago.

Yet, the experience we bring to the play is very different to that of the original spectators, predominantly Athenian males of fighting age and over, possessed of their own culturally specific systems of beliefs and values, far more at ease with the complexities of Greek mythology and drama than we shall ever be. While, like any truly great work, *Antigone* can be enjoyed without knowing anything of the circumstances in which it was intended to be first performed, a knowledge of the background to the drama enhances our appreciation. So, in this introduction, we shall look at four key areas – myth; moral values; history; and Sophocles' contribution to public life and dramatic innovation – before considering the performance context of fifth-century BC Athens, and how Sophocles' words and ideas translate for us today.

The myth of Antigone

There was no one accepted version of any Greek myth. Different narratives were told at different times in different cities by different authors. Sometimes, indeed, to allow him to use the myths to explore specific issues, in different works the same author would embrace two completely divergent traditions, as Euripides did in his treatment of the story of Helen. However, when it came to the myths surrounding the royal family of Thebes, to which Antigone belonged, most people could agree on one thing: it was a family accursed.

It was King Laius who was principally to blame. An obnoxious man, he was (according to late sources) the first human to commit homosexual rape, for which he was punished by the gods. When he consulted the oracle at

Delphi, he was told that he would die at the hands of his son, a fate which he tried to avoid by having the baby boy exposed on a hillside. However, no one can escape fate, and, years later, the oracle came true, when Laius insulted a young man at a crossroads. Blows were exchanged; King Laius was killed; and the assassin, Oedipus, ignorant that his victim was his father, went on to marry the queen – his mother, Jocasta. Together they had four children: two boys, Eteocles and Polyneices; and two girls, Antigone and Ismene.

According to Sophocles' version of the myth, when Oedipus at last discovered his unnatural crime, he blinded himself, and went into self-imposed exile with Antigone. Meanwhile, his sons inherited the throne of Thebes, agreeing to rule in alternate years. However, when Eteocles came to the end of his term, he refused to concede the throne to his brother. So Polyneices took himself to Argos, where he assembled an army to help him reclaim his kingdom. By now Oedipus and Jocasta were both dead, and Antigone was back in Thebes, engaged to be married to her cousin, Haemon, when the invading horde arrived. The attack (described in our play's *parodos*, or choral entrance song) was terrifying, but in the end the Argive army fled, leaving Polyneices dead behind them. But it was not just Polyneices who had fallen. In the heat of battle, the two brothers had fought, and killed each other, a crime against the family every bit as horrifying as Oedipus' incest.

It is in the immediate aftermath of the attack – just hours after it has been repulsed – that Sophocles sets his play. With both 'legitimate' kings dead, their uncle, Creon, brother of Jocasta, has assumed the throne, and his first act has been to issue an edict that, while Eteocles, who died defending Thebes, should be interred with full honours, the corpse of Polyneices, who fell attacking his own city, should be left exposed 'unwept, unburied, so much carrion for birds to glut on'. The penalty for disobeying is death. This, however, does not deter Antigone. For her, moral and religious obligation to her family trumps blind obedience to the state, and it is this clash of loyalties that underpins Sophocles' play.

As Ioanna Karamanou explores in her chapter, other tragedians (Aeschylus in *Seven Against Thebes*, and Euripides in *Phoenician Women*, as well as others, whose work, like Euripides' own *Antigone*, survives only in fragments) chose to explore different versions of the myth. In *Phoenician Women*, for example, both Oedipus and Jocasta are still alive during the siege; and, while Sophocles dramatizes Haemon's resistance to his father, Creon, Euripides highlights the heroic sacrifice of his brother, Menoeceus, whose death saved his city – but who is only alluded to at the end of our play – as well as the role played by the pious Athenian King Theseus in burying the dead. Theseus' intervention speaks volumes. For, to many in historical Athens, Thebes was not just an ancient enemy. Rather, the myths about its amoral, godless and incestuous royal family provided a useful counterpoint, against which to explore the values and moral codes that underpinned their own society.

Moral and societal values in *Antigone*

Despite being set in an alien world – the monarchy of mythological Thebes – *Antigone* is firmly rooted in the moral and societal values of fifth-century BC Athens. By the time the play was first performed around 440 BC, Athenian democracy, born some two generations earlier, was flourishing. Most of the offices of state were held by ordinary citizens, while mass assemblies, held regularly throughout the year, reached major policy decisions, and, although wealthy aristocrats did still manage to wield disproportionate power, there was a general agreement that monarchy – or tyranny (in Greek terms, the often unconstitutional rule of an individual, who is above the law) – was a bad thing and should be resisted at all costs.

Fading memories of two monarchs reinforced this view. The first was the Athenian tyrant, Hippias, expelled in 510 BC, a man who, in the wake of his brother's assassination, ruled with increasing cruelty. The second was the Persian Great King, Xerxes, who overran Athens in 480 BC, destroying its temples and almost conquering the whole of Greece, before being defeated the next year. Like Creon, both set themselves above the common people, expecting total obedience, and executing dissenters, while Xerxes thought nothing of attacking the sanctuaries, which embodied Greek religion.

But despite their distaste for monarchs and tyrants, in the privacy of their own homes Greek men exerted autocratic power over not just their slaves but their children and womenfolk. A free-born Athenian woman was obliged to live under the 'protection' of a *kyrios*, usually her closest male relative. For an unmarried girl, her *kyrios* was usually her father, or, in the event of his death, her adult brother or uncle. After her (arranged) marriage, the role of *kyrios* passed to her husband. If she was widowed or divorced, it returned to her closest male blood relative. The *kyrios* exercised enormous authority over the women of his family, who were, for the most part, confined within the bounds of the house, and who played no active role in the political life of the city. Antigone's defiance of her *kyrios*, Creon, would, therefore, have been distinctly troubling to an Athenian male audience: her disobedience is directed not only against the laws of the state, but against the head of her domestic household.

Against this, however, would have weighed Antigone's determination to bury Polyneices. In classical Athens, the rituals surrounding burial were one of the few areas over which women presided, laying out the corpse, washing it, and mourning. Under normal circumstances Antigone and Ismene would have been expected to conduct the funeral rites for both their brothers. It was only with burial, the Greeks believed, that the spirits of the dead could be released, thereby allowing them to make the journey to the afterlife in Hades (the Underworld).

To deny a corpse burial (an issue that animates not just our present play but Sophocles' *Ajax* and Euripides *Suppliant Women*) was generally considered to be unacceptable. After battles it was the rule that bodies were returned for burial under truce, and so important was it to retrieve the fallen that there were times when a general would concede victory to the opposing side simply to enable him to do so. On only a very few occasions under very exceptional circumstances (for example, after the Battle of Delium in 424 BC, when the Thebans prevented the Athenians from collecting their dead) did a victorious side refuse to allow the enemy fallen to be collected – to the outrage of the rest of Greece. Even when someone had committed a gross offence against his city, he was generally allowed to be buried – though in certain cases the corpse was thrown into a pit, while in others it had to be transported beyond the boundaries of the state before a proper burial could take place.

However, there is evidence that, at times during the fifth century BC, the question of whether to grant burial to enemies of the state was hotly debated. There is even a suggestion that one event, that prompted such a debate, occurred at the very time when *Antigone* was first performed.

Antigone and Samos

Sophocles' biographers connect his writing of *Antigone* with his term serving as general on campaign against Samos in 440 BC. Indeed, they suggest that it was the success of *Antigone*, which so endeared him to the Athenians that they appointed him to the post. Although not impossible, this is unlikely. Ancient biographies were notoriously confused, and it has been suggested that the chronology should be reversed, and that it was Sophocles' experience as general on Samos, which inspired him to write *Antigone*.

For many years, the island of Samos had been a loyal ally of Athens, but in 440 it seceded from her empire. In response, the Athenians sent out their navy, with Pericles in overall command and Sophocles as one of their generals. After a lengthy campaign and siege, the island surrendered, and, while the pro-Periclean Thucydides suggests a relatively peaceful resolution, another historian, Duris (himself from Samos), records that Pericles imposed on the leaders of the revolt the punishment of *apotympanismos*. This meant that they were crucified until almost dead, before being despatched by being beaten with clubs – after which it was forbidden for their corpses to be buried.

Pericles' treatment of the Samians echoed his father's behaviour almost forty years earlier, when he crucified a Persian governor by the shores of the Hellespont (Dardanelles). This was the image, with which Herodotus chose to end his *Histories*, and it is possible that the influence of another episode from Herodotus (3.119) can be felt in *Antigone*. Antigone's speech about the irreplaceability of brothers (ll. 904–20, discussed here by Alex Garvie, Sophie Mills and Ruth Scodel) is strikingly similar to a speech given in the *Histories* by the Persian Intaphernes' wife, which had led many scholars to believe that Sophocles was influenced by it. Like much else about antiquity, it is difficult to be certain, however. Some historians now suggest that Herodotus was writing somewhat later than was previously believed, possibly during the 420s/410s. If this were so, it would change the relationship between the speeches in *Antigone* and the *Histories*, meaning that either Herodotus based his speech on Sophocles, or a later actor, familiar with the *Histories*, interpolated it into the script of *Antigone*.

To return to Samos: it is possible Pericles' *apotympanismos* of the rebel leaders was the catalyst for Sophocles to write *Antigone*. Lurking behind all Greek popular morality was the idea that one should do as much good as possible to one's friends, while unleashing the maximum harm against one's enemies. As several contributors discuss in this collection, this concept lies at the heart of *Antigone*. But it lay, too, at the heart of Athens' relationship with Samos. Samos' oscillation between being a friend and an enemy, and the tensions and ambiguities which that created, are mirrored in both Polyneices' and Antigone's relationships with their family and Thebes, especially since the Greek word for friend (*philos*) also meant family member. In this dualistic world, Antigone, placed in an impossible situation, and torn between loyalty to her dead brother and her still-living family, must renounce the status of *philos* in regard to those alive, become their enemy instead, and endure the bitter consequences – while, like the revolutionaries on Samos, Polyneices has not only moved from *philos* to enemy, but, being refused burial, has suffered the same fate as they did.

Whether *Antigone* preceded the revolt on Samos or (as I suspect) was inspired by it, the play reflects political debate in Athens. Although some scholars resile from any notion of Greek tragedy being connected with contemporary events, politics were so much in the blood of the Athenians that it would have been difficult for any author to dissociate himself from them. Every citizen was expected to play his role in civic life, and Sophocles took up the challenge with great gusto.

Sophocles: Public servant and dramatic innovator

According to his ancient biographers, Sophocles was born in 497/6 BC, the son of an arms manufacturer, and as a youth he was chosen to lead the chorus in the victory celebrations over the Persians at the Battle of Salamis (480). At his debut as a tragedian in 468, he won first prize in the dramatic contest, something he would go on to do on some twenty-three further occasions. He is recorded as writing 123 plays, though today only seven survive in their entirety.

Sophocles was equally active in the political life of Athens. In 442, he was one of the ten commissioners overseeing the annual tribute paid by members of the Athenian Empire, while in 440 he served as a general on the Samian campaign. His relationship with his commander, Pericles, was fraught. Indeed, Pericles quipped that Sophocles was 'an excellent poet but a poor general'. In 413–411, during the Peloponnesian War, thanks to the respect in which he was held, Sophocles served as a 'proboulos', one of ten magistrates with emergency powers. He died in 405 at the grand old age of 91, either choking on a grape pip or suffering a seizure while trying to recite an entire speech from *Antigone* without taking breath, though perhaps both stories are true – until recently reciting speeches with grapes in the mouth was part of an actor's vocal training.

A pious man, Sophocles helped to introduce the worship of the healing god Asclepius to Athens from Epidaurus, in recognition of which, after his death, he received a hero-shrine on the west slope of the Acropolis and was worshipped as 'Dexion' (Receiver). His gravestone, topped by a carved siren (a mythical creature whose singing was legendary) proclaimed: 'I, Sophocles, am hidden in this tomb, who took first prize in tragic arts, the most revered of men.'

Aristotle records that Sophocles said he represented human beings 'as they ought to be', and his tragedies do possess unusual nobility. Theatricality was in his blood. He is said to have instituted three major innovations, increasing the number of solo performers from two to three, increasing the number in the chorus from twelve to fifteen, and introducing 'painted scenery' – perhaps moveable boards, which could form a backdrop. These innovations suggest that he was striving for greater realism in Greek tragedy, though any moves towards naturalism were relative, for it would remain a highly stylized art form.

Tragedy in classical Athens

Antigone was written to be performed at the Great (or City) Dionysia, one of two Athenian dramatic festivals in honour of Dionysus, the god of transformation, whose remit also included wine and fecundity. Held in March/April, the Dionysia attracted audiences not just from Athens but from across the Greek-speaking world. Part religious, part civic, part dramatic, the festival featured a number of competitions in performance arts, including tragedy. Over three days, three playwrights each staged three tragedies (plus one 'satyr play', a riotous coda, which burlesqued many of the themes of the tragedies), after which a jury of ten men chosen by lot voted for a winner. The other two tragedies first performed alongside *Antigone* have not survived: while Sophocles' *Oedipus Tyrannus* and *Oedipus at Colonus* are sometimes said to be part of a 'Theban Trilogy', they were written years later (in around 428 and 406 respectively).

Tragedy may have evolved out of purely choral performances, when first one solo actor, then two, then finally three assumed the roles of characters, usually from mythology. These choral roots explain much about the genre. Greek choruses both sang and danced, and singing and dancing remained a key part of theatrical performance. Indeed, with its often spectacular staging, tragedy resembled modern musical theatre more than 'straight' drama. The chorus was the anchor to the tragedy. After its entrance song (*parodos*), it usually stayed on stage throughout, punctuating the 'episodes' (scenes between solo performers) with so-called odes or *stasima* (singular = *stasimon*), choreographed songs, whose subject matter generally takes us away from the specific action of the drama to explore more universal themes. Because of their musical element (which sadly does not survive), the *stasima* could reinforce the emotional impact of the scenes preceding them, while preparing the audience for what followed.

Like the choral passages, the solo performers' lines were in verse, and while many of their scenes and speeches were spoken in iambic trimeter (translated into prose in my version), episodes of great emotional intensity (such as when Antigone departs for her tomb, and when Creon laments for his dead family) were sung. In this translation, these are characterized by a looser typographical layout. The impact of these highly operatic moments was no doubt increased by the spectacle of their staging. All performers wore masks – those of the chorus were perhaps identical, adding to their aura of anonymity – which allowed the three soloists to change role with relative ease between characters of different ages and genders. The masks may also have amplified the voice, but, because of the acoustics of the open-air Theatre of Dionysus, performers probably sang and delivered their lines 'up and out', much as opera singers do today. In addition, in *Antigone* both soloists and chorus would have been dressed in sumptuous costumes, their long robes probably made out of intricately woven fabric, for audiences appear to have enjoyed a dazzling display, and the wealthy citizens who paid to stage the plays seem to have vied to outdo each other in the extravagance of their productions.

Technology (and the suspension of disbelief) even allowed for certain 'special effects', though only one is utilized in *Antigone*: the *ekkuklema* ('roller-out'), a kind of trolley, which was brought into view through the stage-building's central doors, and on which could be displayed tableaux showing the aftermaths of events which had taken place inside. In *Antigone* it allowed audiences to see the corpse of Creon's wife, Eurydice.

Translating *Antigone* for modern audiences and readers

From what has gone before, it can be seen that there is much about Greek tragedy and the culture that created it, that is alien to the modern world. To appreciate its dramatic impact requires active translation – not just the translation of the text for those who do not read classical Greek, but the translation of ideas and values rooted in fifth-century BC Athens to the context of the modern world. Inevitably these acts of translation involve both compromises and, in some instances, changes to the original meaning. Sometimes these can be nuanced, sometimes whole scale, but every translator must to a greater or a lesser extent impose their own interpretation.

We have already considered the word *philos*, which can mean both friend and family member, balancing which is *echthros*, which can mean both enemy, and one who is not of the family circle. There are no direct equivalents in English, so in most cases the translator must choose which meaning to favour in any given circumstance, while being fully aware that the making of any choice will obscure the fact that the same Greek word may have been translated differently elsewhere, thus removing some of the resonances of the original text. Other examples are flagged up in many of the chapters in this collection.

Equally problematic can be Sophocles' syntax. Delighting in balance, periphrasis and high-flown vocabulary (as Hanna Roisman tells us, *Antigone* is 'the most antithetical of all Greek plays'), it can sound stilted in the extreme if translated directly into English. The play's opening line is notorious. Translated literally it would read, 'O my connected-by-common-origin / kindred, very sister, head of Ismene' – inspiration enough for the beginning of A.E. Housman's infamous parody, *A Fragment of a Greek Tragedy*: 'O suitably-attired-in-leather-boots, head of a traveller'. My version of Sophocles' line, 'Ismene! Sister! Blood of my own blood!', tries to convey the meaning but is far from being literal.

Just a few lines later in my translation, Ismene tells Antigone that she has not heard anything, 'since we lost our brothers. Not since they killed each other. Yesterday.' However, a literal translation would read, 'since we two were deprived of our two brothers on one day killed by a double hand'. Examples such as these are far from rare, so I hope that readers will forgive me if, for the sake of clarity, I have attempted to make Sophocles' dialogue (and poetry) more direct, even though this has inevitably meant sacrificing some of his grandeur.

Even greater decisions are faced by a director wishing to put *Antigone* on stage. Twenty-first century society is so far removed from that of fifth-century BC Athens that many of the values that permeate the play no longer resonate. Whereas (given the status and position of women) the original audience would probably have considered aspects of Antigone's behaviour controversial – her disobedience of her *kyrios*, her brazen willingness to do business outside the confines of the house – today, in the West at least, there is nothing outrageous about it at all. Equally, in modern secular societies, Creon's apparent religious scepticism might seem more acceptable than Antigone's religious fundamentalism.

But if some of the tables have been turned, the issues at the play's heart are still as vital as they were when it was first performed. The opposites still clash. Religious faith still challenges secular rationalism; youth still questions the ingrained certainties of age; the oppressed still stand up to the oppressor. It is part of what makes us human. And it is part of what lets *Antigone* still speak to us that its plotline and its characters can be refitted and adapted to accommodate the changing world in which we live. From versions staged in South America and Japan (discussed by Helene Foley) to performances in occupied Paris, apartheid South Africa, and Amsterdam after terrorist attacks on Paris and Brussels (discussed by Betine van Zyl Smit), to short films such as Fawaz al-Matrouk's haunting *To Rest in Peace* set in Iraqi-occupied Kuwait, the story of Antigone is as alive today as it was when Sophocles first imagined it. And – as the chapters in this book will show – the debate surrounding it is impassioned.

1

Antigone: Right or Wrong?

Alex Garvie

By the end of his play Sophocles makes it as clear as he possibly can that Creon was wrong to forbid the burial of Polyneices and to order Antigone to be killed.[1] When Haemon, Creon's son, and Antigone's fiancé, reports (692–700) that the population of Thebes is secretly on Antigone's side, the view that he is not telling the truth is untenable. In Greek tragedy dramatic convention requires that if an audience is to understand that a character is – or has been – lying, it must at some stage be given a clear indication that this is the case.[2] In this play Sophocles gives us no such indication. More decisive is the intervention of the seer Teiresias, whose regular role in Greek tragedy is to speak the truth and who is regularly treated by the tragedians with the utmost respect. Teiresias is always right. When, therefore, he denounces Creon's treatment of both Polyneices and Antigone, which has brought pollution upon the city that he claims to serve, because the gods are angry and will punish him through the death of his own son, we must take him seriously. So will Creon himself, when he changes his mind and goes off, too late, to give Polyneices the proper funeral which all along, as the male head of the family, he had been responsible for giving him. At the end of the play Creon himself acknowledges his responsibility for all his wrong decisions. In that final scene all the emphasis is on these, and Antigone is almost forgotten. But it seems obvious that, if Creon was so clearly wrong to deny burial to Polyneices, Antigone must have been right to bury him. The view that there is right and wrong on both sides, is unsatisfactory; how can there be any compromise when the question is whether or not to bury a corpse?

Creon, then, is condemned by men and gods and by himself. By the end of the play Sophocles has made his intention clear and apparently incontrovertible; if he had intended otherwise, the end of the play would have been different. One may wonder therefore why, after generations of interpretation by adapters, translators, directors, audiences, and critics,[3] scholars can still debate as to whether Antigone or Creon was right, with some concluding that Sophocles leaves it ambiguous. How could one distinguished scholar, Christiane Sourvinou-Inwood, provocatively go so far as to publish an influential paper entitled 'Sophocles' Antigone as a "Bad Woman"'?[4]

Modern practitioners of Reception Studies provide us with a fascinating account of the different ways in which the play has been received in modern times, from the nineteenth century in which Antigone was presented as a saintly, almost Christian, virginal martyr, to the twentieth century, in which she became increasingly an icon of heroic pacifist resistance to tyranny and oppression and a kind of feminist role-model. We should indeed remember that our own reaction to *Antigone* is culturally determined, and that we should never assume that it was the same as that of the original audience. But when we are told that the meaning of a text is created *only* at the point of its reception, and that it is therefore pointless and indeed misguided to ask how Sophocles intended his original audience to understand his play, this is going too far. That our culture is different from that of the fifth century BC in many respects should not mean that they are different in *all* respects. In studying Greek tragedy, despite the differences, we can still identify with the characters and their problems. It may not always be easy to do so, but that is not a valid excuse for refusing to try.

The great merit of Sourvinou-Inwood's paper on Antigone as a 'Bad Woman' is her declared aim 'to reconstruct as far as possible what the play meant to its original audience, blocking out our own culturally determined assumptions and expectations'. Having candidly admitted (pp. 25–6), however, that Antigone turns out to be right to bury the corpse, and Creon wrong to leave it exposed, she still maintains (pp. 26–7) that 'the fact that in the end Polyneikes does get a proper burial does not entail that he was entitled to it at the beginning, and that Antigone's whole position is vindicated', so that (p. 32) her action is at the same time right and wrong, and that is why she is punished. I do not understand how her deed can be right in retrospect, but wrong at the time when she did it. That the original audience may be led to consider it wrong at the beginning of the play is an entirely different matter. The modern scholar knows from the beginning how the play is going to end, and has the pleasure of observing how skilfully Sophocles constructs his plot in such a way that the question of right and wrong remains undecided until well into the play.[5] The original audience did not have the privilege of reading it, as it were, backwards. If its initial expectation turns out to be wrong, it will not be the only Greek tragedy in which this occurs.

How, then, are we to assess the reaction of the original audience to the beginning of the play? Sourvinou-Inwood's argument is based principally on the role of a respectable woman in fifth-century BC Athens, which was undoubtedly very different from that of women in most modern societies.

Subject to the authority of her father before her marriage and of her husband after it, she played no part in the public and political life of the city. The home and the family, and the production of an heir for her husband, were her realm, and she seldom left the house, except on the occasion of religious festivals. Though women had a part to play in family funerals, especially in their early stages, it was men who normally had the sole responsibility for their organization and conduct. It was, therefore, Antigone's refusal to adhere to the accepted code that made her, in the eyes of the original audience, a 'bad woman'. There are perhaps two flaws in this argument. First, it fails to recognize any distinction between the make-believe characters of Greek drama and real-life people.[6] Second, its implicit assumption that all the spectators of a play react in the same way is likely to be untrue. A production of Anouilh's *Antigone* in the Occupied Paris of 1944 was interpreted by some as pro- and by others as anti- the Resistance. We do not know whether women were present in Sophocles' audience, or, if so, whether they formed a significant part of it, and there is no way of telling what their reaction would have been to Sophocles' treatment of Antigone.

When Antigone begins the play by bringing her sister Ismene out of the house – the women's quarters – into the public space, there is already a hint of the unconventional behaviour that lies ahead. One might dismiss the significance of this entrance altogether, on the grounds that, since indoor scenes are rarely, if ever, presented on the stage in Greek tragedy, the only way in which women can appear at all in this 'make-belief drama' is for them to come out of the house. However, Sophocles himself draws the audience's attention to it by having Antigone explain to Ismene that she did not want anyone inside the house to hear what she has to say. When, having informed her sister of Creon's edict that Polyneices is to be left unburied, and that the penalty for disobedience is to be death by public stoning, she announces her intention to disobey the edict of the king, it is reasonable to suppose that many, perhaps even a majority, of the spectators would disapprove of her usurpation of the masculine role and its potential threat to society.

We have to consider also the reaction of the audience to the edict. In fifth-century Athens, criminals might be thrown to their deaths and left unburied in a deep cleft, but presumably their corpses were out of sight, unlike that of Polyneices which is to remain in full view of any passer-by. In scholarly discussion of this matter it is usually pointed out that, while traitors might be denied burial in Attica, they could be carried beyond the borders of the state to be interred elsewhere. Sophocles himself nowhere suggests that this is what Creon should have done (the stark way in which he presents the dilemma is dramatically more effective), but there was nothing to prevent at least some of the spectators from considering it. Liapis points out that *excessive* funeral rites in Athens were associated with the powerful families, and were thus antithetical to the democratic *polis*.[7] But that can hardly mean that the city was opposed to a burial of any kind. There cannot be many cultures in which the proper burial of the dead, all of the dead, has not been given a high priority. Robinson recalls the production of *Antigone* in Cracow in January 1984 during the darkest days of the post-Solidarity period.[8] The play was still in repertory when a Catholic priest was abducted and murdered by the Government security forces. When the body was found in October, the Government's attempt to bury it in secret was foiled as 400,000 people turned up at the funeral. In Scotland very recently a serious scandal has resulted from the discovery that, in some crematoria, the ashes of new-born infants have not been given the treatment that was considered appropriate. Polyneices is to be left on the ground for the dogs and the birds to eat, the image with which Homer begins the *Iliad* to mark in its most extreme form the horror of the Trojan War. Sophocles himself in his *Ajax*, a play produced according to many scholars before *Antigone*,[9] has Odysseus insist that Ajax, his worst enemy, should be given a proper burial, despite the fact that he has tried to murder Menelaus and Agamemnon, the commanders of the Greek army. The gods, he says, have ruled that *every* human being must receive burial. In Euripides' *Suppliant Women* the revered Athenian Theseus will insist that not only Polyneices but all of the Argive army who died with him should be properly buried.[10] In all cultures, apart from being a matter of disrespect, the principle of Health and Hygiene doubtless plays here an important part, and for a Greek audience the ensuing pollution has a religious significance. So in this play the seer Teiresias (1016–22) will blame Creon for the tainting of the altars by the carrion that the birds and dogs have carried from Polyneices' corpse. In all cultures the feeling of repulsion seems to go even more deeply. Steiner remarks on 'the primal dread of decomposition, of violation by dogs and birds of prey'. He recounts also an episode in Nazi-occupied Riga, in which a young girl was caught trying to sprinkle earth on her executed brother.[11] When she was asked why she had done it, her reply was, 'he was my brother; for me that is sufficient'. This is why Antigone buries Polyneices, and why she is so offended by the refusal of her sister to feel the same way. Nobody has a right to prevent her from doing so. And it was because the infants were *their* children that the parents in the modern Scottish crematoria scandal were rightly so upset.

In *Antigone* a further question for the original audience, and for us, to ponder is that of relationships within this unhappy family. The Greek word *philoi* embraces both family and friends, everyone with whom one enjoys a positive relationship, while *echthroi* are one's enemies, and one is expected, indeed one has a duty, to do as much good as one can to the former, and as much harm as possible to the latter. In tragedy this often leads to problems when the characters get the two categories confused. In Sophocles' *Ajax* it is this that makes so remarkable Odysseus' insistence that his worst enemy Ajax should be given a proper burial. In *Antigone* the confusion is visible already in the prologue. In the almost untranslatable opening line of the play, Antigone addresses Ismene in the affectionate terms appropriate for a sister, but in the enigmatic line 10 she points out in effect that in her family Polyneices has become the enemy of his uncle Creon, with the result that Creon is now the enemy of Antigone, while Ismene should recognize that he is her enemy too. By the end of the prologue, because Ismene has refused to help Antigone in disobeying their uncle, and has urged her not to do so, Antigone declares that not only will Ismene be an enemy of her brother but also that the two sisters are now to become each other's enemy. Ismene has the last word: no matter what her sister does, she will always rightly love her. Her final appeal to Antigone, to join her in keeping her deed a secret, is unsuccessful. Antigone wants the whole world to hear about it. She seems to be glad that Ismene has refused to help her because she looks forward to a glorious martyr's death, with nobody to share the glory.

As a character Ismene seems so much more attractive than Antigone. Indeed she is the one with whom the audience is likely to feel comfortable, while it is uneasy with Antigone. But that does not necessarily mean that she is right, and Antigone wrong. In fact Ismene in the prologue nowhere tells Antigone what she *ought* to do. She shows no interest in the morality of the issue. All of her concern is for the *folly* of what her sister intends to do. Antigone and Ismene as women are too weak to fight against men, especially those who have authority over them. It is dangerous to disobey 'tyrants', a word which in tragedy can mean 'king' without any derogatory sense, but which, in an appropriate context like the present one clearly means 'tyrant' in the modern sense. Ismene does not approve of Creon. The very fact that she will ask Polyneices to forgive her for doing what she is compelled to do, indicates that in her heart she knows Antigone to be right. Ismene's role, then, is not to indicate to the audience how Antigone should behave. Rather it is to establish the way in which a normal woman would behave, and to set this against the way in which *Antigone will* behave.

The complexity, then, of the issues presented in the prologue makes it very unlikely that all the original spectators shared the same reaction to them. Many may well have disapproved of her, while others admired her for her courage in deciding to behave not like a normal woman. Some might have wished that she had been kinder to her sister, while others might have wondered whether her intention was completely altruistic. What all must have noticed is the significance of the departure of the two girls at the end of the prologue – Ismene through the door into the women's quarters of the house, Antigone via the side passage that leads to the public male world, to the corpse of Polyneices.

The first episode begins with the arrival of Creon, who announces to the Chorus the irreproachable principles on which he, as the new king, intends to govern.[12] When, in the middle of the fourth century, the orator Demosthenes quotes Creon's lines with apparent approval he reminds *his* audience that his opponent Aeschines has appropriately played the part of Creon in a recent production of Sophocles' play – appropriately because in Demosthenes' time Creon has become a byword for a bad politician. Aeschines, therefore, is just as bad as Creon whose hypocrisy Demosthenes' audience will take for granted.[13] At this stage of the play, Sophocles' audience cannot have been nearly as certain as this. However, if it had already seen his *Ajax*, some might remember how in that play Menelaus presents an equally plausible account of his devotion to democracy, despite which the spectators already knew him, as a hated Spartan, to be an anti-democratic villain. In *Antigone* the inappropriateness of the sentiments to the character is revealed more subtly. But when Creon stresses the duty of a ruler to choose his friends correctly, always putting the interests of his city before those of a personal friend, some will realize that the theme of friends has already been shown in the prologue to be problematic. The second part of his speech begins with a remarkable *non sequitur*. He informs the Chorus that 'closely related to all of which' [i.e. to his excellent principles], he has proclaimed that Eteocles is to be honourably buried, but that Polyneices is to be left for the birds and dogs to eat. The Greek word translated here (192) 'related' means literally 'sibling, cognate, kin'. In the context of this play in which family relationships are so important, some at least of the audience will be unconvinced by Creon's assumption that to leave a corpse unburied is so closely related to all the virtues of a good king.

In this speech Creon begins to reveal a characteristic which will become more and more important as the plot develops: he likes to speak in trite maxims to demonstrate his conviction that he *knows*, rationally and intellectually, what is right and what needs to be done. Contrast Antigone who is guided almost entirely by her feelings. In the brief stichomythia (line-by-line dialogue) with the Chorus-leader that follows his speech he takes it for granted that anyone (masculine) who might hypothetically disobey his order must be motivated by a base desire for a reward. Throughout the play he will assume the worst of anyone who opposes him. It may be significant too that he seems to expect opposition and perhaps looks forward to it. More striking is the attitude of the Chorus-leader in this stichomythia. In Greek tragedy the Chorus is normally of the same gender as the principal character, and much of its role consists in supporting, advising, and comforting him or her. If in this play Antigone is the principal character (but see below), it is, then, unusual in that its Chorus is male. We shall not expect it to sing an ode in which it laments the subjection and generally inferior status of women in society, as does, for example, the female Chorus in the third ode of Euripides' *Medea*. However, this male Chorus is less than enthusiastic also about the male Creon's proclamation. Its response is simply, 'You have the power to decree whatever law you wish for the living and the dead alike . . . No one's so foolish as to want to die' (213–14 . . . 217; trans. Stuttard). Later in the play the Chorus's attitude to Antigone may seem at times to be inconsistent. But its character is of no interest in itself; the dramatist is happy for it apparently to respond differently to the different situations in which the characters find themselves.

With the arrival of the Guard we move immediately from the consideration of a hypothetical act of disobedience to the news that someone, unknown, has in fact buried the body. Only after the Chorus has sung an ode will the true identity of the miscreant be revealed to Creon and the Chorus. Sophocles has carefully constructed the sequence of events, though at the risk of raising a slightly awkward question in the minds of the audience. Antigone, we learn, has paid two visits to the corpse. On the first she sprinkled dust over it in a symbolic burial, which ought, one might think, to be sufficient for her purpose. Why, then, does she return to it, and why, when she discovers that the dust has been cleared off by the guards, does she repeat the process, only to be caught doing so?[14] Perhaps, though Sophocles does not tell us, a symbolic burial is not enough for her; Polyneices is still at risk from the birds and dogs. Or was Antigone disappointed because the first time she was not caught, and was therefore in danger of being deprived of her martyr's glory? This is only speculation. What matters is that it allows Sophocles to show us the reaction of Creon and the Chorus to the news that the body has been buried by someone, before they know who that someone is. The audience waits expectantly for their reaction when they learn that the someone is a family member, and, worse still, a woman. The Chorus-leader's response to the Messenger's first speech is very short; he wonders tentatively whether a god may have been responsible for this mysterious burial. The audience knows better, but the guess is not unreasonable. We shall shortly hear from Antigone herself about the unwritten laws of the gods, which require that all the dead should be properly buried. Will the Chorus be of the same mind when in the Messenger's second speech it discovers that the malefactor is a woman?

Much further from the truth is Creon, who pours scorn on the Chorus's surmise. He 'knows' that those who carried out the burial were hired by *men* in the city who were politically disaffected, and did not want to keep their necks under the yoke [of slavery]. What has happened to Creon's fine principles? Always ready to think the worst of everyone, he goes on to preach a long sermon on the harm that the love of money can do to a city. It is not surprising that the Guard was so reluctant to bring the news to Creon, or that, in the light of Creon's threat to hang him if he does not come back with the name of the perpetrator, he will be so relieved to return to the stage with Antigone as his prisoner.

Between the two Messenger speeches the Chorus sings one of the most celebrated of Sophocles' choral odes. The theme is the amazing intellectual and technological skills with which men have created a highly civilized society. If Creon had not left the stage he would no doubt have congratulated himself on his own share in that development. He would, however, be less happy to hear the conclusion of the ode, in which the Chorus points out that there is also a moral sphere, in which men have been less successful. The Guard enters from a side passage with Antigone; Creon through the door from the house. The Guard tells his story of how Antigone was arrested while restoring the dust on the corpse and pouring libations over it. He is sorry for Antigone – for the audience a significant clue to the opinion of the common man – but this pain is outweighed by his relief at being saved from hanging. The rest of the first part of the episode is occupied by the long-awaited confrontation between uncle and niece. It is clear from the beginning that neither is going to yield. Antigone has no interest in the offence committed by Polyneices against his city. It is now for the first and last time in the play that she refers to the unwritten laws of the gods, which must take precedence over the proclamations of mere mortals. But for most of the argument she talks about her feelings; her present plight does not cause her pain, but to leave her brother unburied would have done so. What greater glory could she have won than that of burying her brother?

The Chorus-leader's two-line comment on her first long speech is disappointingly unsympathetic; all that he can say is that Antigone is just as headstrong as her father Oedipus. On the other hand, while there may still be some spectators to sympathize with Creon's declaration that 'As long as I'm alive, I'll have no woman tell me what to do' (525), it is hard to believe that anyone will subscribe to Creon's comparison of Antigone to a horse that needs to be broken in, or to a slave. When they disagree as to whether the people of Thebes are on the one side or the other, we shall have to wait until the Haemon scene (see p. 11) for confirmation that Antigone is right. So far, however, the audience may feel that Antigone has had the better of the argument. As this section comes to an end and we prepare for the arrival of Ismene, whom Creon has summoned, having wrongly decided that she shares Antigone's guilt, Sophocles arouses some misgivings by reminding us of the theme of tangled relationships (522–5). 'An enemy can never be a friend, not even when he's dead', says Creon, to which Antigone replies somewhat enigmatically, 'My nature is not to join in hating but in loving'.[15] We know that she loves her brother, but in the prologue we have already seen her love for her sister turn into hatred.

So Ismene enters, and the final section of this long episode begins. The first part of it consists of line-by-line dialogue between the two sisters while Creon listens (sardonically?) to them; the second consists of line-by-line dialogue between Ismene and Creon while Antigone almost certainly remains silent. Ismene, as the conventional female, sheds the tears that Antigone refused to shed. But she is no longer quite so conventional in her behaviour. She promised in the prologue to love her sister to the end, so she now wants Creon to believe that she shared in the burial, so that she may share also in her sister's death. Antigone refuses to let her do so. When she says '*my* death's enough' (547), and 'save yourself' (553), is she genuinely trying to spare Ismene from her suffering? Or is she being sarcastic, and does she really want to hurt her as much as possible? It is difficult to see how such lines as, 'Ask Creon. He's the one you care about' (549), could be spoken sincerely, or 'Don't worry. You're going to live' (559), when Ismene has just said that she wants more than anything to die. The original audience would be guided by the actor's delivery and tone of voice. For us it raises questions, not about whether Antigone was right to bury Polyneices, but about her state of mind when she did so.

As the episode draws to a close, the question of relationships takes a new turn. 'Poor Haemon', says Ismene, 'Your father does you such discredit!' (572). The original audience is as surprised as we are to learn for the first time that Creon has a son, Antigone's fiancé; for Haemon is probably Sophocles' own invention. The editor of the first printed edition of *Antigone* in 1502, followed by a few modern editors, decided to attribute the line not to Ismene but to Antigone, who ought to be more upset than her sister by the thought that she was about to lose her marriage to the fiancé whom, one would hope, she loved. In modern editions the attribution to Ismene is usually and rightly kept, not only because the intrusion of Antigone here would upset the symmetry of the line-by-line dialogue, but because the question that Sophocles wants to leave in the spectators' minds is evidently, 'Why is it *not* Antigone who brings her fiancé into the argument?' The episode ends as the two girls are led off into the house.

After an ode from the Chorus, the Chorus-leader announces the arrival of Haemon himself, and wonders how he will react to the loss of his marriage. Haemon, as the dramatic link between Antigone and Creon, is part of the tragedy of both, as well as having a tragic end himself. Each in turn delivers a long speech, before the argument becomes more excited in line-by-line dialogue. After a polite start, in which each acknowledges that he is the *philos* of the other, that relationship soon begins to deteriorate. Creon concentrates on the danger of anarchy in a city, but this time adds to it the related danger of being defeated by a woman. Haemon begins by acknowledging his admiration for his father's judgement, but suggests that on this occasion he is wrong, and that it would be wise for him to change his mind. The Chorus-leader, non-committal as usual, says that there is much to be said on both sides. Creon, however, is furious, and adds a new prejudice to his repertoire: is he at his age to be taught what to think by a young man? When Haemon, less tactfully than before, goes on to demolish his father's arguments by exposing the despotic nature of his government, Creon responds by contemptuously calling him a woman's slave. Can anyone in the audience still believe that Creon is right?

To a modern reader or audience Haemon's attitude to Antigone may seem disappointing. He tells us nothing about what *she* means to him. Does he really love her? We should guard against the often implicit assumption that romantic and conjugal love were invented by Hollywood or in the Romantic period. Certainly Greek tragedy does not often present the kind of emotional good-bye scene in which one partner in a love-affair or a marriage is about to die. Does it make a difference that, of course, in *La Bohème* and *La Traviata* the women's parts are played by women? But the normal Greek attitude to the status of a woman in marriage (see p. 13), does not preclude the possibility of genuine affection between the two partners. Euripides' *Alcestis* does feature such a farewell scene, while in Sophocles' *Trachinian Women* it is the woman's love for her husband that leads to tragedy for them both. In real life the poignant funeral *stelae* of deceased husbands or wives should remove any doubts. Haemon concentrates entirely on the political arguments because it is there that his father is most vulnerable, and there that he can hurt him most. But the fury that he displays when, having heard his father's threat to put Antigone to death before his eyes, he vows that Creon will never see him again, surely indicates his love. If there is still any doubt about it, it is immediately resolved by the subject of the Chorus's ode that follows – not just friends and enemies, but Eros, the god of sexual love, who played a central part in a Greek marriage,[16] but who in tragedy wreaks havoc in human life.

Creon has not been entirely untouched by the quarrel. He ends the episode by announcing, for the first time, two changes of mind. The first is fairly minor: Ismene is to be spared. The audience probably never expected that she would die with Antigone. More important is that Antigone is no longer to be publicly stoned to death (35–6). Instead she is to be walled up alive in a rocky cave, with a little food to keep her alive long enough, he hopes, for him to avoid being held responsible for the pollution that might result from her death. He is beginning to feel worried. The effect that this will have on Antigone is even more striking. As the Chorus finishes its ode on Eros, the sight of Antigone being led out of the house to her death causes even the Chorus to weep in sympathy. At first Antigone and the Chorus engage in an excited lyric dialogue, which is eventually interrupted by a sardonic Creon. Antigone ignores him while she delivers a long speech, before she finally departs to be seen no more. The Greek audience would compare her passage to that of a bride on her journey to her new home, according to the belief that an unmarried woman would wed Hades in the next world. Antigone can still look forward to being reunited with her loved ones, her parents and her brother, in the Underworld, but her tone is largely one of lamentation. Public stoning, she had thought, would bring her glory. But, when the now sympathetic Chorus tries to reassure her, she no longer believes it. All that she can see is that she is now going to die alone with nobody to witness it, and nobody to lament her, and so she has in effect to sing her own dirge. She was not on stage to hear Haemon's report that the Theban people approved of her deed. Nor will she hear the judgement that Teiresias will deliver; that her action was in accordance with the will of the gods. By the end of the play Creon knows it, and so does the audience. But Antigone dies without ever having it confirmed to her. The Chorus, for all its sympathy, is still inclined to blame her for her action, and, when it rejects her attempt to compare herself with Niobe, who became a goddess, she takes offence at its lack of understanding.

If the gods were on her side, she wonders, why are they letting her suffer for it now? But does she ever regret doing it? In a strange passage (904–20) she maintains that she would not have done it for any other relation; for only a brother, given that the parents are also dead, is irreplaceable. Some older editors deleted it as a later interpolation, based on a story in a different context in Herodotus. More recently various attempts have, with considerable success, been made to show that, given the Greek view of the role of a woman when she marries (p. 13) and of the potential for divided loyalty between her natal and her married families, Antigone's argument is not as illogical or irrelevant for the original audience as it may seem to us.[17] That may well be true, but even the original audience may still have been troubled by the cold calculation that it involves. Apart from her earlier appeal to the unwritten laws of the gods (p. 18) this is the only occasion on which Antigone tries to give a rational explanation for her behaviour. Creon is still on stage to hear her, but she is not really addressing him or the Chorus. Her audience is the tomb, which will be her only marriage-chamber (891), and she is no longer arguing but lamenting. She is also addressing herself, as she, not very successfully, tries to convince herself that she acted rightly.

In some Sophoclean plays (e.g. *Oedipus the King*) the one principal character stands out from the often ordinary, conventional people, whose attempts to persuade him or her to listen to common sense and to yield to the virtue of moderation, he or she resists to the end. The labelling of this character as the typical 'Sophoclean hero' has recently fallen out of favour, no doubt because it seems to convey the inappropriate ideas of 'hero-worship' and of the character as a role model for the audience. In other plays (including *Antigone*) it is less easy to determine among two or even three major characters which of them is the principal character. However, there is never more than one character to whom the above description applies. Creon does ultimately change his mind, but Antigone remains true to herself until the end. What, then, are we to make of the enigmatic lines, almost the last words that we hear her speak (925–8), in which she seems to leave open the possibility that she could have been wrong? 'If that's what the gods think, too, I'll soon find out the error of my ways. But if the crime is Creon's I hope the punishment he suffers will be no less than the one he's imposed on me – unjustly'. Surely Antigone means that the first alternative, that the gods approve of Creon's behaviour, is to be rejected as a blatant impossibility, while the second one, that Creon was wrong and she herself right, remains her conviction to the end. One cannot, however, be quite sure that everyone in the audience took it this way. In *Oedipus the King* Oedipus declares explicitly at the end that he is glad that he has discovered the truth against all the other characters who think that it would be better for him not to have done so. We admire him for it. Antigone is less positive. All her concentration is on the suffering that she is now enduring as a result of her action. Either way, she never explicitly says that she wishes that she had not buried her brother.

After the Messenger has reported her suicide and that of Haemon we hardly hear of her again. In the final part of the play the suffering of Creon is increased by the further suicide of his wife Eurydice, introduced for that purpose alone by Sophocles. Haemon's body is carried on to the stage for the audience to see, and that of Eurydice is brought out from the house, but not Antigone's. Yet her suffering is more tragic than Creon's. He has to endure it because of the wrong that he has done, while hers is the result of doing what is right, and she goes to her death without understanding why. It would be wrong to dismiss Haemon's suffering as mere collateral damage. He loves Antigone, but she has not mentioned him once in the whole play, not even when she laments the fact that she will die without having married or brought up a child. She complains that her bridegroom will be Acheron the river of Hades, a common way of describing the fate of an unmarried girl. At 1236–41 the Messenger provides a little comfort by informing us that Haemon had died in time to embrace Antigone so that the two corpses lay in each other's arms. This the Messenger interprets to mean that Haemon did achieve his marriage rites in Hades. He embraced her, but can she be said to have embraced him? And can we forget that it was beside Polyneices that she had hoped to lie in Hades? Cairns neatly describes the situation as 'a bizarre triangle of love and death'.[18] Nothing is said about poor Ismene at the end of the play, but we may remember her appeal to Antigone, 'What kind of life's ahead of me with you gone?' (see p. 19). If Creon suffers for doing what is wrong, and Antigone for doing what is right, Ismene suffers for doing nothing.

There is more pessimism than optimism at the end of the play. As far as the future is concerned there is a greater sense of closure than is sometimes the case; Antigone and Haemon are both dead, and the shattered Creon has no future to contemplate. Few scholars would now argue that Sophocles' aim was to teach his audiences that moderation in all things was the greatest of virtues, that sin was always punished and good behaviour rewarded. It would be equally wrong to maintain that he wrote his plays to promote some kind of revolutionary civic or social programme for Athens. But he does present his audience with questions, which it is not his job to answer.[19] Why, for example, do the gods apparently punish, or at least not reward, people for doing the right thing? Why can the relationship between friends and enemies so often lead to such problems? How is it that those who do the right thing can be those whom you would least expect to do it? Why can those who base their behaviour on rational judgement turn out to be wrong, while those who base it purely on their feelings are the ones who get it right? Why did Sophocles compose three choral odes, the first on the theme of man's intellectual capacity and achievements, the second on that of the irrational power of Eros (see p. 20), and the third a hymn to Dionysus, the god par excellence of the irrational? Holt describes the Festival on which tragedies were produced as one in which 'rules are broken, anti-social feelings unleashed, in a civic setting, on a Dionysian holiday'.[20] I should be reluctant to abandon entirely my belief that Sophocles has something serious to say that is relevant to real people in his audience, and that some at least of his spectators changed their opinions by the end of the play.

Notes

1 With this categorical statement I am glad to find myself in agreement with Cairns (2016), the author of the most recent, thorough and reliable

discussion of most of the matters discussed in this chapter. It is gratifying also that I have so much in common with Sommerstein in this volume.

2 For this important principle see van Erp Taalman Kip (1996) 517–36, especially 521–4.

3 For the reception of *Antigone* see especially Hall and Macintosh (2005); Mee and Foley (2011); Cairns (2016) 115–53.

4 Sourvinou-Inwood (1990) 11–38 and also (1989) 134–48. She is followed more recently by Hame (2008) 1–15; see also Liapis (2013) 81–118. For Hall (2011) 51–63, especially 62, the world of the play reflects the Athenians' democratic view of their Theban enemy.

5 For detailed analysis of this process see for example Holt (1999) 658–90; Liapis (2013) 81–118; Cairns (2016) especially 53, 57.

6 For the importance of this distinction see especially Easterling (1987) 15–26 and (1997) 21–37; Holt (1999) 658–90, at 670, 686, 688; Cairns (2016) 44–5 with n. 56.

7 Liapis (2013) 82.

8 Robinson (2011) 201–18, at 203.

9 Garvie (1998) 6–8. The dates of both plays, however, are highly uncertain. *Antigone* is usually placed, but on unreliable evidence, in the late 440s, while *Ajax* has been dated in every decade from the 460s to the 430s. The latest scholar to provide a thorough discussion is Finglass (2011) 1–11, who tentatively puts the two plays in the 440s, but is inclined to think that *Antigone* comes before *Ajax*. If this is correct, it is still significant that in two plays that belong to the same period of his life Sophocles presents the same view of the burial of the dead.

10 This version, in which burial was to be denied to all the Argive commanders, was used earlier by Aeschylus in his *Eleusinians*. In our play, lines 1080–3, which seem to point at it, are probably interpolated. See Brown (2015) 1–26.

11 Steiner (1984) 33 and 108. For the grisly details in our play see also Holt (1999) 680.

12 Liapis (2013) makes out a particularly good case for Creon and his political principles at this stage of the play.

13 Hall (2011) 58; also Cairns (2016) 43 with n. 50.

14 I am not convinced by Bonnie (2013) 161–70, that on the first occasion it was Ismene who buried the corpse.

15 Stuttard in his translation interprets this line to mean, 'I don't want to hate either of them! I want to love them both!'

16 Cairns (2016) 108.

17 Murnaghan (1986) 192–207; Foley (1995) 135–50 and (1996) 49–73; Trapp (1996) 74–84; Cropp (1997) 137–60; Griffith (2001) 117–36, at 131.

18 Cairns (2016) 106.

19 Goldhill (1986) 106; Foley (1996) 66; Liapis (2013) 110.

20 Holt (1999) 690.

2

Antigone as Others See Her*

Alan H. Sommerstein

Most readers of Sophocles' *Antigone* today, most audience members at modern productions of the play or of adapted versions of it, and most of those responsible for these productions and adaptations, see Antigone as a heroic figure, defying the authority of the state, at the cost of her life, in order to do a last service to her dead brother in obedience to what both she and the prophet Teiresias regard as the laws of the gods. Her uncle, guardian and ruler (and prospective father-in-law) Creon tends to be viewed unsympathetically, and directors often present him as a quasi-fascist figure; at any rate he has issued a decree that is declared by Teiresias to have been impious, and the gods punish him appropriately, even if excessively, for his undue exaltation of state over family by destroying his whole family (that is, his wife and his one surviving son).

There are, it is true, some disturbing features about Antigone. She gives the impression that she positively wants to be caught (which will mean certain death): when her sister Ismene promises to keep her intentions a secret (84–5), Antigone tells her, on the contrary, to proclaim them to everyone (86–7), and after having given her brother a symbolic burial, undetected, before daybreak, she came back to the spot in the middle of the day (415–17) to make an offering, and did not seem at all put out when she was arrested (433). She explains this attitude in her first major speech to Creon (460–6): she knew that disobedience would mean death, but her miseries in life were such that death would be preferable; she is impatient for the sentence to be carried out (499), and presently she tells her sister 'You've chosen life. I've chosen death' (555). The Chorus-leader had said that nobody was so foolish as to be in love with death (220); that expression seems to describe Antigone very well. In the end, after her sentence has been changed from stoning (36) to a horrendously slow death by starvation in the darkness of an underground prison, she bitterly laments the fate that she had previously embraced

* This chapter should be read in conjunction with the preceding one; it reaches similar conclusions by a somewhat different route.

(806–75, 901–28, 933–4, 937–43), and her ultimate suicide is not proof of a second change of mind, since she is then only choosing an easy death in preference to a hard one, not knowing that Creon is even then on his way to release her. Her initial eagerness for death (despite knowing how much she is loved by Ismene – and, as we shall later discover, also by her foster-brother and fiancé Haemon) may well seem unreasonable, and her subsequent revulsion from it humanly intelligible but hardly heroic.

Of her own feelings towards Haemon we are told nothing,[1] but we can see how she behaves towards Ismene when Ismene refuses to join her in defying Creon's decree. She may say later that she was not born to join in hatred but in love (523), but her treatment of Ismene seems to give the lie to this. Her first reaction to Ismene's refusal is to say that even if Ismene were to change her mind she wouldn't now want her as an accomplice (69–70), and presently she makes it plain that she hates Ismene (86–7; cf. 93). After Antigone's arrest, when Ismene comes under suspicion and makes her false confession, Antigone rejects Ismene's attempt to share her fate and calls her one who loves only in words (543); and when Ismene makes the moving plea 'What kind of life's ahead of me with you gone?' Antigone produces the most cutting, and the most unjust, response she could have found: 'Ask Creon. He's the one you care about' (549). Creon may think – wrongly, we know, by Sophoclean standards[2] – that an enemy ought to be hated even when he is dead (522); Antigone seems to think that kinsfolk need not be loved unless they are dead.

More radically, the question has been raised, notably in a famous article by the late Christiane Sourvinou-Inwood,[3] whether we may not actually be meant to disapprove of Antigone's action in defying the decree. It is agreed that the decree itself is presented as wrong in the eyes of the gods: the words of Teiresias can leave us in no doubt about this. But is an individual citizen entitled to disobey the decision of the *polis*? And, more than that, is a woman, who is not even a member of the citizen body, entitled to take the law into her own hands in defiance not only of the *polis* but of her own male guardian and legal representative (*kyrios*), who is none other than Creon?

Many may feel that the best answer to these questions is that given by the hero of Aristophanes' *Acharnians* (540), adapting a line from Euripides' lost *Telephus* (fr. 708): 'if you say "that was the wrong thing to do", you should also say what was the *right* thing to do'. If the gods are offended by Polyneices' being left unburied, then acquiescence in Creon's decree is tantamount to acquiescence in possible future divine punishment of the whole community, so that it is arguably everyone's *duty*, for the community's sake, to defy the decree; and if, as seems to be the case, no one except Antigone is prepared to take the risk of doing so, the duty must be hers. That argument, however, is not explicitly raised in the play, and I wish to take a rather different route.

Between Antigone's first appearance at the very beginning of the play and her final exit at line 943, she is for most of the time the centre of attention, and everyone who appears on stage (and also, as we shall see, an important group who do not) expresses some kind of opinion about her actions – in prospect, in retrospect, or both. We can reasonably assume that if the dramatist expects us to censure Antigone's actions, they will have been censured within the play by some person or persons other than Creon – who, though he is the ruler of Thebes, with some claim to speak on behalf of the *polis*, is also the individual whose will has been flouted, and who can hardly be taken as a reliable authority, seeing that his policy is condemned by Teiresias, and that he then abandons it and attempts to reverse its results.

Two of the other characters, Ismene and Haemon, are equally clearly biased in favour of Antigone. Ismene, unlike Antigone, loves the living more than the dead, and Antigone is her only close relative left alive. She clearly thinks that it is wrong for Polyneices to be left unburied, since she begs the forgiveness of the dead for failing to see to his burial (65–8); but she feels herself to be the victim of *force majeure* on the part of the *polis* authorities. This is not strictly true, as Antigone shows; it is *possible* to defy the authorities – but only if one is prepared to accept death as the likely consequence. Ismene is not, and in explaining why, she lays stress on the fact that her father, mother and brothers have all died in shameful circumstances, all *autoktonountes* (cf. 56), slayers of themselves or of their closest kin, so that she and Antigone are the last survivors of their *oikos* (58) and should not disgrace it further by an even more miserable death. In her eyes they have a duty to survive; Antigone recognizes no such duty. In conformity with this view, when Antigone reiterates her determination, Ismene promises to keep the matter secret (84–5): this is not what Antigone wants, but it is what Ismene in fact does until after Antigone's arrest, when Ismene makes the utmost efforts, in the face of Antigone's scorn and contempt, either to save her or to die with her, and again shows what she thinks of Creon's decree by unnecessarily and falsely confessing to having violated it, and by speaking of her own prospective death as a tribute of honour to Polyneices (545). Ismene's position is not that it is wrong in principle to bury Polyneices, but that it is madly imprudent to do so against the will of the *polis* or of its ruler.[4]

Haemon is betrothed to Antigone; both Creon (648–51) and the Chorus (781–800) clearly think he is deeply in love with her, and we are given no reason to suppose them mistaken. He is careful, however, not to put any favourable view of her forward as his own; instead (688–700, 733) he reports what he has heard of the opinions of the general public. We shall assess this report presently.

There remain one person and two groups of persons who have no particular reason to be biased for or against Antigone. The individual is the

Guard, who first reports that Polyneices has been symbolically buried by an unknown hand, and then apprehends Antigone and brings her before Creon. In doing so, he says (436–9), he feels both pleasure and pain: pleasure at having escaped from danger himself, but pain at having brought 'friends'[5] into trouble. That is, he regards Antigone as a friend, despite what she has done, and regrets being the cause of her suffering. His narrative, too, betrays sympathy for her: he lays great emphasis on her distress at seeing that Polyneices' body had been stripped of its covering of dust, and while he of course states the fact that she had violated the prohibition (395–6, 402, 404–5, 434–5) he utters no word of condemnation.

But the Guard is a minor character. Much more significant are the Chorus of Theban elders. Many spectators and readers see them as being loyal to Creon and hostile to Antigone right up to the point when they hear the reports and warnings of Teiresias. There is, however, ample evidence that this attitude is only a mask.

A constant refrain in the play is that almost everyone in Thebes is afraid of offending Creon. The Guard was reluctant to come to Creon with his first report, feeling sure he would be punished (223–36; cf. 269–77), and Creon tells him that if the culprit is not discovered, the entire company of guards will be executed in a particularly cruel way (305–12). Haemon says that the ordinary citizens do not dare to speak their minds openly for fear of Creon's displeasure (688–92). And crucially, this also applies to the elders, despite their status as councillors of state (cf. 159–61). Antigone says that they would approve her action if they were not silenced by fear (504–5, 509); Creon denies this assertion the first time it is made (507), but when it is repeated he simply ignores it and goes on talking as if he could be sure that what they say in his presence represents their real opinion (510). We, and the elders, have already had a taste of his anger; when they tentatively express dissent, wondering if the first covering of the corpse was due to divine intervention (278–9), he retorts 'Stop! Now! Before you anger me, before your words show that you're not just old but senile!' (280–1) – and they say nothing for the rest of the scene. From that point on we can expect them to be very guarded in what they say when Creon is present, though they may be able to express themselves more freely in his absence. And, as we shall see, the dramatist himself to a great extent puts a curb on their mouths by keeping Creon on stage, unusually and without any dramatic necessity, during at least two, probably three, choral odes.

The elders have a long and unbroken record of loyalty to the throne through three generations (165–9). But when they hear Creon repeat his proclamation that the body of Polyneices shall not be buried or lamented by anyone, but shall 'lie unburied for the birds and dogs to feed on, a mutilated corpse for all to see' (204–6), their response contains no hint of approval:

'Creon, if this *is* how you wish to treat Thebes' enemy and Thebes' protector . . . You have the power to decree whatever law you wish for the living and the dead alike.' (211–14). It reminds one of nothing so much as what the Duke of Buckingham says to the newly-crowned Richard III, when Richard tells him that he wants his two young nephews dead: 'Your grace may do your pleasure.'[6] Buckingham is evading an implicit request from Richard that *he* should arrange for the princes to be murdered. Creon's next words (215) are the beginning of what would have been an explicit request for the elders to assist in the enforcement of his decree – and they evade it, pleading that they are too old (216). Creon retreats a little, asking them only not to be indulgent to a violator (219); the reply, 'No one's so foolish as to *want* to die', while of course ironic for the audience (that is exactly what Antigone apparently *does* desire), also implies that they fear for their own lives if they disobey Creon's command. We have seen how their slightly bolder intervention at 278–9 is slapped down by Creon, after which they are silent until the end of the scene.

Probably at 326, possibly at 331, Creon goes back into his palace; we know this because his return to the stage is announced at 386. The Chorus sing the famous 'Ode on Man' (332–75). Only its last few lines are directly relevant to the current situation, and even they are expressed in very general terms:

> The man who respects the laws of his country
> and the oaths [lit. sworn justice] of his gods
> deserves the highest honour in the city;
> there is no place in any city though for anyone
> who arrogantly, recklessly, commits his life to wickedness.
> A man like that's not welcome in my house
> and I could never sympathize with him.
>
> 368–75

Who, or what type of person, is being marked out for the elders' approval, and who for their condemnation? The person being commended can hardly be one like Creon; his decree may now be one of 'the laws of [the] country' – the elders' first response to it shows that they recognize that Creon's proclamations have the force of law – but they clearly have doubts whether it embodies the justice of the gods, seeing that they have wondered aloud whether its violation was the gods' work. Contrariwise, the violator himself (everyone at this stage assumes that the deed was done by one or more men) may or may not have been fulfilling the will of the gods, but is certainly disobeying a lawful state decree. So neither of them meets the criteria the Chorus have set for commendation.

What of the type that is condemned, the audacious evildoer? The language could be applied to the unknown violator of the decree, or it could be applied to Creon. A recent commentator, Mark Griffith,[7] sees the potential double meaning, and argues that the first interpretation is to be taken as that intended by the Chorus, and the second is an ironic one perceived only by the audience. I am not so sure. Creon is not present, and the elders can express themselves freely. They have made it pretty evident that they disapprove of Creon's decree and think it may well be contrary to the will of the gods. And to go against the gods' will is certainly audacious (and dangerous), and could very properly be described as 'baseness' or 'not something to be proud of' (*mē kalon*). That interpretation is arguably likely to be closer than the other to what a group of old, wise and pious men could reasonably be expected to think.

To the elders' amazement, Antigone is now brought in under guard. They can hardly believe that it is she who has violated the decree, but if it is, they categorize her action as folly (*aphrosynē*, 383), which by normal standards it certainly is (since it means her life is forfeit), whatever one may think of it in moral or religious terms. It is not the sort of expression Creon would have used; when it is his turn, he speaks, twice over, of *hybris* (480, 482). Creon appears almost immediately afterwards, and the Chorus make no comment on the Guard's narrative: they know better than, for example, to underline his statement that the dust-storm that concealed Antigone's arrival was a divine intervention (421). They speak first at 471–2, when their comment on Antigone's first speech to Creon is that her nature is 'headstrong' and unyielding: that is very true (especially when she has just told Creon to his face that he is a fool, 470), but it implies nothing about the merits of the case she is making about the relationship between Creon's decree and the laws of the gods. They make no comment on Creon's angry reply (473–96), and their only other utterance in the scene is a chanted (anapaestic) comment on the entrance of Ismene (526–30). Ismene is now herself under accusation (488–96), but the Chorus remark only on her discoloured face and (twice) on the tears she is shedding for her sister.

At the end of this scene (577–81) Antigone and Ismene are taken inside, but Creon remains where he is: the Chorus address him (627–8) when Haemon is seen approaching. The Choral ode 582–624 is therefore sung in Creon's presence. It may be summarized as follows.

Strophe 1:	When the gods are hostile to a family, it is utterly ruined.
Antistrophe 1:	Thus they are destroying the last survivors of the house of Labdacus through 'thoughtless words [and] minds possessed by madness [lit. an Erinys]'.
Strophe 2:	Zeus is the unchallengeable ruler of the universe; no arrogance of (male) men can restrain him; great wealth always leads to disaster.

Antistrophe 2: Many (male) men are deceived by hope, and evil seems good to them as the god drives them unknowingly towards ruin.

The first strophic pair, proceeding as usual from the general to the particular, does indeed comment on the fate of Antigone (and Ismene), and does see them as partly responsible for it, but the only identifiable fault they mention is folly in *words* (603), which both of them indeed showed in the preceding scene, Antigone by her insolent defiance of Creon and Ismene by making a false confession; nothing at all is said about Antigone's *actions*. And the second strophic pair is not about her at all; both its stanzas speak specifically of *male* humans (*andres*),[8] and the references to great wealth and to deceptive hope do not fit Antigone in any way – the Chorus have heard from Antigone herself that she expected nothing except death (460–8, 555). I would not wish to assert that the Chorus are to be understood as having Creon in mind; but they have never actually rejected Antigone's claim that Creon has challenged the laws of the gods.

The Chorus do then (681–2) express approval of Creon's first speech to Haemon, which includes the shocking (to Athenians) statement that the authorities of the *polis* must be obeyed in matters small and great, just and unjust (666–7) – this in direct contradiction to the oath taken by every Athenian on coming of age, that he would obey those who exercised authority 'reasonably' or 'sanely' (*emphronōs*).[9] But then even Haemon, who is about to express a radically different view, begins his speech by saying that he could not, and would never wish to, say that Creon had spoken wrongly (685–6). Haemon is certainly being tactfully insincere, and so therefore may the Chorus be: a prudent precaution, one may feel, when dealing with the man who recently sentenced Ismene to death for grieving (488–92). And when Haemon has told Creon that the Theban public are against him, and that he ought to relent, the Chorus urge Creon to learn from him, though they cover themselves by also recommending Haemon to learn from what his father has said (724–5). Their statement that both have spoken well – more literally, that there has been good speaking on both sides – does not commit them to the view that *everything* said on either side has been good.

The angry quarrel between Haemon and Creon, and Haemon's dark words before his departure (751, 762–5), alarm the elders, who draw his attention to the matter without making any recommendation (766–7). Creon professes unconcern (768–9), though inwardly he is sufficiently disturbed that when the Chorus make bold to ask whether he really means to execute *both* his nieces, he instantly stands on his head and reprieves Ismene (771).

Does Creon exit after announcing his ghastly sentence on Antigone? Nothing in the text positively indicates an exit after 780 or an entrance at 882.

More importantly, Creon has ordered that Antigone be brought outside (760–1), and has said he will have her entombed in a remote place (773–6): if she is to be brought out and then taken away, it makes no sense that Creon, instead of waiting for his attendants to bring her, should go inside and then reappear not together with her but eighty-two lines later. Creon, then, again remains on stage; he is in fact present without a break from 387 (when he enters to find that Antigone has been brought to the palace) until 1114 (when he exits for the purpose of releasing her from her prison-tomb).

The Chorus sing a short ode to the power of love (781–800), which has certainly been one determinant of the behaviour of Haemon; this enables them to avoid making any comment on the fate of Antigone. But when they see her brought out on her way to 'her marriage bed of death', they feel themselves carried beyond the bounds of law (801–2) and cannot restrain their tears (802–5). She immediately addresses them (806); what can they say to her? They make four replies to her impassioned lyrics; the first two are in chanted anapaests, the last two in a simple lyric iambic metre.

The two anapaestic passages (818–23, 834–8) are attempts at consolation. The Chorus first tell Antigone that she has won glory by dying not from disease or violence but by her own choice (*autonomos*); then, when she compares herself to Niobe, they reply that while the comparison is not quite proper (since Niobe, they say inaccurately, was a goddess), it is still 'wonderful' to have a fate even partly comparable to hers. Antigone understandably regards this as contemptuous mockery (838–40), but we will hardly imagine it to have been intended as such.

A very different note is struck in the two short lyric responses (853–6, 872–5), where the elders come as close as they ever do to endorsing Creon's position. They tell Antigone that she has 'dared to go too far' and 'crashed against the hard wall of justice'; yet even now they mitigate their condemnation by suggesting that she is paying for something done by an ancestor. And rather similarly in the antistrophe, while saying that Antigone has been destroyed by her own emotions, they also say that she acted honourably in honouring her kinsfolk (873). These utterances are perhaps not quite in character for the elders as we have seen them so far, even allowing for the presence of Creon: consistency here gives way a little to the desire to have Antigone, the last time we see her in the play, feel completely isolated and utterly friendless (876–82). After this, until Antigone's final exit, the Chorus are kept silent except for a brief anapaestic comment on her last major speech (929–30), to the effect that her attitude has not changed.

Antigone is led off, but Creon still remains on stage; he is already present when Teiresias arrives at 988, otherwise Teiresias, who has come to give him information and advice, would certainly be made to ask where he was. Yet again, then, the Chorus can only say what is safe to say in his presence, and in an ode that has often been found puzzling (944–87) they address themselves to the absent Antigone (949, 987), and reflect on some famous myths that present analogies of various kinds to Antigone's fate. We need not explore the possible broader relevance of these to other aspects of the drama; it is sufficient to note that by choosing this subject the elders avoid making any direct comment at all on what Creon has done to Antigone.

And then comes Teiresias. During his confrontation with Creon, the elders say nothing. When he has gone, we hear again from the Chorus-leader the same words he had spoken three hundred lines earlier upon the exit of Haemon (1091 ~ 766: 'he's gone, sir'). This time he is able to remind Creon of his own statement that in the past he had always followed Teiresias' advice and it had always proved to be sound (1082–4 ~ 993–5). Creon knows it is true (1085), and a moment later he collapses and is asking the elders what he should do. They tell him: release Antigone and bury Polyneices, without a moment's delay (1100–4).

All in all, it appears that Antigone was right in her reading of the elders' minds. They thought Creon's decree was wrong; they sympathized with Antigone's motives for disobeying it, and were deeply saddened by her plight; they never unequivocally condemned her, and certainly never said or implied, as Creon repeatedly does (484–5, 525, 578–9, 678–80, 740, 746, 756), that as a woman she has no right to resist decisions made by men; but they felt unable to speak freely in the presence of Creon,

So, according to Haemon (690–1), do our last group of neutral commenters – the ordinary people of Thebes. Having listened to their talk, he says, he can report (694–9) that the city is grieving for Antigone as 'more than any woman in the world ... not deserv[ing] to die in such a squalid way for doing something which should earn the highest praise' by refusing to leave her dead brother to become carrion for dogs and birds. He adds a sentence in direct speech (699): 'Doesn't she deserve the highest [lit. a golden] honour?' This might in principle be his own comment, but since he says immediately afterwards that these mutterings are spreading through the city (700), line 699 is much better taken as a quotation of something being said among the citizens (and modern editors ought to print it between quotation marks). Public opinion, then, according to Haemon, is entirely on Antigone's side, and thinks that, far from being punished, she should have been rewarded, perhaps with that regular symbol of civic commendation, a golden crown.

Now it is very easy to suggest that Haemon, being himself so much in love with Antigone, 'would say that, wouldn't he?' – or at least to take Griffith's agnostic position (on 692–3) that his claim 'may or may not be valid or oversimplified'. But if Sophocles wanted us even to entertain that view, he would certainly have put it in the mouth of Creon, who does in fact believe that Haemon has become the slave of his erotic passions: if Creon doesn't think his son is lying or deluded in his assessment of public opinion, why should we? In line 733 Haemon repeats his assertion that the people of Thebes do not regard Antigone as a villain. That was the moment for Creon to say something like 'So *you* say, but you are deceiving yourself'. Instead he says 'So Thebes wants to tell me what to do now, does it?' (734). To that, for an Athenian, the only legitimate answer would be 'Yes, that is the people's right – unless you want to be called a tyrant'; which is more or less the answer that Haemon gives, though by the conventions of *stichomythia* he has to string it out a little (735–9). To his final gibe, 'You'd do a great job ruling ... in an empty land' (739), Creon has no answer except to change the subject and accuse him of being the ally of a woman. We have thus been given no reason at all to believe that Haemon's report is not essentially correct.

Antigone's stand, then, has broad support both among the Theban elite (as represented by the Chorus) and among the Theban masses. It is also supported by the gods, who, as Teiresias reveals (1068–9), condemn, and will punish, Creon's treatment of her. The Athenian audience may well at first have been uncertain how to view her: Polyneices was, after all, a traitor, and Creon's first speech (especially 175–90) may have made as favourable an impression on fifth-century Athenians as it did some ninety-nine years later on Demosthenes (*On the False Embassy* 246–7). But the cautious response of the elders to his decree, their suspicion that the gods may be against it, Creon's irrational treatment of the Guard and Ismene, the increasing evidence that it is dangerous to openly disagree with him about anything ... all this will have made many spectators rethink their position well before they hear about Theban public opinion and Creon's contempt for it, let alone about what the gods think of his actions. Creon may assert that Antigone is the only person in Thebes who sees things her way (508): the play will show that, on the contrary, he is the only person in Thebes (or the only one we know of) who does not, and that not only was he wrong, but Antigone was right. That, we discover, was both *vox populi* and *vox dei*.

Notes

1 Line 572 ('Poor Haemon! Your father does you such discredit!') should be assigned to Ismene; see Sommerstein (1993/2010).

2 See especially the argument between Odysseus and Agamemnon in *Ajax* 1332–73.

3 Sourvinou-Inwood (1989).
4 Ismene has a significant tendency to confuse these two entities. Sometimes she ascribes the decree to the city or the citizens (44, 79), sometimes to Creon or 'the government' (47, 67), and once (59–60) to both in the same breath ('if we break this law . . . if we defy the power of these powerful men').
5 Greek *tous philous* is much stronger than Stuttard's translation 'somebody you know'.
6 Shakespeare (1999), *King Richard III* IV.ii.22.
7 Griffith (1999) 180–1.
8 Stuttard translates this word at 604–5 but not at 616.
9 See Siewert (1977).

3

Assessing the Character of Creon

Brad Levett

The figure of Creon in Sophocles' *Antigone* has elicited a wide range of responses from modern scholars and readers. Moreover, the play's original audience, insofar as they had a different value system from ours, would have had their own particular responses to him. In what follows we will look at how the character of Creon is written in such a way as to arouse a complex response from audiences then and now (if at times for different reasons and in different ways), with a particular focus on the ethical issues he raises for any spectator or reader.

Two general points to start: First, any ethical system arising organically over time within a society will contain the potential for conflict between agents attempting to abide by the ethical system in question. The attempt to follow one societal rule can, in a particular set of circumstances, involve compromising another, different, rule. In many ways, this is the core of the ethical element of Greek tragedy. Time and again in this genre we see agents who agree on basic principles, but come into fatal conflict in their application of these values. In *Antigone*, we can readily see that both Creon and Antigone attempt to abide by the central Greek ethic of 'helping friends and harming enemies'. This ethic can be understood as a founding principle for society, since it strives to create cohesive groups that work together to advance the interests of those in the group, with the logical (if harsh) corollary of the need to strike out at one's enemies. (Note that the Greek term for 'friends', *philoi*, covers a broad range of relationships, from family members to friends to comrades-in-arms to business associates.) Creon's injunction that Polyneices is not to be buried is motivated by the desire to harm an enemy (e.g. 198–210, 518–22). Yet so too is Antigone's defiance of his edict based upon the ethic, since she still views her brother as part of the in-group defined as 'friends' (e.g. 73, 521). The situation reveals the sort of difficulties that can occur: one person can at one moment be defined differently by different people (Polyneices as friend, Polyneices as enemy), and individuals can move from one category to another, just as Creon and Antigone, relatives, come to regard each other as enemies. Moreover, not only can different principles come into conflict, as they clearly do when Creon focuses on the ethic of punishing enemies to the point that he neglects his religious and family obligations, but even a given ethic such as 'helping friends and harming enemies' can come into conflict with itself. For Creon's adherence to one prong of the ethic, harming enemies, results in harming friends, as a result of the deaths of Antigone, Haemon and Eurydice. Thus, as a simple starting point based on the genre's exploration of complex ethical issues, we might expect its characters to be more ambiguous than not.

Second, another simple but important point to keep in mind is that our responses to the characters can and do operate in a complex fashion on different registers. On the most basic level, we can respond emotionally to a character in a way that may not line up with our rational assessment of the character's behaviour. Hence, for example, we might well be impressed with Antigone's dedication to her brother and her willingness to die for her values, while still criticizing the manner in which she pursues her ethical objectives. And of course, an individual can have an ambiguous response even within one given register of response. For example, we might be impressed with Antigone's dedication to her brother while being put off by her swift emotional rejection of her sister, Ismene. Thus, there is a potential divergence of response not only between different audience members, but even within a given audience member.

A central question to ask first is the issue of the ethicality of Creon's decision to deny Polyneices a burial. This can be answered in two ways. Within the internal logic of the play itself, there is no doubt that he has acted improperly in this regard, since we learn later through the seer Teiresias that the gods condemn his action (998–1032). But would the historical audience have assumed this from the beginning of the play? The answer in terms of the religious beliefs of the fifth-century Athenians is a bit more complicated. It was certainly a standard Greek religious belief that dead bodies should be buried in order to send their souls to the underworld, and that Hades demanded this as part of his due. However, it was not completely unheard of to punish certain types of criminals, such as traitors like Polyneices in fact, with a lack of burial. Yet, presumably because it involved what was potentially a religious transgression, this 'refusal' of a burial could be understood in different, less absolute ways. For instance, it could mean not being buried on Athenian soil, and in fact quietly allowing the family of the dead individual to collect the body and have it buried somewhere outside of Attica. In this regard, it may be important to remember that Creon is leaving the body to rot on Theban land. Most important, however, is the fact that Creon's edict gives no room at all for any sort of compromise. His decision to make the punishment death for anyone attempting to bury the body, and indeed to put guards over it, does not allow much possibility for a peaceful resolution. Finally, note that Creon, since he is now the head of the house of Oedipus, is in fact the individual who would normally be responsible for giving Polyneices a proper burial.

Yet if the play eventually shows Creon to be in the wrong in this regard, he is not simply or absolutely wrong in all his motivations, decisions and actions, just as Antigone is not simply correct in her own behaviour, despite being correct in her recognition of the need for her brother's body to be buried. In what follows we will see that it is a combination of a stubborn nature and an inability to carefully disentangle ethical obligations that is central to Creon's downfall.

When Creon comes on stage for the first time he sounds quite reasonable and reassuring. First, he acknowledges that he is new to rule and needs in effect to prove himself (175–90). The Athenian audience may have seen this as similar to their own practice in the democracy of assessing politicians before and after their terms of office. Whereas in the democracy it was typically the elite (aristocratic and/or wealthy individuals in society) who held the more important political positions (just as Creon is a noble related to the royal family), they were understood, in part by such reviews, to be accountable to the *demos*, the people as a whole. Thus, there is the suggestion at this point that Creon's emphasis on the need for loyalty to the state involves a recognition of the importance of the collective body of citizens that composes the state.

Second, his principle that one should value the interests of the state over those of the family, on the surface and in context, might seem entirely reasonable to any audience. We have just had the violent imagery of the opening song of the Chorus, describing how Thebes narrowly avoided being destroyed by Polyneices and his borrowed Argive army (100–61). The song notes that this conflict resulted from two royal princes fighting over who should rule the state (110, 144–7). Hence the citizens of Thebes (and any audience) might well feel that in the recent past the concerns of the royal family have been far too dominant over those of the city. Indeed, put very simply, the democracy in Athens developed out of previous forms of government based on rule by elite families (aristocracy, tyranny), and so Creon's emphasis on the good of the state over that of (elite/royal) families is again in line with the values of his historical audience.

Yet warning notes can already be heard in this first speech. Creon, much like Antigone earlier, tends to talk in ethical absolutes. Creon would *never* value a friend more than the state; he will *always* honour good men and punish the wicked, etc. (187–90, 207–10). Yet it was understood that in democratic Athens one had obligations to a number of individuals and institutions: family, state, the gods. Creon's opposition between loyalty to family and loyalty to the state may make some sense in relation to the issue of the royal family's recent behaviour, but not as a general principle. It was expected that one would strive to meet one's obligations to both the family and the state, and not to simply choose one over the other. Creon's tendency towards extremes is also seen, as mentioned, in the obsessive measures he takes to try to ensure that no one disobeys his edict. It is also perhaps a sign that the Chorus, who have been summoned in particular to support the new ruler (164–74), do not praise Creon's decree, but merely note that as the king, he has the power to do as he sees fit (211–14).

From these first hints at an autocratic nature, the play will gradually reveal further aspects of tyranny in Creon's character and rule. This can be seen, and criticized, by any audience, but for the Athenians it would have been particularly worrying. In democratic Athens, the figure of the tyrant was a staple of political discourse, and in particular was used as a foil to democracy. The Athenians (specifically the adult males who held citizen rights) prided themselves on the freedom accorded them by being equal participants in a ruling collective, whereas tyranny and monarchy were viewed as essentially slavery for everyone except the ruler.

This characterization can be seen in the excessive fear of the Guard, who comes on stage to reveal that he and his fellows have failed in their task of preventing the body from being buried (223–36). The Chorus, upon being told the uncanny tale of how the burial occurred, suggest that this reflects divine approval, but Creon angrily rejects this out of hand as foolish (278–89). He then groundlessly accuses the Guard of potentially being involved in the burial for the purpose of profiting himself, and threatens him with death if he does not find the real culprit. Volatile anger, a tendency to see conspiracies abounding and the use of violence are all stereotypical behaviours for a tyrant in Greek thought. The tyrant, unsure of his power – typically because it is ill-gained or maintained unethically – fears being deposed and so lashes out in anger. Moreover, Creon's specific comment that there are individuals who will not bear the yoke of his rule, suggesting the image of the populace as mere chattel owned by the king, is particularly revealing (290–2).

When the Guard returns with Antigone, having caught her re-performing the burial, the same anger, stubbornness and tendency to extreme measures is revealed in Creon's behaviour. And we are also shown, importantly, how these characteristics make Creon unable to disentangle his ethical obligations. When Antigone first explains her reasons for defying his edict, she speaks of the higher obligation to respect the rules of the gods, one of which is that the dead must be given a burial (450–70). In his immediate response, Creon makes no reference to this point at all, but instead focuses on the fact of Antigone's disobedience, emphasizing that she is related to him (484–9; see also 659–60). Creon is now the head of Antigone's family, in Greek its *kurios* ('guardian', 'one who holds power'), and of course he is also her king. And finally, as he will almost obsessively emphasize (e.g. 577–81, 648–51, 746), she is a woman and so should not have the audacity to resist a male. Hence Antigone's disobedience can be understood to upset three accepted forms of authority.

This is one of those areas in which modern and ancient responses will differ considerably. Modern audiences will typically reject the legitimacy of these forms of authority, especially the one based in misogyny: if Antigone's position is ethically correct, there is no reason that her gender should affect the issue. Yet the Greeks had a very hierarchical sense of the relations between individual classes of entities in the world, whether it be between animals, humans and gods, or between foreigners and Greeks, or between women and men. It is a historical reality that men in Athens were accorded more power and worth. Yet if an ancient audience would probably agree that Antigone should not be opposing her male *kurios*, this does not mean that they would accept Creon's response as simply correct. The very same basic principle of hierarchy, in the form of female obedience to male interests, certainly holds true for the relationship between humans and gods. Antigone specifically mentioned that the rules of the gods supersede those of human governments (450–5), but Creon ignores this by focusing on the issue of feminine disobedience. But the two issues can and should be distinguished. There is no necessary reason that Creon could not punish Antigone for disobeying his edict (presumably with some punishment less extreme than death, which is hardly required) while recognizing the sensible principle of according to the gods their due respect, just as he is demanding respect from Antigone on the basis of his position as her king and *kurios*.

Of course, his extreme response to Polyneices' treachery has already painted him into a corner. And yet later, after Creon's confrontation with his son, Haemon, we are in fact given a glimpse of another aspect of the character that will become important for understanding him. Whereas at first he thought to punish Ismene also with death, assuming her to be a part of the plot to bury the body (which we the audience know to be far from the truth), under the influence of the Chorus's comments he backs down and decides not to execute her (770–1). This ability to relent and change his mind will return later, if too late, when he finally heeds Teiresias' warning.

In his conflict with his son Haemon the tyrannical elements of Creon's character and rule are fully revealed. Fixated on his authority, he immediately asks Haemon to maintain proper loyalty to his father (639–47), which was certainly a standard value in ancient Greece, much as Creon himself suggests – Haemon readily agrees to this basic principle, but tries to rationally explain why Creon is making a mistake in his treatment of Antigone. First, while Haemon also owes his father his obedience, as a male he avoids any confrontation on the level of gender, which, given the way that Creon repeatedly returns to this level of conflict, seems to play an overly large role in motivating the king's behaviour. Rather than reiterating Antigone's basic point of the divine requirement of burial, he emphasizes two other arguments. Taking a more pragmatic and political approach, he notes that he has learned that the people of Thebes disagree with Creon's decision. Why should the royal daughter be killed for doing something so glorious as giving her brother his due burial (692–700)? While potentially anachronistic, Haemon's assumption that Creon, a monarch, is failing in his obligations to the people of Thebes would have reverberated well with the democratic principles of the historical audience. His reference to his desire that his father 'fare well' (701) in his career suggests straightforwardly that it would be advantageous to Creon's own continuing rule that he respect the views of his subjects. Yet here Creon, in the bitter exchange that follows, veers wildly into statements of extreme totalitarianism. He complains again about the need for obedience, this time from the younger towards the older (726–7), and from the citizens towards their ruler (734). His most outrageous defence for the political obedience he is demanding is his claim that a ruler in effects *owns* the state (737–8), which naturally would have been highly offensive to the original audience (and indeed it reminds us of the metaphor of 'yoking' used earlier).

Second, Haemon importantly emphasizes the need to be both rational and flexible in one's decision making (683–4, 705–11). As he says, obedience is not the issue if the point made by the one with less status and power is itself sensible and advantageous (728–9). He uses two powerful metaphors to emphasize the need to be able to change one's mind towards the better course of action once one has recognized it (712–17). He notes how those trees that are supple and bend in the face of a storm survive, whereas those that do not bend but resist the gales end up being uprooted and destroyed. This effectively makes the principle of the need for adaptability and flexibility a natural one that applies in a universal fashion. The second metaphor, of the helmsman changing course in a storm in order to save the ship, brings the general principle into the specific realm of the political. The metaphor of the state understood as a ship was extremely common in Greek thought, and is certainly relevant here: Creon is the helmsman who is now facing a storm of political disapproval and must change course in order to save himself and the city.

Thus we can see that Creon's errors result from a stubborn and intransigent disposition that makes it difficult for him to properly distinguish his various ethical duties. His tendency to see things in extreme terms causes him mistakenly to privilege one value over another, rather than trying to balance them. As mentioned, giving the gods their due in the form of allowing Polyneices some form of burial does not preclude keeping the state strong or treating his family properly. Equally important, and related to the excessive selfishness that is characteristic of the figure of a tyrant, we have seen that he also misrepresents ethical obligations by tending to see them unilaterally in terms of the obligations due *to him*, without a corresponding amount of attention given to his own obligations to others. It is important to emphasize that to the Greek audience he is not wrong in the particular values that he does hold, as they would have readily agreed with the need for obedience to the state (and to authority more generally), but in *how* he holds and attempts to act upon such values. He is precisely lacking the flexibility needed to negotiate the series of ethical responsibilities and benefits involved in ancient Greek life (and indeed, in anyone's life). This is especially true if we consider how, under the democracy at Athens, the franchise was held by many more people (if certainly not all) than it had been held by previously under earlier political systems, and as a result the need to acknowledge and respect the rights of others was now more extensive.

It should be carefully qualified that while the play presents Creon as having tyrannical aspects to his character and behaviour, it does not paint him as a simple caricature. He does not, for instance, display the overwhelming appetite for personal pleasure that was one of the most common traits associated with tyranny. We have already noticed that, both generally speaking and in the specific context of a city restoring itself after foreign invasion, his desire for strong political rule is completely reasonable in itself, and seems to be related to a genuine desire that the city prosper. Perhaps most importantly, if Creon were to be understood as a simple stereotype of the evil tyrant, this would make the play's ending, in which we are invited to feel pity for Creon's suffering, very hard to explain.

Haemon, being unsuccessful in persuading his father (and perhaps ironically showing something of the same extreme nature) becomes enraged and storms offstage with threats of violence (762–5). We then return to the religious issue when Teiresias enters and lays it out as directly as possible that Creon is in the wrong (998–1022). As he powerfully describes it, Creon has completely reversed the natural order by entombing a living individual and leaving the dead to rot above ground (1064–71). He also repeats Haemon's point on the need for flexibility in one's decisions when one has made an error (1023–32). Creon at first stubbornly stands his (mistaken) ground, momentarily reaching the point of outright blasphemy, claiming he will oppose Zeus himself before he allows Polyneices to be buried (1039–41). He again, like the figure of the tyrant, sees conspiracies against him where there are none, now accusing Teiresias of plotting against him for personal gain (1033–39). The prophet leaves in anger, warning that Creon's own loved ones will be harmed as a result of his foolish acts. It is at this point that Creon finally bends. Under the guidance of the Chorus, and despite his desire to remain fixed in his position, he decides to free Antigone from the cave she is entombed in and to give a proper burial to Polyneices (1091–114), thereby correcting the reversal of norms that Teiresias mentioned. The reason for his reversal seems to result straightforwardly from the fact that he now recognizes, due to the prophetic authority of Teiresias' warning, that his actions may have detrimental effects. His mistaken view that the gods could not possibly want the body of a traitor to be honoured with a burial has been directly refuted by the portents the gods themselves have revealed through their prophet Teiresias. Interestingly, Teiresias specifically noted that not only was Creon bringing ruin upon himself, but that the city itself was 'sick' due to his behaviour (1015). Thus, Creon's over-zealous attempt to strengthen the state at all costs over other ethical values results, in fact, in harm to the state, since the gods will not prosper a city that does not acknowledge their rules.

While the Chorus seem to suggest that Creon should free Antigone first and then bury the body of Polyneices (1100–1), we learn from the Messenger that Creon does the reverse. This may simply reflect the play's emphasis on the crime of not burying the body, and the fact that Antigone would not, in the normal course of things, be in immediate danger. Yet the decision to bury the body first, when of course nothing more harmful can be done to it by delaying its burial slightly, presumably also represents yet another failure of judgement on Creon's part.

When the Messenger arrives to reveal the disasters that have occurred, it is important to recognize that he begins by framing his account of Creon's downfall as an object lesson about the vulnerability of human life (1155–71). He mentions the Greek truism that you can never be sure of your happiness and prosperity due to the reversals of fortune to which human life is ever susceptible. Again, presenting Creon as an example of humanity more generally would make little sense if we were meant to understand him simply as the evil tyrant who suffers his just downfall. Similarly, the play's focus on Creon's lamentation after the revelation of the deaths of Antigone, Haemon and his wife Eurydice would also make little sense. Certainly all involved, including Creon himself, recognize that he bears responsibility for the disasters, but the emphasis is on his mistaken judgement and not any evil intentions. As the Chorus say at the end of the play, good sense is crucial for prosperity, and there must be respect for the gods (1348–50), the original lack of which aptly explains Creon and his fate.

Their last lines also emphasize a final important aspect of Creon's characterization. They say that the arrogant suffer great blows and so learn wisdom with age (1350–3). Creon's change of heart at the end of the play distinguishes him from his counterpart, Antigone (and indeed from the majority of Sophoclean heroes). The two characters, while championing different values, are very similar in their extremely one-sided pursuit of a particular view to the neglect of others. For just as Creon should balance his commitment to the state with his obligations to the gods and family, so too should Antigone balance her dedication to her brother with loyalty to her *kurios* and king. However, although she deeply laments for her suffering and the various calamities that have afflicted her family, during her final scene when she exits to her entombment and eventual death she does not seem to suggest that she wishes she had acted otherwise (891–943). This could simply reflect the fact that, in her current situation, she has no possibility of changing her course, but in truth she has stated from the beginning that she is willing to suffer death in the pursuit of her values (72, 95–7). Perhaps in one sense she has 'learned' the true extent of her own suffering and that of her family, but she has not come to a new ethical understanding in the sense that Creon has come to know that his previous actions and decisions were both unethical in important aspects and indeed detrimental to his own best interests. Now, the play's final lines can be read negatively, if they are understood in the sense that a person can learn *only* by suffering. This basic notion is certainly a common one in Greek tragedy. Yet even if suffering is required to learn, it nevertheless does produce learning. Moreover, the presentation of such an act of learning by characters enacting a drama before a mass audience suggests the idea that this audience can itself learn from Creon's mistake, that the cycle of learning through suffering need not be contained within the tragic life of one individual, but shared among the group as a means to learn from the experiences of others. Creon's change of heart came too late, despite being warned repeatedly of his errors in judgement and of the consequent need to be flexible in his ethical behaviour. Yet the simple point that he is indeed able to change his mind reflects our own ability to learn from him, and from tragic drama more generally. Thus, while modern audiences may often not particularly like the character of Creon, insofar as we may find some of his ethical positions and decisions offensive, and while any audience will be able to find fault in Creon's decisions, we can nonetheless feel for the suffering that results from his human fallibility, and as a result see in his downfall the possibility for our own learning and ethical improvement.

Suggestions for further reading

For a recent, and excellent, study of the play, see Cairns (2016), especially Chapter 2 for many of the issues discussed here, and Chapter 5 on the play's diverse reception. On the play's ethical issues, see Nussbaum (2001): Chapter 3, in particular 54–63 on Creon and his ethical inflexibility; and Blundell (1989): Chapter 4, especially 115–30 on Creon, with 123–6 on his tyrannical aspects. While there is no consensus on just what degree of blame Creon and Antigone bear for the tragedy, scholars are often more critical of Creon. For a stronger defence of Creon, see Sourvinou-Inwood (1989). On the 'Sophoclean hero' and her or his intransigent ethical nature, see the seminal study of Knox (1964), especially 10–44 on the general character type, and 67–75 on how Creon does and does not fit the pattern. For the relationship between tragedy and its historical/social setting in democratic Athens, see Hall (1997), and on that between elites and *demos*, see Ober (1989). On the issue of refusal of burial in Athens, see Parker (1983): 45–8.

4

Images and Effects of Incest in Sophocles' *Antigone*

Sophie Mills

Non-incestuous families look outwards. Their choices of marriage partner move them outside their family grouping as they make new connections with new families. If all goes well, these connections are beneficial to all concerned, and they ultimately strengthen both the individual families and society as a whole. Incestuous families look inwards and choose the wrong people as sexual partners, damaging both the immediate family and less immediate relationships. Certain members of the family have secrets that cannot be easily shared; certain things cannot be said, or if said, are hushed up or ignored. Additionally, incest is not only by its nature often intergenerational (father/daughter, uncle/niece and so on), but it often transcends the generation in which it starts, so that a child abused by an older relative can go on to be an abuser him or herself, whether to relatives or to others, and the cycle of abuse is repeated in the next generation.[1] An incestuous relationship can thus seep both horizontally, damaging the proper bonds between family members,[2] but also vertically as damage done in one generation is replicated in some way in the next. It is the opposite of the outward-looking family relationships, which have more positive horizontal and vertical effects.

The family of Antigone in Sophocles' play exhibits many characteristics of incestuous families. Everything in Oedipus' family is turned in on itself, as mother and son are also husband and wife, and children are also their father's half-siblings. The Greek prefix *auto-* ('self-') is repeated throughout the play (e.g. 1, 51, 55–7, 172, 306, 863–5, 900, 1175, 1315) and this is a family whose crimes and sufferings are decidedly self-inflicted.[3] These twisted connections damage them as individuals and the proper family bonds between them, and, because they are the royal family of Thebes, they also damage their city.[4]

At the start of the play, Thebes has just undergone a civil war caused by strife between Oedipus' two sons Eteocles and Polyneices, and Ismene's description of the way that the brothers turn their violence against one another at the gate of Thebes, by running each other through with their swords (*Ant.* 55–7; cf. 14) encapsulates the incestuous way that Oedipus' family turn in on, and destroy each other: 'think . . . of how in one day by some cruel twist of fate each of our brothers killed the other! At their own hands!' Civil war between brothers is an analogue of incest, as combatants turn inwards on themselves the aggression that, in Greek thought, should more properly be turned on enemies: in Aeschylus' *Eumenides*, for example, one of the benefits that the Eumenides promise to Athens is an end to civil war with the implication that the presence of war against external enemies will harness natural aggressions in the city and turn them outwards (Aeschylus *Eumenides* 975–87). Although Creon and his wife and son are technically not part of Oedipus' incestuous union with his mother Jocasta (Creon's sister), they are still part of the broader family, and the corruption caused by Oedipus has spread to him. As the chief male of this family and ruler of his city, the decisions for good or ill that Creon makes within his family will affect the city at large (cf. 659–62). By the end of the play, his wife, son and three out of four of his nephews and nieces are dead and there is no sense that Thebes can easily regenerate.

Incest in one generation can damage the next ones. While the characters of Greek literature frequently address one another by referring to their parents' names, in *Antigone,* the repeated connections of Antigone with her father Oedipus take on an extra significance given their uniquely problematic family connection. Almost the first thing Antigone mentions at the start of her play is the 'sins of Oedipus' (2); at 379–80, she is described as 'poor Oedipus' child', while at 471–2, the Chorus comment: 'Her father was headstrong. The girl is headstrong, too.' The Greek word used for father and daughter here is *ōmos,* which literally means 'raw', but in an extended sense of 'savage', it may hint at Oedipus' two fundamental familial transgressions of parricide and incest.[5] In an ode almost in the middle of the play (582–625), the Chorus offer an extended reflection on Oedipus' family, and how the ruin rolls down its generations relentlessly like the endless waves of the sea. In Antigone's long exchange with them (806–943) as her death comes ever nearer, the Chorus repeatedly ascribe the misery in which she finds herself to her origin from Oedipus. At 853–6, they tell her:

you dared
to go
too far
  child
and
you crashed against

the hard wall
  of justice

you're paying
the blood-price
for some ancestral crime

Her 'daring' must primarily be the burial of Polyneices, but it is hard not to reflect beyond the initial meaning of the Chorus' words and interpret her transgression as somehow related to, and of a piece with her father's original transgressions. In her reply to them (858–71), though elsewhere in this scene (e.g. 838–41) she is quite antagonistic to the Chorus, she agrees that her family origins are the cause of her troubles now:

grief for my father
  a grief that never fades
grief for the heavy fate
  that crushes
  all my family

a father
  sleeping with his mother
a mother
  sleeping with her son
a union
  whose result was me

and now
  curs'd and
  unmarried
i am going
  back home
  to them

and my brother too
you made a luckless marriage

and now you're reaching out
  beyond the grave
to kill me too

When Antigone is trying to persuade Ismene to help her bury her brother, she claims that she is offering her a test of whether or not she is *eugenēs* ('worthy of your noble birth', 38), but no offspring of such a union could ever be regarded as truly well-born. Polyneices and Eteocles are also repeatedly damned for their origin from an incestuous connection, most memorably by Ismene (55–7) and again by the Chorus (143–7):

two
  cursed
  brothers

both levelled spears
which both
  sank home
and so
  shared birth
became
  shared death

Their incestuous beginning is deeply tied to the identities of Oedipus' children and is repeated throughout the play, as though it encapsulates something innate about them, something that they can never slough off. The corruption born of Oedipus' original act transcends its generations, bringing ruin to all, and in fact can only stop when almost everyone over whom it has fallen is dead, at the end of the play. Because they are the children of Oedipus, the most polluted man in all of Greek mythology, that pollution clings to them without hope of release and keeps working in their lives to devastating effect.

Incest can arise from flawed perceptions of acceptable sexual partnerships and the confusion of categories or lack of appropriate boundaries between adult and child.[6] Just as Oedipus' choice of sexual partner was wrong (though unwitting) and he was destroyed for it, so Creon and Antigone somewhat more consciously confuse other categories through flawed perception. By so doing, they will destroy themselves and their family: indeed, at 622–4, the Chorus state that

the bad course
appears good
  to those god
  wishes to destroy

As Oedipus' brother-in-law, Creon is not as directly connected with the incestuous family group created by his sister's union with Oedipus as Eteocles,

Polyneices and their sisters are, but the corruption in the house will prove uncontainable and spills over onto his line as well.

At the start of the play, Oedipus is dead and the city has been saved from destruction by Polyneices, one of his two sons who attacked it. Both the Chorus in their *parodos* (100–61) and Creon are optimistic that the dark days of Thebes are at last over, but Oedipus' sins will prove impossible for the next generation to escape through Creon's disastrous decision to refuse Polyneices any sort of burial, and this initial flawed decision has ramifications that he cannot imagine until it is too late to halt the consequences. Eventually the corruption engulfs his wife and son, and Thebes will have endured one more disastrous ruler. In his first speech (162–91), however, Creon expresses sentiments about leadership that many of Sophocles' audience would have found acceptable and even admirable: in fact, one fourth century source, Demosthenes 19.247, actually quotes his words as a paradigm of good counsel for leaders. But at 192, Creon links these acceptable principles with the very different principle that it is acceptable to treat Polyneices' corpse with disdain and cruelty: the word he uses to link the two principles to one another is *adelpha* – literally, 'as brothers of', using a word with particular resonance for this problematic family. While the word is not uncommon in Greek, the word sounds 'off-key'[7] in the context of what he is about to say. After his first bad decision, Creon becomes increasingly embattled and determined that he is right and Antigone and her defenders are wrong: the more resistance he experiences, the firmer he is in his decision to uphold the original decision. In a sense, he has created his own reality in which he is convinced that his point of view is right: in incestuous or sexually abusive houses, perpetrators frequently claim that what they are doing is normal and right.[8]

Creon's initial decision is born of flawed perception and from a confusion of categories, even as it attempts to create clear demarcations between the two brothers. But it is not so simple to distinguish good brother from bad brother with complete clarity, given the circumstances preceding their war with each other, or to make their fates such opposite ones. More importantly, the rights and wrongs of leaving a corpse unburied in the world of the living, depriving its owner of the right to journey to the world of the dead, clearly transcend human judgement and, as Antigone says (449–55), are a matter for the gods as well, and Creon does not have the power that he thinks he has to determine such matters. He confuses other categories as well, so that he treats people as animals to be yoked (291–2), as iron to be shattered or as horses to be bridled (473–8) and claims the free people of Thebes as his own slaves (478–9; cf. 738).

The moral intuition of others in the city, according to both Antigone and Haemon, is that Antigone is right to resist Creon's judgement and bury her brother. The horrific punishment that Creon undergoes in the loss of his wife and son would tend to support this judgement. That said, we are only told that the city supports Antigone by potentially unreliable claimants,[9] and in fact, the Chorus, who at least partly represent the people of Thebes, seem notably unsympathetic to her. Moreover, while Antigone believes that the gods agree with her decision to bury her brother, their response to her proves more complex than she assumes it will be at the start of the play. While ultimately, Creon is punished, and she is therefore vindicated, the complete lack of comfort or encouragement the gods offer her while she is alive for apparently following their orders is striking. By the last time we see her, she is at last uncertain of her position (925–8) and claims: 'I did the moral thing, but they're calling me immoral' (924; cf. 74), a phrase that sums up an essential ambiguity about what she does.

The ambiguity surrounding Antigone's burial of her brother has been the subject of countless scholarly articles, and for centuries the relative merits of Creon's and Antigone's positions have been debated without any universal consensus.[10] One reason for this lack of consensus may be because this central question of the play is connected with the incestuous nature of Antigone's birth. Her corrupted beginnings cannot ever be transcended, so that even though she is right to go against Creon's decree and bury her brother, she simply cannot be allowed to live to adulthood and fulfil her destiny as a woman to marry and reproduce. There is too much corruption in her family to let any more generations replicate yet more disaster. Antigone and even her sensible and virtuous fiancé Haemon therefore will not bring another accursed generation born of Oedipus' stock into the world. Thus in the second half of the play, Antigone replicates symbolically her own father's incestuous journey backwards rather than forwards. A normal path for a woman in Greece is out of her father's house, into the house of another male where she will give birth to new children in a new family alliance. But Antigone will not be married, she will not have children, and the last time we see her is on her way going into a cave where she will spend a living death apart from all company or humanity. Her journey into the cave is a journey to Hades and the land of the dead, Hades' chamber, and it is also a journey into a womb-like but barren place. In a similar fashion, when he married Jocasta, Oedipus too went backwards into his own mother's womb in the initial act from which his cursed children came into the world. Antigone even hints at this at 863–8:

a father
  sleeping with his mother
a mother

sleeping with her son
a union
whose result was me

and now
curs'd and
unmarried
i am going
back home
to them

Antigone is extremely attached to her dead brother. Already at a very early stage of the play, she is fixated upon the fact that it is *her* brother (45–6) who has died, expressing a strongly possessive attachment to him which makes the details of Creon's proclamation of no concern to her. Later in the play, at 900–3, she emphasizes her exclusive responsibility for tending the dead corpses of both her brothers, but especially Polyneices: 'When you died, I held you in my arms. I laid you out. I poured offerings at your grave. And Polyneices, too. Just now I honoured you as best I could.' While it was normal for women to tend the corpses of the dead, Antigone implies that she and she alone performed this task. Twice in the play, the smell of Polyneices' rotting body is mentioned, at 1080–3 and by the guard at 412, for whom it is deeply unpleasant. But Antigone was apparently entirely undeterred by that smell when she buried her brother, even though she would have been in very close proximity to it. Familiarity with, and even embracing, the smell of bodily corruption is another analogue for incestuous corruption.[11]

While she spends all her time and emotion on her dead brother, she speaks harshly to her living sister: she says she will hate her (93) if she refuses to help with the burial, and later in the play, when Ismene is belatedly trying to support her and share in her punishment from Creon she is cold and sarcastic (543, 549) and refuses to imagine that Ismene herself might also regret their brother's treatment. Her relationship with Haemon is similarly strange. While later in the play, she laments in general terms her failure to marry and have children, she never mentions her fiancé by name or shows any apparent love for him or regret that she will lose him. Although Haemon never mentions Antigone specifically in his speeches either, he is attached enough to her to quarrel with his father over her and eventually to kill himself over her corpse, and others vouch for his love for her (568–72, 627–30, 632–3).

Some of the language she uses to describe her relationship with her dead brother is striking. In lines 73–6, she states, 'I'll lie with him, a loving sister with her loving brother.' The word she uses for 'lie with' – *keisomai* – does not automatically have sexual connotations, but when seen through the filter of an incestuous family incapable of normal, fruitful relationships it may acquire them, especially as it is used twice in four lines, so that the unusual repetition emphasizes the bond and the physical closeness of their bodies.[12] She describes her act here as being one of 'a law-breaker perhaps, but one with principles' (74; cf. 924), a paradoxical phrase that exemplifies the way that Antigone confuses, or mixes categories. Antigone's incestuous nature drives her to confuse categories and makes her love the corpse of a dead brother more intensely than a live sister or fiancé.

One especially striking image that encapsulates the intensity of Antigone's feelings towards her brother comes at 423–5 as the guard describes her reaction to discovering Polyneices' bare corpse. She makes a sound like a mother bird lamenting her empty nest.[13] In itself, this is not an unusual image for a grieving woman.[14] The image of Antigone as mother and Polyneices as baby bird is obviously touching, but its implications in the context of their ancestry are also complex and even sinister.[15] Antigone is not a mother, and will never be one. Instead, her dead brother is the 'chick' to her mother bird, and, resembling her father, she confuses the categories of parent and offspring. At 905–12 she attempts to explain her single-minded devotion to burying her brother:[16]

> Because – even if I'd been a mother and it was my *children*, or if it had been my *husband* who'd been killed, whose corpse was lying out there decaying, even then I'd *never* have done what I did. I'd never have gone against the power of the state. And why not? What law would I be following? I could marry again if my husband died. I could have a child by someone else. But my mother and father are both dead, and I can't get another *brother*! Ever. So that's the law – the law of nature.

For Antigone, husbands and children are replaceable and brothers are not, but since marriage is about the unions of two different houses, so as to create new bonds and a social unity in the city, it is potentially subversive and perverse for a woman to privilege a relationship with her own brother over such considerations. However, this is just what we should expect from a woman who is herself not the normal product of two separate households but just of one.[17] The normal relationships beyond the family that would be proper for a non-incestuous family are not as attractive to her as the primary relationship that she has formed before ever reaching the stage of leaving home and creating a new, exogamous, healthy union. The argument Antigone makes here also resembles that of the Persian Intaphernes' wife, who chooses to save her brother from death rather than her children or husband (Herodotus 3.119.4–6): if the traditional dating of Herodotus' *Histories* is correct (see Introduction), it is possible that the audience would have recognized this as a perverse choice associated with the Persian 'other' and condemned Antigone for it.[18]

The corruption in the heart of the Theban royal family and in their ideas of marriage and productive relationships recurs in Creon's dialogue with Ismene at 568–72. At 568, she points out that Antigone is his own son's fiancée, apparently aghast that Creon is not taking this into account, but Creon replies that there are 'other furrows' for him to plough; apparently the object of Haemon's affection does not matter, which again suggests a kind of confusion, as though choice of sexual partner has no real meaning. To this, Ismene points out that her sister and Haemon are uniquely suited, and when Creon continues to refuse to take this into account, in her next line (572) she addresses Haemon directly, lamenting his heartless treatment by Creon. Manuscripts ascribe this line to Ismene, but the editor of the first printed edition of Sophocles gave it to Antigone and many editors and translators have followed that lead, on the grounds that the line is more appropriate in the mouth of Haemon's fiancée. But it would be highly unusual in Greek tragedy for a *stichomythia* (dialogue between two characters) to be interrupted by just one line from another, and preserving the manuscript's attribution of the line to Ismene shows once more the essential oddness of Antigone's relationship with Haemon.[19] Not she, but her more conventional sister Ismene is able to feel sympathy for Haemon and acknowledge their prospective union. Haemon's fate is especially sad: though he tries to reason politely with his father and help him to change his mind (635–761), he fails and ultimately falls prey to rage, violence and irrationality (762–5, 1231–9). Although he is not directly in Oedipus' incestuous line, even he is infected with the corruption and will not be allowed to live.

The perversity of the relationship of Haemon and Antigone is perfectly expressed in the messenger's description of Haemon's death (1234–41).

> And then . . . poor boy . . . furious with *himself* . . . he didn't hesitate . . . he strained his muscles hard and drove the knife to half its length into his own ribcage. And then, before his senses failed, he hugged her to him in a last embrace. He fought for breath. He gasped. He coughed a stream of blood which trickled black down her white cheek.
>
> They're in each other's arms, both dead. The poor boy's married now in death.

In a horrible perversion of his once-imagined wedding night with Antigone in the palace at Thebes, Haemon penetrates himself with his own sword and spurts out, not white sperm and the possibility of new life attendant on it, but red blood, as the dying man coughs and defiles the white cheek of a dead woman in the marriage chamber of Hades. Everything is sterile here, a simulacrum of what it should be.[20]

Secrecy is endemic to incest,[21] because if an incestuous relationship is brought to light, that is usually its end. Secrecy depends on people not talking about a topic or silencing those who attempt to do so. In Sophocles' other Oedipus plays, attempts to silence questions of Oedipus' origins and identity are notable: in *Oedipus Tyrannus*, both Jocasta and the shepherd – who knows who Oedipus really is – beg Oedipus not to go further in his inquiry or try to divert the conversation (*OT* 1060–72, 1144–69), while at the beginning of *Oedipus at Colonus*, Oedipus' true identity is only dragged out of him by the insistence of the Chorus (*OC* 208–23). There is less obvious silence in the *Antigone* – in fact, Antigone actively rejects Ismene's urging her to bury her brother silently (84–5) – but Creon's account of the royal succession at Thebes is striking in the way that he glosses over its extreme complexity, so as to imply a normal and uneventful path from Laius through Oedipus to his sons to himself (165–9).[22] Critics have also noticed the way that the guard is so unwilling to speak to Creon: his language is rambling and it takes some 20 lines before he will reveal what has happened, so that Creon has to drag it out of him (223–47): as an ordinary Theban, he is affected by the troubles of the royal household and he is frightened of the king's tendency to anger and blame (cf. 388–95).

Because of her attachment to her brother and other dead family, Antigone's boundaries between life and death are not clear-cut, so that she consistently expresses a desire for death throughout much the first part of the play: 70, 462–6, where she connects her desire to die with being 'surrounded on all sides by suffering'; cf. 555, 559–60. In the second half of the play, she frequently says that she is going to marry Death (cf. 653–4) or describes the rocky cave where she is to be entombed as a 'marriage chamber'. At 804, the Chorus states that she is approaching the *pagkoitan thalamon*, the 'marriage bed of death' (cf. 832–3) and Antigone echoes this phrase at 810–16:

but hades
  where we all must lie [*pagkoitas*]
  for all eternity in death
is drawing me
  down
  alive
to the shores
of the river acheron

no marriage songs
  for me
no hymn sung
  for my veiling
no
  i'll be
  the bride
  of acheron
  and death

While the analogy between marriage and death for women is commonplace in Greek thought, and it features in epitaphs for unmarried women,[23] it takes on a rather different connotation when used by a woman who claims to seek death and gives so much of herself to a relationship with a dead brother. She complains that she is unlamented by loved ones (847, 876, 881–2). All normal affections are over for her, but this is hardly surprising given that her primary emotional relationship is with a dead brother. At 891 she addresses her cave: 'My tomb. My marriage bed! My rock-cut home.' The real marriage to Haemon and the new home with him, which were her prospects at the start of the play, are far away. Instead, she describes herself both as the bride of death, while also lamenting that she is 'unmarried' (867), and will obtain

no tears
no family
no marriage now

just sorrow

(876; cf. 916–18). She is both bride and not bride and laments that she is neither among the dead nor the living (851–2; cf. 868). In this, of course, she is the mirror image of her brother, also somewhere between this world and the underworld. Both have been tainted by the confusion of categories endemic to this incestuous family.

Antigone gives up her own life in favour of her dead family, and at 898–9, she imagines their response to her arrival in Hades: 'I have such hopes! My father hugging me so tenderly. My mother loving me.' Perhaps she is trying to console herself by imagining their imminent welcome to her now that she realizes that death really is near at hand. At the beginning of the play, Antigone had seemed so certain that she was right, refusing to entertain any counter-argument against her position, that it is reasonable to imagine that she also assumed that she would eventually be vindicated by the gods before her death. No such vindication has taken place and at 902, she seems to complain that the reward for tending Polyneices was after all illusory: 'Just now I honoured you as best I could. And now I face my punishment. But I was right to honour you.' By 925–6, her doubt that she made the right decision is clearer, in some of the last words she says in the play: 'Well, if that's what the gods think, too, I'll soon find out the error of my ways.' But when viewed through the filter of the incestuous nature of Antigone's family her earlier words at 898–9 also indicate once more the excessively close connection that Antigone has with her relatives that makes her unable to function normally in the world of the living.

The corruption of relationships and of decision-making that has run through the play is given powerful and graphically unpleasant physical expression by the report of Teiresias after Antigone has gone to her fate. He is blind, but he heard from the birds, who are traditionally the prophetic messengers from gods to men, 'a horrid screeching, angry and cacophonous. I could tell that they were tearing at each other, ripping at each others' flesh with talons dripping blood' (1001–3). The birds are doing to one another what Oedipus' sons did to one another before this tragedy began, and while that civil war is over, Thebes' trials are far from finished. Teiresias, the prophet whose insight is far greater than Creon's or Antigone's, is actually frightened by what he hears and attempts a sacrifice to communicate with the gods once more, but no fire blazes up on the altar. 'Instead, from the embers, a sticky discharge oozed, dripping from the thigh-flesh folded round with fat, smouldering and spitting. The gall sack burst, exploded, shooting bile high in the air, and the liquefying thighs were left bare as the fat contracted' (1005–11). The image is repulsive, and uses words such as *mudōsa* ('sticky', 1008; cf. *mudōn*, 410) and *etēketo* ('oozed', 1008; cf. 906), which recall the references to Polyneices' putrefying corpse earlier in the play. The rites have failed: Thebes is sick[24] and quite literally God-forsaken as a result of Creon's obstinacy. The altars and hearths of the entire city have been tainted by the birds and dogs with the remains of the rotting corpse of Oedipus' sons (1016–18). When Creon refuses to take Teiresias' warning seriously, the prophet warns him explicitly of the consequences of the confusion of categories that he has made by keeping a live person dishonourably in the tomb and a dead person above earth 'giving it no rites of burial, giving it no gifts of burial, giving it no sacrament whatever.' The form of this line (1071) in Greek – *amoiron, akteriston, anosion nekun* – resembles the form of Antigone's own description of her unnatural life at 876, *aklautos, aphilos, anumenaios* ('no tears/ no family/ no marriage now') and the description of Polyneices' fate at Creon's hands, *aklauton, ataphon* ('unwept, unburied', 29). Creon can expect that one of his own family will be sacrificed in recompense for what he has done. At 1080, Teiresias goes further and warns that what has happened in Thebes is having repercussions even beyond it: 'every hostile city seethes with hatred for you, every one whose mutilated citizens you've left unburied for the dogs or beasts or for the birds to flap their wings and carry back the stench of their pollution to their cities and their altars.' The corruption is seeping far and wide and threatens to go far beyond the royal family of Thebes.

Even when he does at last repent and agree to end the sufferings of Antigone and Polyneices, Creon has gone too far down the wrong path for him to return satisfactorily and without further damage to his family and city. The Chorus privilege the rights of the still living over those of the dead, and urge Creon first to go and release Antigone from her cave and then bury her brother's corpse (1100), but Creon reverses the actions, burying the body and only afterwards going to the cave. It is true that he could not have been expected to know that Antigone will kill herself, and meanwhile the source of pollution is spreading frighteningly,[25] so it is perhaps not fair to blame him entirely for this decision. Equally, his quandary here over which action to take first is entirely of his own making: like Antigone at the beginning of the play, he is caught in a trap where no decision is trouble-free. Soon a messenger arrives on stage and reveals what has happened (1155–71), describing a man who has fallen as Creon has fallen as 'a dead man walking' – a telling description in the light of the pervasive imagery of confusion of life and death in this play.

Only once Creon has buried Polyneices' mangled body does he go to the 'marriage chamber' (1205) to find Antigone. He hears crying: the word used at 1206 (*kōkumatōn*) recalls the word used of Antigone (*anakōkuei,* 423) when she first viewed her dead brother, and will be picked up in the messenger's description of Creon's reaction on first seeing his son in the cave (*anakōkusas,* 1227). In the last chamber, they find Antigone hanging, while Haemon holds her. The reasonable, persuasive Haemon of most of his previous encounter with Creon is no more. Now he is maddened by grief, and while Creon was angry with what he saw as his insubordination earlier in the play, this is nothing to what he sees now: his child is rolling his eyes, spitting at him and, far from being the eloquent and persuasive young man of the earlier scene, he says nothing and can only draw his sword and turn it upon himself, leading to the extraordinary image partaking of death and sexuality (1234–41) that was discussed earlier. Oedipus' two sons turned inwards by turning their violence on one another, Haemon turns a sword upon himself, and Eurydice will also kill herself with a sword (1315) when she hears of Haemon's death, all of them the victims of a series of actions and decisions in which they had no original part but which came to determine their own fate, as the effects of these relentlessly overwhelm them in a pile of corpses at the end of the play. Creon is distraught, and fully accepts that his actions led to what has taken place, even as he says at 1340 that he 'didn't mean to kill' either his son or wife. In this, of course, he resembles the one who began Sophocles' account of this terrible and sad family. Like Creon, Oedipus did not mean to do what he did. The history of an incestuous family has a horrible habit of repeating itself.

Sophocles' rendition of the Oedipus story was not shaped by modern psychological understanding, but by highly traditional Greek ideas, such as that of the ancestral curse and of the effect of *atē* (584, 614, 624–5), the 'inescapable complex of delusion, error, crime and ruin.'[26] But incest itself is a kind of *atē*: one crime begets another as the abused turn into abusers, often with dire effects that spread beyond the original family grouping to others and leading to many damaged relationships between family members or their partners and children or other people in their orbit. Sophocles' treatment of the *Antigone* story transcends its time and culture and one can only admire the depth and complexity of insight that he brought to his portrayal of this family: *polla ta deina* ('there is/ much that is/ miraculous', 332) indeed.

Notes

1 Cooper and Cormier (1982). It is not inevitable that an abused child turns into an abuser, but children who have been abused are statistically more likely to be abusers themselves than those who have not.
2 Kluft (2011); Gelinas (1983).
3 Griffith (1999) 132; cf. Benardete (1999) 2.
4 Sourvinou-Inwood (1989) 140.
5 Tyrrell and Bennett (1998) 72; Segal (1981) 34, 224–6.
6 There is no simple cause of incest or other sexual abuse, but current research suggests that a cognitive element may influence such behaviour: Faupel (2014); Courtois (2010) 39.
7 Griffith (1999) 160.
8 Young (1997).
9 Sourvinou-Inwood (1989) 146.
10 Griffith (1999) 28–34 offers a notably even-handed approach to the question in which neither Antigone nor Creon is entirely culpable or innocent.
11 Cf. Benardete (1999) 53.
12 Griffith (1999) 135.
13 The word used for 'nest' is *eunē*, a word that is frequently used of a marital bed in Greek: Homer *Iliad* 24.130; Sophocles *Trachiniae* 109.
14 For example, Sophocles *Trachiniae* 105 and *Ajax* 629; see also Aeschylus *Agamemnon* 49–59.

15 For other sinister readings of the image, see Tyrrell and Blake (1998) 66–8.
16 On the difficulties of this passage and earlier scholarship discussing it, see Neuberg (1990).
17 Beer (2004) 77. See also Benardete (1999): 111–13 who sees Antigone as another Jocasta in this passage.
18 Sourvinou-Inwood (1989) 146.
19 Griffith (1999) 217.
20 See also Seaford (1987) 120–1, comparing the similarly shocking and perverse imagery of Aeschylus *Agamemnon* 1389–2.
21 Allen (2012); Kluft (2011).
22 Benardete (1999) 23–4.
23 Seaford (1987) 106 n. 11; Neuberg (1990) 68–9.
24 Goheen (1951) 41–5 discusses the imagery of sickness and healing that runs through the play.
25 Griffith (1999) 329.
26 Griffith (1999) 219.

5

The Two Sisters

Hanna M. Roisman

Sophocles is known for his antithetical style, which probably reflects contemporary sophistic rhetoric, and *Antigone* is the most antithetical of all Greek plays.[1] The tendency to set up contrasts can be seen both in the balanced debates with which *Antigone* abounds and in its character drawing. The binary relationship between characters has already been pointed out by many scholars, who tend to emphasize the conflict between Antigone and Creon. However, it is the secondary characters, such as Ismene, that often reveal the intricacies of the major figures, partly by allowing them to explain their motivations, although the lesser roles themselves are not devoid of individual characterization.[2] The contrast between Antigone and Ismene is secondary to the clash between Antigone and Creon, but without the subsidiary arguments between the sisters, we would not be able to understand fully how Antigone's rigidity and passionate idealism leads to her antithetical discourse with Creon. It is the opening encounter with Ismene that reveals Antigone's most profound characteristics.

I will discuss the interaction between Antigone and Ismene first, drawing some comparisons with the interplay between Electra and Chrysothemis in Sophocles' later play *Electra*. Antigone and Ismene spar together in two scenes, in the prologue (1–99) and at the end of the second episode (526–81). Between their disputes the audience hears Creon's proclamation before the Chorus, his interactions with the Guard before and after Antigone is caught (162–445), his confrontation with Antigone (446–530), and the intervening choral odes.

I. *Antigone* starts with the protagonist's address to her sister Ismene. The scene takes place in Thebes in front of Creon's palace, which was once the palace of Oedipus, the father/brother of the sisters. The city has just been delivered from a great peril. It had been besieged by an Argive army, the allies of Polyneices, who came to retrieve his rule from his brother Eteocles, then in control of the city, but on the day before that on which the play is set, Polyneices and Eteocles slew each other in battle. Six other leaders of the besiegers were also killed, and the besieging host has fled in the night. At dawn Antigone asks her sister to come with her out of the palace, in order that they may converse alone. She tells Ismene that their uncle Creon, the brother of their mother Jocasta, is now the ruler, and has issued orders that Eteocles, who defended the city, be honourably buried (see below), but that the body of Polyneices, who attacked the city, be left on the plain outside the walls of Thebes, for dogs and birds to mangle. Any citizen who dares to disobey the edict will be stoned to death. Antigone declares to Ismene that she is resolved to defy this order and bury their brother Polyneices. She seeks Ismene's help in her undertaking. Ismene vainly tries to discourage her sister, but Antigone goes forth, alone, to execute her decision. With no helper, however, she is able to offer only a symbolic burial by covering Polyneices' corpse with a light film of dust (256). Knox suggests that this symbolic burial may have brought with it 'a sense of inadequacy', which in turn brought her back a second time and in broad daylight to pour libations on the corpse.[3]

Antigone's approach to Ismene could be seen as spontaneous and impromptu,[4] yet it is also nuanced. Antigone craves Ismene's support: after all, she needs someone to help her lift the body and lower it into a properly dug grave. To that end, she does everything she can to be convincing. She is very careful in her first ten lines not only to announce the news to her sister, but also to establish their common ground, a standard tactic in persuasive rhetoric. The first line both establishes their close relationship and expresses affection. She calls Ismene *koinon autadelphon* which literally translates as 'my connected-by-common-origin / kindred, very sister', in our translation: 'Ismene! Sister! Blood of my own blood!' Every word in this opening line suggests endearment, but *koinon* may also allude to common interests. Thus the elaborate expression of endearment establishes an atmosphere of unity and mutual support, which Antigone underscores in the next five lines. She speaks of their common past of suffering and endurance. The awkward, twisted syntax of lines 2–3, with the double question, communicates Antigone's current anguish and draws attention:

> Has Zeus — wait! Tell me! Can you think of any punishment that Zeus is not afflicting on us two [*nôin*], the last survivors, for the sins of Oedipus?

The grammatical form *nôin* she uses underscores further her *koinōnia,* her spirit of oneness or solidarity with Ismene. Greek has a grammatical system to indicate a dual number in addition to singular and plural, often used of pairs that the speaker considers a unit. It does not have to be employed for two persons instead of the regular plural, and Sophocles uses both systems to indicate a pair.[5] The dual, however, is often used for emphasis, and in our case the grammar contributes to Antigone's purpose of forming a tight union with Ismene, in the hope of making Ismene identify with her goals. Where the dual does not fit, Antigone uses the possessive adjectives '*your* sorrows and *mine*' (6) to cement their common lot. In the passage above, Antigone uses the dual when she asks Ismene whether she knows of any evil emanating from Oedipus that Zeus has not yet inflicted on the two of them, 'the last survivors' of Oedipus' house. Further along, both sisters speak of themselves and their two dead brothers in the dual (13, 21–2, 50, 61–2), since they think of themselves and their brothers as an inseparable unit. Creon uses the dual for the sisters as well, calling them 'two demons' before realizing that in fact they were not like-minded at all regarding the burial (533). However, once Ismene refuses to aid in burying Polyneices, Antigone stops using the dual, in a grammatical reflection of the rupture between her and her sister, thus reinforcing her isolation for the rest of the play.[6]

After making their shared experience and lot abundantly clear, Antigone moves to the news:

> Have you heard of this new edict (*kērygma*) that they're saying the General's just broadcast to the city and the people (*pandēmōi polei*)? Do you know anything about it? . . .
>
> 7–8

Antigone's announcement to Ismene is a remarkable piece of rhetoric. A few points are of particular interest. First, Antigone does not use the word *nomos*, 'law' (usually a written law),[7] for Creon's edict, here or anywhere in the play, but the more temporary term 'order' (*kērygma*), literally 'an announcement', an emergency decree announced by a herald. In contrast, however, Ismene will refer to the decree as a *nomos* (in line 59). A second point of interest is that Antigone does not refer to Creon as *tyrannos*, a civil ruler, the title their father carried as a ruler of Thebes, but calls him *stratēgos*, a general, the natural term for a fifth-century Athenian to use in designating a military commander. By so doing, Antigone emphasizes Creon's military role, the crisis just past, and his resulting broad sweep of authority. Thus from the start Sophocles presents Antigone putting 'her proposed act of burial in the worst possible light'[8] by making clear that she intends with full awareness to disobey an edict categorically demanding observance.

Antigone seems to frame her report carefully. She uses the rhetorical device of *hypohora*, in which the speaker poses a question, the answer to which she knows and proceeds to give the answer to. She also prefaces her report by noting more than once that what she is relaying she has not heard first hand: she has heard 'rumours' (*phāsi* 'they're saying', 7, 27, 31; *legousi* 'they're saying', 23). This insistence, however, is unnecessary, since it would be obvious to Ismene that Antigone could not have been on the battlefield where the edict must have been first announced.[9] It is only later that Creon comes and announces it to the Chorus, to the city elders, and thus to the public. Why does Antigone emphasize the derivative nature of her information? Is she highlighting her superior knowledge of the outside world as a rhetorical strategy? Or does she mean to provide cover for the confused report she is about to present to her sister?

The confusion starts in lines 7–8 when she says 'they're saying' that the proclamation was made 'just now' (*artiōs*), implying that whatever was ordered by Creon is for the future, but in line 25 she says that the rumour is ('I've heard' [= 'they're saying'] 23) that Creon 'has already *buried* (*ekrypse*) Eteocles, with all due rites and ceremony'. (I would like to thank F. Ahl for drawing my attention to the use of the past tense.) How could that be? The usual understanding of Creon's proclamation is that it concerned what *should be done* rather than what had already been performed. Indeed, when Creon comes out and repeats his decree to the Theban Elders (192–210), he states what he wants to be executed, i.e., that 'Eteocles will be laid to rest . . .' while Polyneices 'no one is to bury him or mourn him' (194–206).[10] It is odd that neither those who heroize Antigone[11] nor her detractors[12] discuss the discrepancy between what Antigone has just relayed as having already happened to Eteocles' corpse, and Creon's proclamation to the elders about what he wants to see happening to the brothers' corpses. Is Antigone herself confused, or is she trying to mislead and manipulate Ismene on purpose, and if so, why?

It is possible of course that Antigone is so distraught that she identifies the proclamation with what it mandates. One could also assume, however, that presenting the proper burial of Eteocles as a *fait accompli* in contrast to the abandonment of Polyneices to rot and feed the birds, while in line with the antithetical style of the play, is not a mere slip of the tongue. The statement makes the situation appear more dire and more alarming, calling for immediate action on the part of the sisters. That is to say, Antigone wants to hurry and incite Ismene to take action at once. This slight prevarication would not necessarily mean that Antigone is an altogether crafty or person, but simply a sister who wants at all costs to give her fallen brother a proper burial, and therefore does everything she can think of to achieve that goal. In fact, such dishonesty might not indicate much beyond the usual depiction of female characters as turning intuitively to guile when confronted with powers they cannot control.[13] After all, it is clear that Antigone feels utterly helpless.

After the death of her father and brothers, Creon is not only her legal 'guardian' (*kyrios*, Just, 1989, 29–38), being her maternal uncle, but also her political ruler. Furthermore, he is set in opposition against one of her beloved brothers, and therefore against her, as she sees it. Thus, true to her gender, she desperately misleads, even if slightly, the only person who might help her, apparently thinking that truth would not suffice. The repeated careful claim that what she relays is second-hand (7, 23, 27, 31) might suggest that this misinforming of Ismene was indeed not entirely accidental or innocent, but it also shows that even a slight lie, as trivial as it might seem, is so unnatural to her that she feels the need to distance it by attribution to a nebulous rumour.

Indeed while the various rhetorical devices she employs may or may not have been intended to indicate calculation on Antigone's part, they are not unintentional on the part of the playwright: a similar misleading of a sister is replicated in his much later *Electra* (probably between 420 and 410), where it is likely to be part of the heroine's intention. After the Paedagogus/Messenger's description of the alleged death of Orestes in the chariot-race, Electra in desperation comes up with the idea that she and her sister will attempt revenge for their father's murder themselves. She must therefore convince the timid Chrysothemis to join her in the endeavour. After describing their common affliction after Agamemnon's death, Electra tells her:

> But now he's [Orestes] gone, I count on you
> not to shrink from killing, along with me, your sister, the man
> who by his own hand murdered our father:
> Aegisthus.
>
> *El.* 954–7, trans. Roisman

The fact that Electra suggests only Aegisthus without mentioning their mother Clytemnestra deserves our attention. She even puts his name into an enjambment (i.e., she moves it after a line break to the following line) to underscore his presence, making him the sole target of the revenge. As in the case of Antigone, one could see the omission of Clytemnestra as an unconscious slip of the tongue, but it could also be viewed as an underhanded attempt to deceive Chrysothemis in order to convince her to participate in the scheme.[14] Indeed, from previous statements, it is clear that Electra viewed her mother as a full partner in Agamemnon's murder (*El.* 97–9, 205–6, 585–8) and, moreover, that she hadn't temporarily forgotten about her, since she mentioned Clytemnestra only a few moments earlier, in the gratuitous statement that the news of Orestes' death was not displeasing to his mother (929). Later in the play, she admits that she and Orestes planned all along to kill their mother (*El.* 1154–6). Electra's focus here on Aegisthus, the male enemy, better enables her to depict the revenge as a heroic act on the part of brave women, while avoiding confronting her sister with the horror of killing her own mother.[15] Antigone's shading of the truth could be a precursor to Electra's.

Antigone and *Electra* are the only two extant plays where we see pairs of sisters, and in both plays there is at least the possibility of intentional deception. In *Electra*, the later drama, the deceit is more cunning than in *Antigone*, but the presence of misinformation in *Antigone* argues that we might read Antigone's confusing and agitated presentation of the news as purposeful. She is, however, less calculating than Electra, and her inclination to be intuitive and emotional is seen again in her first encounter with Creon, when she brings up the notion of *agrapta k'asphalē theōn nomima* 'the gods' unwritten and established laws' (454–5).

Up to this point, Antigone, Ismene, Creon and the Chorus have each used the word 'law' (*nomos*) to defend their various positions. Antigone uses it in her attempt to sway Ismene to revere the 'law' (23), meaning the rights of the family, and bury Polyneices. For Ismene *nomos* is synonymous with what the ruler decrees, and therefore she follows Creon's edict (59). Creon promulgates his *nomoi* ('manifesto' ['laws'], 191) in his opening address to the elders, and both the Chorus (381–2) and Creon (449) use the term to chastise Antigone as she is led in by the guard. It is noteworthy that until now Antigone has not raised the idea of 'unwritten laws' in support of the burial, even though she had the opportunity to do so: she could have pointed out the extent to which Creon's law/edict defies the unwritten laws of the gods both in her answer to Ismene when the latter identified *nomos* with Creon's edict, and when she, Antigone, tried to convince her sister to collaborate with her. However, she did not. One gets the impression that while Antigone knew why she needed to bury Polyneices – because he is her kin and custom and propriety demand that she bury him (23–4) – she had not yet formulated for herself the theoretical grounds of objection to Creon's edict. Until this point she has busied herself with the burial and pouring libations, having no time for reflection on her stance and motivation. Her act was motivated by instinct and an emotional impulse rather than by reason. It is now, however, as she is escorted onstage by the guard and listens to both the Chorus rebuking her for transgressing Creon's *nomoi* (381–2), and as she hears Creon identifying his 'proclamations' (*kēruchthenta*, 447) with 'laws' (*nomoi,* 449), that she rebels wholeheartedly against the assertion that Creon's broadcasted 'edict' (*kērygma,* 8) is a *nomos*, a 'law' she should obey. The formulation of the idea and phrase 'unwritten laws' have not been developed by her beforehand, but borrowed on the spot from what she hears as she is forcefully led in. Creon's 'law', *nomos*, does not measure up to what she sees as the prevailing laws: the timeless and eternally valid laws, divinely sanctioned, in distinction to the positivistic laws created by men (450–60). These laws do not need to be written or pronounced because they were always there and are taken for granted. She is not opposing the laws of gods against those of men: for her, they are a continuum. By refusing to give proper burial to Polyneices, Creon has transgressed the human sphere of influence, and therefore his edict – or as he would like to call it, his 'law' – is invalid. By obeying the laws of gods she also obeys what she thinks is her duty dictated by kinship. She has acted not from a set of considered principles, but from a semi-articulated idea of devotion to those of her own blood and from an assumed divine awareness. The scene is a forerunner of the one before the execution of her sentence, where Antigone makes a long speech in which she tries to reason out her own motives, as if to clarify to herself why her way was the right one (891–928; in spite of their oddity, no compelling scholarly grounds exist for athetizing lines 904–20, Neuberg, 1990). What is important to note here is that Antigone is reacting to what she hears rather than acting on considered principles. Faced with Creon's legalese, she answers in legalese with carefully selected words. She has twice heard the word *nomoi* referring to the edict, and counters with *nomos*'s derivative *nomimon*, which conveys better the original meaning of *nomos*, 'what is customary', the neuter plural of which, *nomima*, meant usually 'customs'.[16] Her idealistic integrity and knowledge of right and wrong is intuitive. Antigone is reactive, acting on the spur of the moment rather than calculating her best arguments beforehand.

II. The first encounter presented two disparate characters. Antigone's stubborn rigidity, imperviousness and unflinching courage are contrasted with Ismene's pragmatic, realistic and sensible approach. Like her later doublet Chrysothemis, Ismene does not buy into Antigone's attempts to convince her. Her reasoning is sensible and unidealistic: the burial is prohibited by Creon, and there is an edict to that effect. She identifies Creon's decree with the will of the people (78–9), and, reminding Antigone of their family history of suffering, death, disgrace and humiliation, asks whether they too, the last survivors of their family, must die, and die ignobly (49–60). Like Chrysothemis, she points out that they are women, and as such cannot resist those with greater power (61–4). Finally she says she is convinced that the dead will understand that she is constrained by circumstances and cannot participate in his burial (65–8, 78–9).

Ismene does not want to die. She does not want the family to be extinct, and she wants to be like any other citizen. She considers what Antigone wants to do as *amēchanon*, which can mean 'impracticable, unmanageable, impossible', but also 'lacking in resources'. The word appears only six times in the extant Sophocles, five of these in *Antigone,* with three of them in the mouth of the perplexed Ismene (*Ant.* 79, 90, 92, 175, 363; cf. *El.* 140). By telling Antigone 'You've set your heart on the impossible (*amēchanōn erāis*)' (90), Ismene wonderfully captures Antigone's main motivation, and her own as well. She explicitly states that she does not have it in her to act against the will of the people, or as she puts it, she is *amēchanos* 'lacking in resources' (79) for such an act. The difference between the two sisters – between the ruthlessly daring Antigone and Ismene's 'avowed temperamental incapacity to disobey the edicts of rulers'[17] – is reflected in their attitudes towards the impossible.[18] Ismene gives in to the powers that rule her, to what she deems impossible to overcome. Antigone sees the 'impossible' as a challenge she must rise to. Indeed, Ismene depicts her as one who 'hunts after impossibilities' (92).

Thus in the first hundred lines Antigone has shown herself 'to be loving, egotistic, devout, cruel, idealistic, exhibitionist and unfeminine. Some critics have even found her guilty of dreams of incest, of necrophilia or a death wish'.[19] Does Ismene's inability to measure up to her sister's intransigence and extremism necessarily make her a faintheart? That is unlikely. Ismene does not strive to be heroic, and unlike Antigone she does not believe that declining to risk her life for Polyneices is unforgivable in the present circumstances (65–8). Her reasoning is both more nuanced and more cogent than Antigone's rather fanatical absolutism. By infusing subtlety into his characterization of Ismene, Sophocles successfully exposes the frightening simplicity of Antigone's thinking, through her reactions to what Ismene says.

The prologue also features the theme of 'right thinking', which runs throughout the play.[20] Antigone, Ismene and Creon all think that their own way of thinking is the right one: this is what makes their clashes so terrible and so uncompromising. Thus Ismene voices her admonition to Antigone to think rightly as early as line 49, where she tells Antigone to 'think' (*phronēson*) about the fate of her family, while Antigone reacts to Ismene's reasonable persuasion by presenting the burial of Polyneices as a privilege Ismene has now forfeited (69–77; cf. 538–9). Her line of thought demands a heedless devotion. The theme of 'right thinking' also appears in *Electra*,[21] where the difference between the timid Chrysothemis and rebellious Electra is highlighted when each urges the other to 'think rightly', while meaning completely different things by the term. Electra means 'think morally' (*El.* 346), Chrysothemis 'think sensibly' (*El.* 394, 890, 1038; cf. 384). Ismene, however, differs from Chrysothemis in terms of what she designates as 'right' or 'wrong' thinking. Chrysothemis admits that justice is on Electra's side, not in her own recommendation to do nothing (338–9), and also that her own choice not to pursue vengeance has its benefits. As she says 'But if I'm to live as a free person, I must heed those in power in everything' (339–40). Ismene, on the other hand, refuses to see Antigone's action as one that is completely necessary, right, or just. She is sure that the dead would find no sense in disobeying those in power (67–8) and that Antigone's act would result in eradicating the family completely, proving more disastrous than not burying Polyneices. Unlike Chrysothemis, who is not harmed by Electra's intransigence, Ismene seems to realize the danger Antigone's act would bring upon her. Such awareness would explain why she is raging in the palace; and her suspicion proves correct.

III. The two sisters differ not only in their assessment of their circumstances and about how to react to Creon's edict, but also in how they view friends and enemies. At the end of her initial approach to Ismene, Antigone differentiates between 'friends' (*philoi*) and 'enemies' (*echthroi*), a distinction that becomes the focus of the debate of the prologue. In her first speech, Antigone says: 'Don't you know that sanctions more appropriate to enemies (*echthrōn*) are being imposed on our own family (*philous* 'friends')?' (9–10). The word *philos* means 'friend' but also 'near and dear', while *echthros* denotes an 'outsider', 'enemy', more specifically 'personal enemy'. *Philos* is also the Homeric possessive adjective meaning 'one's own',[22] which introduces the same personal element that *echthros* has. Thus, for Antigone, Creon's edict is an affront to what is 'hers'. Her world view has a personal centre: whoever counters her wishes or disagrees with her principles is her personal enemy, and this is what Creon has become to her by proclaiming the edict.

For Antigone the issue of burial is a personal matter with no connection to the *polis*. When she explains to Ismene what Creon has done, she says: 'Creon has no right to keep me from my [own] family' (48). The emphasis falls on 'my own' (*tōn emōn*). Polyneices, as her brother, belongs to her, and Creon cannot separate them. Her religious duty to bury kin pales in comparison to her realization that what was/is hers has been disrespected. She tries to incite Ismene to the same thinking when she tells her:

> This is the edict (they say) that the 'good and noble' Creon has announced
> — for *you and me*, yes, yes, *for me*.

On Antigone's double mention of herself, Brown notes:

> It is not often in Greek tragedy that we are invited to assess a speaker's motivation and character from such implicit clues as this. There is a note of fierce pride here: Antigone takes the decree as a personal insult, assuming without hesitation that she, at least, could not possibly be expected to obey it.[23]

Similarly, O'Brien writes: 'An.'s repetition here conveys her incredulous indignation that Cr. should think she would obey such an order. The phrase also shows she fully understands that she will pay dearly for her piety to her brother's corpse.'[24] What needs to be added is that she tries to include Ismene in her self-identification with Polyneices, but Ismene resists her emotional urging.

Antigone does not give up at once, however. When Ismene asks if she is going to bury Polyneices in spite of the prohibition, Antigone tries again to pressure her sister into her own way of thinking:

> He is *my* (*emon*) brother – and *yours* (*son*), too – and with you or without you I *will* bury him. *I* shan't be seen to have betrayed him.
>
> 45–6

However, Antigone's repeated efforts are to no avail. For Ismene, Creon's edict does not resonate as a personal harm. She sees herself as part of the *polis*, and Creon has forbidden the *polis* to bury Polyneices (44, 47). Furthermore, while at the very beginning of Antigone's address to her, Ismene echoes her sister's reference to her brothers as *philoi* ('family', 11), she does not use this term for them again, either in the prologue or later in the play.

The first encounter between the sisters ends in a stalemate. Antigone does not persuade Ismene to participate in the burial of Polyneices, and Ismene fails in her efforts to dissuade Antigone from attempting the impossible and failing miserably. When we see the sisters together again, we shall see further into Antigone's intransigence and Ismene's despair.

IV. When Creon blames Ismene, too, for the burial, as Antigone's collaborator, and Ismene declares she is willing to bear and share the blame if Antigone agrees, Antigone rejects her, saying that she and Ismene do not share in solidarity (*koinōnia*), because Ismene refused to do the deed (538–9, 546). She then withdraws from Ismene what she once had thought unified the two of them (1). She accuses Ismene of being a *philē*, a loved one who belongs to her, in words only (543).

While Antigone brings her fate upon herself, Ismene is forced by Creon to accept death, and when Antigone gives her an option for escape, she still chooses, for no clear reason, to die with her sister. Some think she wants to die because she dearly loves her sister,[25] an argument supported by her claim that she cannot live without Antigone (548, 566). This could be true of course, but it is also noteworthy that Antigone has locked Ismene into an impossible position. Creon's description of her acting in the palace 'like she was deranged. As if she'd lost her senses' (*phrenōn*, 492) surely indicates strong emotion, perhaps that she felt trapped and desperate. After her first meeting with Antigone she not only understood that she could not dissuade her sister, but also that Antigone would die if she buried Polyneices. Being realistic and pragmatic, Ismene had no heart to disobey the edict, and her care for the dead and unburied, even in her second encounter with Antigone, does not go beyond the four words in line 545, when she asks Antigone to allow her *ton thanonta th' hagnisai* 'give the dead the honour that I owe them' – said most probably only in order to appease her sister (see below). Yet she must have understood that the train of events set in motion by others would leave her with no immediate family. As she can do nothing to prevent the collision, in maddened frustration she chooses to die.

When Ismene returns to the stage after Antigone's capture, Creon asks her if she was party to the burial or knew nothing about it (534–5). The double question is significant because of Ismene's choice to ignore the second half. She could have told the truth – that she knew about Antigone's intention but took no part in the burial – but this would hardly have made her less culpable in the eyes of Creon. Instead she chooses to be actively implicated in the burial, although she qualifies her statement by saying: 'If she [Antigone] agrees!' (536). Why did she feel compelled to add these words? Two possibilities come to mind. Ismene may be motivated by her love for Antigone. If she believes that Creon won't execute them both, she hopes to save them both by claiming a share of blame. A more subtle interpretation is suggested by Kamerbeek[26] – that for dramatic effect, Sophocles constructs the attempt to save Antigone in incremental stages. This construction necessitates Antigone's active participation in the conversation, which Ismene secures by offering to die with Antigone and at the same time trying to involve Antigone in her [Ismene's] own death. Ismene is giving Antigone an opportunity to show some repentance, which might mollify Creon and thus save both of them. Once her offer falls on deaf ears, Ismene attempts to get on Antigone's good side: '*I'm not ashamed* to stand beside you . . . to face whatever sentence he hands down' (my emphasis, 540–1). Kamerbeek correctly points out (on l. 540) that she actually means '"I make it a point of honour" to partake in your sufferings.' However, Antigone's offensive reply that she does not love one who shows her love only in words (543) tells Ismene that she must have underestimated the degree of her sister's inflexibility. Antigone does not allow Creon the slightest opportunity to retreat from his position. Desperately, Ismene tries again, this time bringing up what is dearest to Antigone—the proper rites for Polyneices. She claims that by dying with Antigone, i.e., sharing blame for the burial, she can also share retroactively in the rites Antigone has performed for their brother (544–5). Ismene certainly knows that in actuality she never touched the corpse or physically performed any of the ritual entailed in burial. Antigone's sharp retort accords with the senselessness of the request, when she says that Ismene should not claim as her own a deed she never put a hand to (*ethiges*, 546). Creon was clear in what he forbade: burying the corpse with proper rites, that is to say, among other things, touching it.[27] To Ismene's horror, what has transpired in her exchange with Antigone is not only that Antigone refuses to take her cue for defence, but in her replies has completely exculpated Ismene in the eyes of Creon. Since Antigone has not controlled the line of conversation,[28] it is unlikely that she intended to absolve Ismene; all she intended to do was to refuse her the honour of martyrdom. Yet she has done both; and when Creon agrees with the Chorus that Ismene should be spared, he repeats Antigone's claim that Ismene did not touch the corpse (*thigousan*, 771). What Ismene has achieved is a complete exoneration – of herself alone.

Ismene's offer to die with Antigone is a courageous act. For a person who admits to wanting to live, a decision to die voluntarily is certainly not timorous or spineless, as Ismene is commonly accused of being. She could not anticipate that Antigone's replies would save her life. Indeed, before the Chorus intervenes, Creon is still willing to put her to death as well (668–71). In a subtle and brave way, she plies the craft of a politician in trying to save her sister. When she understands that Antigone will not cooperate with her, she turns to Creon, bringing up the last card she has: Antigone's engagement to Haemon. This argument fails as well. If anything, it hardens Creon's resolution to kill Antigone, whom he now sees as an evil woman he does not want to be the bride for his son. Ismene fails, not because her strategy isn't smart, but because she is between two people rigid in their doctrinaire positions. Her sister is too engrossed in her own emotions to cooperate, and for Creon family counts much less than it does for either sister. Ismene has thus failed twice in spite of her best efforts. She is not the protagonist; we tend not to discuss secondary figures in the same terms as the great tragic characters, but hers is a true tragedy of intent and purpose.

Ismene's act of courage is not as simple and obvious as Chrysothemis'. The relationships of the two non-heroic characters with their 'heroic' sisters are also slightly different. Chrysothemis agrees that Electra's way, seeking revenge at all costs, is the right way, and she would have done the same, had she the power. As things are, however, 'to lower my sails', she says, is the right choice, and she would like Electra to do the same (*El.* 333–40). When she secretly replaces Clytemnestra's libations for Agamemnon's tomb with gifts from herself and Electra, as Electra requests, she does not do anything contrary to her beliefs, nor does she endanger herself significantly. The sisters see eye to eye on what larger action ought to be taken, but only one, Electra, pursues it. This is not the case with Ismene and Antigone. Ismene does not see the burial of Polyneices as categorically necessary. She is sure that those below would understand her need to obey those in authority as trumping her obligation to pay them the proper rites (65–7). Risking her life in order to save both Antigone and herself for what she neither did nor believed in doing displays her courage as much as her love for Antigone. Her despair at the thought of living without her sister is a mark not of selfishness, but of the deep love she feels for the only remaining member of her family. Ismene emerges as a much more noble and respectable figure than Chrysothemis. As Winnington-Ingram has stated: 'Ismene is infinitely more interesting, subtle and attractive than the time-serving Chrysothemis.'[29] All the same, she is doomed to oblivion. The last we see of her is when she is taken inside with Antigone in line 581, and the last we hear about her, although not by name, is in line 771, when Creon retracts his death sentence on her. She is the sister who will live, according to Antigone (555), and yet when Antigone is walking to her death, she sings: '... leading men in Thebes look on me now *the last of the royal family* ...' (my emphasis, 940–1). For Antigone, Ismene seems not to exist anymore. Is Antigone so focused on the loss of her brother and her own impending death that she has forgotten Ismene altogether (909–12)? Has she written Ismene off because she sees Ismene's refusal to help her bury Polyneices as a collaboration with Creon (549)? Sophocles does not tell us, and we will never know. It is noteworthy that nothing is said of Chrysothemis, either, after her last confrontation with Electra and her entrance into the palace in line 1057, except for Electra's general comment on the women in the house as: 'useless, burdensome women who are always in the house' (*El.* 1241–2). It may be that we are meant to see Ismene and Chrysothemis as silent and conforming women who have done nothing on their own[30] and are forgotten because they do not measure up to their 'heroic sisters'. However, would their obscurity be understood as entirely bad by the spectators? Or is the playwright anticipating by ten years Pericles' definition (as quoted by Thucydides) of female excellence: 'greatest [glory] will be hers who is least talked of among the men, whether for good or for bad' (Thuc. 2.45)?

Antigone and Electra, on the other hand, have much more in common. Bernard Knox states that the two share 'the distinction of being the most intransigent of the Sophoclean heroes'.[31] Both are self-willed, unrelenting, stubborn women who are determined to do what they think is right. Yet between these strong sisters there are also some differences. While there is innocence and basic integrity in Antigone, who must be younger than the Sophoclean Electra, there is none in the latter. Antigone chose to bury her brother on the spot: a natural and instantaneous decision fortified by the need to give her kin the proper rites. Her act does not involve deliberately harming any of her family. Ismene's dismissal of the absolute need for the burial only underscores Antigone's determination to perform the funeral rituals and her obsession with accomplishing them, as shown by her return to pour libations. Whether this action is explained by her sense of inadequacy arising from not having actually interred Polyneices[32] or by the dramatic effect of having two impacts from the burial,[33] it draws attention to Antigone's absorption in personal relationships and her indifference to politics, to the point of self-immolation. Electra, on the other hand, is caught between two strongly held moral imperatives: the duty to avenge her father and the injunction against killing a parent. In this case, vengeance means killing the person who gave her life, an instinctively heinous act that violates the most basic of human ties and obligations. There was no way out for Electra. Antigone might have escaped after her first symbolic burial of Polyneices. She might also have followed Ismene's lead by showing remorse and trying to soften Creon. That she dared not only to act but to maintain the rightness of her action is probably the reason Antigone has captured the world's attention and still serves as a symbol and example for any defiant person, whether a rebel or an idealist. To a large extent it is the very *choice* to act, thrown into relief by Ismene's quite reasonable refusal, that makes Antigone a heroine universally acclaimed.

Notes

1 O'Brien (1978) 1–3.
2 Kirkwood (1994) 100–1; Bowra (1952) 79–82.
3 Knox (1964) 64.
4 Kirkwood (1994) 120–1.
5 Morwood (1982) 2–3.
6 O'Brien (1978) 2–3.
7 Knox (1964) 94–9.
8 O'Brien (1978) on l. 8.
9 Blundell (1998) on l. 34.
10 For such understanding, see e.g. Brown (1987); Blundell (1998); Lloyd-Jones (1998); Grene (1991) ll. 211–24; Willink (2007) who suggest emending *ekrypse*, in a way that will accord with Eteocles' future burial.
11 E.g. Winnington-Ingram (1980) 117–49; Gellie (1972) 29–52, 117–49; Kitto (1954) 126–7, (1956) 149–78; Lesky (1979) 104–5; Whiteley's reply to Sourvinou-Inwood (1989).
12 E.g. Agard (1937); Minadeo (1985); Sourvinou-Inwood (1989) esp. 138–42.
13 Zeitlin (1996) 356; cf. Eur. *Andr.* 565–7, where Andromache's lying is gratuitous.
14 For the various views, see MacLeod (2001) 142 n. 7.
15 Roisman (2008) on line 957.
16 Knox (1964) 97.

17 Gellie (1972) 31.
18 O'Brien (1978) on l. 90.
19 Gellie (1972) 32.
20 Cf. Griffith (1999) 41–3.
21 Roisman (2008) 102–4.
22 Knox (1964) 80; Griffith (1999) 41.
23 Brown (1987) on l. 32.
24 O'Brien (1978) on l. 32.
25 Gellie (1972) 31; Winnington-Ingram (1980) 134–5.
26 Kamerbeek (1978) on l. 552.
27 Cf. touching the corpse in Soph. *El.* 1136–42, Eur. *Phoen.* 1669–70, 1693–4, 1699–700.
28 *Pace* Adams (1957) 51.
29 Winnington-Ingram (1982) 237.
30 Lefkowitz (1981) 4.
31 Knox (1964) 67.
32 Knox (1964) 64.
33 E.g. Kitto (1956) 152–8; Kirkwood (1994) 70.

6

Antigone's Change of Heart

Ruth Scodel

At *Antigone* 806, Antigone makes her final entrance, and she delivers an extended lament (806–82) for her coming death and failure to marry, in lyric dialogue with the Chorus:

> no marriage songs
>   for me
> no hymn sung
>   for my veiling
> no
>   i'll be
>   the bride
>   of acheron
>   and death
>
> 806–16

Her invitation to pity is conventional. Yet Antigone has earlier seemed positively to welcome death. In her initial argument with Ismene, she has shown no concern at all for her life. She has insisted to Creon:

> In fact, I count it as a benefit to die before my time. When you live like me, surrounded on all sides by suffering, how can death *not* be a benefit? For me, to face death is inconsequential.
>
> 461–4

To Ismene, she says 'You're going to live. But me? I chose long ago to die' (555).

Yet in this scene, the previously fearless heroine sings as if in losing her life, she loses something of great value. Scholars have discussed the inconsistency, but it has been less important in their discussions than another apparent contradiction. To Creon, she delivers a grand speech on the unwritten laws:

> To my mind, 'edicts' that a mortal man like you imposes have no authority to supersede the gods' unwritten and established laws. No! They're eternal – not just for today or yesterday – and no one knows when they were first laid down.
>
> 453–7

Later, however, she says that she acted according to a much narrower reasoning:

> Because – even if I'd been a mother and it was my *children*, or if it had been my *husband* who'd been killed, whose corpse was lying out there decaying, even then I'd *never* have done what I did. I'd never have gone against the power of the state. And why not? What law would I be following? I could marry again if my husband died. I could have a child by someone else. But my mother and father are both dead, and I can't get another *brother*! Ever. So that's the law – the law of nature.
>
> 904–12

This passage has led to endless discussion, and indeed some have wanted to remove these lines as an actor's interpolation.[1] They are clearly adapted from the story of the wife of Intaphernes that Herodotus tells (3.119; Herodotus very probably gave public performances of his work-in-progress in Athens in the 440s). When the men in her family were arrested and condemned to death after plotting a coup against King Dareius of Persia, Dareius allowed Intaphernes' wife to choose one relative whose life would be spared. She chose her brother, because she could have another husband or son, but would never have another brother, since her parents were dead.

This reasoning is counter-intuitive and paradoxical even in Herodotus – that is the point of the anecdote. Fifth-century Greeks loved clever and surprising arguments. The adaptation in *Antigone* seems strange, since it is hard to see how the irreplaceability of a brother compared to a husband or son would provide a reason to bury him. Antigone's change in reasoning here has been a topic of intense discussion because political and ethical questions have so often framed how we approach the play. Antigone's lament has not demanded quite so much attention, because it seems to indicate an emotional rather than an intellectual change.

Interpreters have tried to explain the emotional change, of course.[2] Creon says 'Even the brave try to escape when they come face to face with death' (580–1), so perhaps Antigone responds to the imminence of her death, which she did not really imagine earlier. Her lament emphasizes the peculiar nature of her death. While she had previously identified the penalty set by Creon as public stoning (36), now in reality she will be entombed alive to die of thirst and starvation, in a suspension between the living and the dead that excludes her from either. Perhaps Sophocles simply preferred the pathos of the lament, so standard a feature of tragedies, to consistency of character.

John Gibert, in his book *Change of Mind in Greek Tragedy*, excludes *Antigone*, because the change in her feelings and her reasoning occurs only after her decisive act.[3] Gibert puts the change in Antigone in the same category as Clytemnestra's evocation of the *daemon* of the house in Aeschylus' *Agamemnon* and Orestes' vision of the Furies in *Libation Bearers*. Clytemnestra, after murdering her husband, argues that she did not really commit the murder – a vengeful spirit of the family killed Agamemnon in her shape. Orestes has in turn killed his mother, and then sees angry goddesses who torment him. These characters, he suggests, understand more fully what they have chosen and the consequences of their choice. They may perceive more clearly the alternatives to the choice that they made, as Antigone's lament implicitly acknowledges that she might have married and had children. These scenes do not, however, resemble tragic episodes in which characters change their minds about future actions. It is surely important that Antigone changes her attitude only after her action. She is not quite like the other tragic figures whom Gibert cites, however, since her lament directly contradicts her earlier insistence that death would be a good thing for her.

She also never, anywhere in the play, gives any sign of seeing her choice as irrational. This is especially significant because other characters repeatedly, very explicitly, make this accusation. The Greek of Ismene's 'know that even though I think you're wrong' is more literally 'know that even though you are irrational' (99). Creon says 'One's just shown herself to be irrational; the other's been irrational from birth' (561–2), and the Chorus sings about the destruction of the family

by thoughtless words
by minds
  possessed
  by madness

601–3

Antigone never accepts this argument. Near the end of the lament, the elders of the Chorus say:

you dared
  to go
  too far

They suggest that the cause of Antigone's fate lies in divine anger at the family:

> you're paying
> the blood-price
> for some ancestral crime

The spectator is likely to infer that they are continuing in the line of thought of the earlier song. Divine anger has disturbed Antigone's mind, rendering her incapable of distinguishing good from bad. Antigone responds to the suggestion that her family history has led to her own early death, addressing her brother:

> and now you're reaching out
> beyond the grave
> to kill me too

She does not, however, in any way accept the Chorus' interpretation. Polyneices is killing her because his war against Thebes was the cause of his death and Creon's decree. Antigone may list the horrors of the family as a way of explaining why the gods have not intervened to help her, but she does not even consider the possibility that she has been unreasonable.

This chapter will argue that both inconsistencies can be better understood if we think carefully about what exactly Antigone changes in her presentation of herself, applying some of the categories of 'Attribution Theory', the branch of social psychology that examines how people explain both their own motives and those of others.[4] Sophocles did not know about modern experiments that reveal some of the characteristic biases in attribution, but his culture was extremely sensitive to rhetorical self-presentation. All claims about motive in Greek tragedy are likely to have a rhetorical dimension. Speaking characters are often trying to persuade others to a particular course of action, and their accounts of their motives and those of others are likely to be rhetorically inflected. Simultaneously, except when they are overcome by emotion, they are engaging in 'impression management', seeking to present themselves in a way that controls a social interaction in a positive way. In highly emotional situations, they may express themselves hyperbolically. Even when a character is using persuasive rhetoric or engaging in impression management, however, the spectator generally accepts that the motives that characters present are genuine unless there is a reason to suspect deceit, although they may be incomplete or exaggerated.

Figure 6.1 presents the psychologist Bertram Malle's account of the possible attributions for actions that speakers regard as intentional.[5] They can offer three kinds of explanation: a reason (belief, desire, or valuing), an

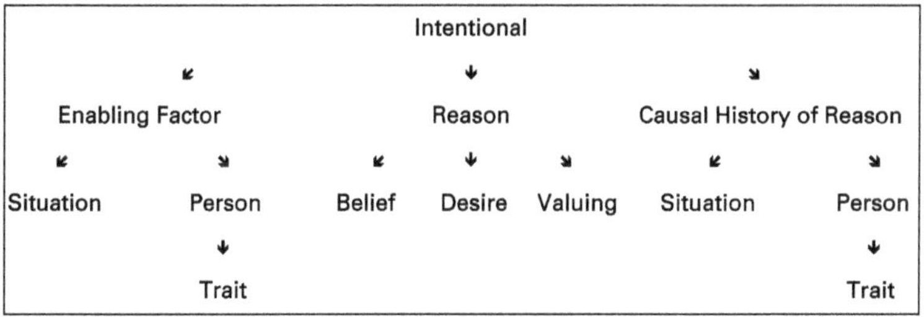

Figure 6.1

enabling factor, or a 'causal history' – not the reason itself, but factors that led to the reason. (Unintentional actions are explained by causes, not reasons.) So if we asked a spectator of the play to offer an opinion about why Antigone hanged herself, the answer might be that Antigone did not want to die slowly (Desire), or that Antigone always acts quickly and fails to consider all possibilities (Causal History of Reason: Trait), or that her belt was readily available (Enabling Factor: Situation). Experimentally, people offer more belief reasons for their own actions than they do for the actions of others, and they are less likely to hedge them by marking them as beliefs. Belief reasons seem the most rational.[6]

Antigone's reasons for her actions, both before and after the burial, are Belief reasons. However, there is one significant ambiguity in Antigone's beliefs in the first part of the play. When Teiresias says that the entire city is polluted and unable to communicate with the gods because of Polyneices' corpse, he must imply that *all* corpses should be buried. Antigone herself, however, never distinguishes a general principle about funeral rites from the obligations of family. It is easiest to understand her, however, if we make this distinction. On this view, Antigone believes

1. The gods want all the dead to receive funeral rites.
2. The relatives of the dead, and only the relatives, are normally obligated to provide them.

There is abundant evidence in Greek literature that someone who accidentally encountered an unburied corpse could feel required to carry out a burial ritual under the threat of pollution. The Guard refers to such an assumption when he describes the first burial:

> The corpse was covered, not like a proper burial, but with the thinnest film of dust – like it was someone trying to avert a curse.
>
> 255–6

This supernatural danger, however, only applied to strangers who were in close proximity to the dead. Greeks were not expected to worry about the funeral rituals of outsiders. Antigone speaks about the unwritten laws of the gods:

> It wasn't Zeus' law. Zeus didn't broadcast it! No! And *Justice* didn't lay down laws like this for mankind either – Justice who shares *her* kingdom with the gods beneath the earth. To my mind, 'edicts' that a mortal man like you imposes have no authority to supersede the gods' unwritten and established laws. No! They're eternal – not just for today or yesterday – and no one knows when they were first laid down. Me, I had no intention of failing in my obligations to the gods, just because I was afraid of some *man*'s whim!
>
> 450–9

Her unwritten laws probably include both that the dead should be buried and that relatives should perform the burials.

Ismene does not offer counter-reasons, evidently agreeing that Polyneices should receive burial. Because Creon has forbidden the burial, however, Ismene invokes another set of reasons why she will not participate. These could be summarized as:

1. Creon is a legitimate authority who should be obeyed
   1A. Women, especially, should not oppose male authority
2. The death penalty provides a sufficient reason not to fulfil the usual obligation, and both gods and the dead will therefore be forgiving
3. Burying Polyneices is impossible.

The first is a Belief. The second and third are Enabling Factors, but they also depend on beliefs. Antigone simply disagrees with Ismene's underlying belief on the first point, as her speech on the unwritten laws shows. She also disagrees on the third, when she says 'Don't say that' in response to Ismene, 'But there's no point even starting the impossible'. Antigone clearly does not believe that it is impossible. However, she also appears to believe that even if she believed the burial to be impossible, she should still attempt it, so she discounts impossibility as an enabling/disenabling factor. This makes sense only because her reasoning about her own death is unusual.

The speech to Creon quoted already indicates a valuing reason. Antigone sets a very low value on her own life. Her valuing, though, could easily be framed as a belief and put in syllogistic form:

> Major premise: Life is worth living when an individual is not surrounded by evil circumstances.
> Minor premise: I am surrounded by evil circumstances.
> Therefore my life is not worth living.

To Ismene in the prologue, she offers a different, revealing formulation: 'For such a noble cause I'll die a noble death.' The word translated 'noble' implies in Greek 'famous': Antigone desires to die in a way that will cause her to be positively remembered. She values such a death. Although Ismene sees a violation of Creon's edict as an act against the citizen body (in 79, 'But to go against the power of the state'; 'state' is literally 'citizens'), the kind of nobility Antigone wants requires public validation. Glorious death is a Greek aristocratic good. Whether we call Antigone's view of her likely death a valuing or a desire, it again depends on a belief – the belief that burying her brother is the noble thing to do, and that others will admire and praise her for it. To choose to die when the alternative is to show oneself a coward is a rational choice, because it is better to die with a good reputation than to survive without one.

At the very beginning, Antigone frames Ismene's choice whether to help her as a revelation of moral worth:

> And in a moment you'll show me what you're made of – if you're worthy of your noble birth or if you're just the runt of a great family
>
> 37–8

This 'showing' will not be confined to Antigone. The city and the future will see Ismene's character. The topic recurs in Antigone's central scene with Creon:

> But . . . What could I have done to win myself a better reputation than bury my own brother? Everyone here would agree with me, if they weren't so frightened.
>
> 502–4

We do not have enough information to know how Antigone weighs her reasons – the low value on life itself, the high value on reputation. The two are in some tension with each other. Someone who chooses to die because she does not want to live will not receive much credit for the heroic choice of honour over life, for it is precisely because life is so precious that risking it for honour is admirable. But whenever continuing to live rather than die entails a loss of honour, the choice to die is both rational and honourable.

People change their judgements both because external circumstances change and because they themselves change. When Antigone sings her lament, the audience has heard confirmation from Haemon that people in Thebes are praising her, 'Doesn't she deserve the highest honour?' Haemon may not be an unbiased witness, but nothing contradicts his account. Antigone, however, has not heard any praise.

When she said that the elders of the Chorus have failed to support her only because they are afraid, she may have been trying to provoke them into less cowardly behaviour. If they protest at all (it is uncertain who speaks 574, 'So that's your decision? She must die?'), their intervention is feeble. She, of course, does not know that when the Guard first reported the burial of Polyneices, the elders tentatively suggested that the gods might have been involved:

> Sir, I've been wondering for some time . . . Sir, I've been thinking: might this be the gods' work . . . sir?
>
> 278–9

Creon responded with a rant about how impossible it is that the gods should care about their enemy Polyneices, and the elders apparently accepted this argument. Antigone may be wrong in attributing their reluctance to speak for her entirely to fear (a Causal History attribution), although the spectator may well agree with Antigone that they have been intimidated (perhaps as an Enabling Factor). The spectator probably attributes a belief to the elders that Creon has a legitimately very wide field of authority, whatever doubts they may harbour ('You have the power to decree whatever law you wish for the living and the dead alike') and a desire for civic order in Thebes at almost any cost. Furthermore, once they learn that Antigone is responsible for Polyneices' burial, they attribute her actions to a trait of her character ('Her father was headstrong. The girl is headstrong, too', 471–2) and to an irrationality caused by divine anger at her family. Her reasons therefore do not matter to the Chorus, any more than they matter to Creon. Even if they thought Creon's decree was a mistake, and even if they suspected that the gods might have intervened on behalf of the corpse, they cannot sympathize with Antigone.

Interpreters have wondered whether Creon's decision to have her entombed instead of stoned indicates he is concerned that the populace would not be enthusiastic about executing her, since stoning is an expression of the community's rejection of the offender.[7] From Antigone's perspective, the decision deprives her of her one opportunity to impress the people. Her desire for reputation suggests that she hoped for a public spectacle. So the change in the nature of her death is not just horrifying because it puts her in a strange, intermediate position between the dead and the living, and because her end promises to be slow and agonizing. It seeks to make her invisible, and so removes one of her reasons for being willing to die. By the time she delivers the lament, then, Antigone is no longer confident that she will receive the fame that she expected. That leaves only her cost-benefit argument.

It is important that she offers her other reason for being willing to die, the argument that death is a positive benefit in her situation, only to Creon. Her utter contempt for him gives her a motive to claim that he cannot actually do her any meaningful harm, and she can make that claim only by defining death as not a loss to her. To be sure, even if the claim is driven by her will to defeat Creon rhetorically, she surely believes, at the moment she speaks it, that she truly believes this. In her very opening lines to Ismene, she has enumerated the consequences of the sins of Oedipus: 'Pain, torment, shame, dishonour – we've experienced them all.' From the play's opening, Antigone is in an extreme situation, where the deaths of both her brothers have compounded the misery of her origin in incest. She could easily feel that death is the best outcome for her.

Nonetheless, in the prologue she speaks only of noble reputation rather than of the advantages of death. Hence Ismene does not try to convince Antigone that Antigone would benefit from remaining alive, and she does not mention her prospective husband. The goods of life are not an argument against noble death, since they render the death even more noble. In arguing with Creon, however, Ismene raises the issue of Antigone's intended marriage to Haemon. 'How can you kill her? She's engaged to marry your own son!' Scholars disagree about who speaks the ensuing lines, especially 572, 'Poor Haemon! Your father does you such discredit' (most often assigned to Ismene).[8] Whether or not Antigone actually speaks about Haemon, the argument about her marriage suggests that her calculus in favour of death is not the only reasonable calculus she could make. Once she has defied Creon, she does not need to maintain this extreme position. Without regretting her decision to bury her brother, she can acknowledge that she is losing something of value in dying. Indeed, since dying-for-glory and dying-because-life-has-nothing-to-offer are not entirely compatible, she needs to make this rhetorical move.

One reason for Antigone's lament, then, is rhetorical. To some extent, her lament may be directed at the gods. Greeks do not always assume that the gods will respond to human suffering without prompting; the lament brings Antigone's case to their attention. If she had repeated her argument that she had nothing to lose by dying, she would have no real case to make to the gods. However, we may also legitimately infer that she stresses what she is losing, presenting herself as more like a conventional woman, in order to move the Chorus to her side. She appeals to their Theban identity:

this was my fathers' country
you are my country's citizens

If the old men were sufficiently moved by pity, they might, by lamenting with her, put her in the heroic narrative that she has sought. Ironically, however, the elders react to Antigone's lament by promising her fame for the unusual *manner* of her death:

but it's with
  fame and
  honour
that you leave us
  on your journey
  to the dead

Antigone wanted to be famed for burying her brother, and the prospect of a slow and lonely death has nothing glorious about it. The elders offer her honour, but this honour has nothing to do with her actions. She compares herself to Niobe, the traditional image of endless grief, and again the elders treat the similarity as a source of glory:

and yet how wonderful
it is
for a woman
  like you
for a woman
  dead
  like you
to be spoken of
  as sharing in a fate
  that's equal to a god's
not only when
  she lived
but when
  she died

Antigone complains that they are mocking her. For Antigone, evidently, fame for the wrong reason is worse than no fame at all. After Antigone and Chorus exchange their very different views of how the family's history has affected her, the elders conclude:

honouring him
   was honourable

but the powerful
   won't let
power
   be challenged

you were angry
and you knew
   exactly
   what you did
and that
was your undoing

Although they seem to concede that her action could be considered honourable (the Greek is more literally 'showing reverence is a sort of piety'), they immediately undercut any such concession by insisting on the power of the powerful. They clearly mean that respect for power should have been more important than any other consideration and that whatever ethical considerations entered into her decision should not have been significant. They do not mean, in saying she knew what she did, that her actions were a rational choice entitled to respect. On the contrary, if they attribute a rational choice to her, it was the choice to subordinate rationality to anger. She 'knew what she did' in that she knew what the consequences would be, but still followed her emotions. They seem in essence to be saying that even if she acted in defence of real values, since she knew that she would be executed if she buried Polyneices, she has no basis for complaint. If she has sung her lament in the hopes that she could move the Chorus from loyalty to Creon, she has failed. So it is not surprising that in her final song she feels utterly alone:

no friend
no family
   to mourn me

876–7

Antigone, then, has abandoned the analysis that made death preferable to life. She acknowledges that she will die prematurely ('before my life's been lived', 896). The only representatives of the community with whom she has contact, the members of the Chorus, do not offer the kind of glory for which she hoped. 'I'd never have gone against the power of the state', is literally 'against the will of the citizens' (907). Earlier, she sharply distinguished Creon from everyone else, probably rightly. Now, however, she has come to believe that everyone thinks that she was wrong. The audience knows better, and we may be surprised that she does not consider at least Ismene and Haemon as potential mourners. We may think that Antigone, in her loneliness and frustration, is indulging in hyperbole, but we may also wonder whether she is not wrongly attributing to Haemon and Ismene the same subservience to Creon that she has seen in the Chorus. She will receive no funeral ritual herself, and she may assume that Creon will forbid any display of mourning.

At the end of her last speech, she turns to the gods:

> Which of the gods' laws have I broken? Or should someone as ill-used as me look to the gods at all? Will no one come to my defence? I did the moral thing, but they're calling me immoral! Well, if that's what the gods think, too, I'll soon find out the error of my ways. But if the crime is Creon's, I hope the punishment he suffers will be no less than the one that he's imposed on me – unjustly.
>
> 927–8

This speech shows clearly why Antigone cannot maintain her willingness to die. Only the gods can at this point vindicate Antigone. Since she believes that she will not receive appropriate honour from mortals, only divine intervention or vengeance against Creon will provide her with the glory that she requires. The warrior who chooses to face death above dishonour does not have his honour questioned, and he generally has no need of divine anger against his killer, because his community recognizes and honours his action. Antigone, in her final song, calls on the Chorus as witnesses:

> gods
>   who gave us birth
>
> they are taking me
>   away
>
> i've no more time
>   to live
>
> you
>   are the leading men in thebes
> look on me now
>   the last of the royal family

suffering
  at the hands of such as him
because
  i held the sacred
  in respect

She knows that they will not see her as she wants to be seen. But they are the only witnesses she has, and if the gods finally intervene, they will be the carriers of Antigone's reputation.

In her last speech, since the elders insist that she was wrong to have defied Creon, Antigone accepts their premise that Creon's edict was an expression of the public will. She does not, however, surrender her belief that she was right. The Chorus has insisted that her choice was driven by her inherited nature, not by reasons, and although Antigone herself has referred to her inherited character (523, 'I don't want to hate either of them! I want to love them both!' implies that this desire is genetic), she does not regard it as a tendency to irrationality. On the contrary, for her the family past is a cause of difficulty and trouble, but also of pride, of nobility she seeks to equal. Even if the Chorus were to agree that the edict was wrong and that she was objectively right to defy it, she cannot really win glory unless she deliberately chose her action. So she must defend her own rationality. She also at this point has adopted the position that her death is a terrible thing. This is necessary if she is to ask the gods for vengeance, and if any such vengeance is to win her fame.

So she narrows her defence in a final attempt to prove that she acted rationally. It is true, as some critics have pointed out, that Antigone can more easily say that she would not have performed the burial for a son or husband because she has no son or husband.[9] However, it may not be important whether Antigone's self-attribution here is accurate or not. The audience cannot judge how she would have acted had the circumstances been different. Antigone's earlier arguments have been ineffective. The elders may endorse the edict itself and evidently believe that the only reasonable course was obedience, so Antigone claims that she violated the edict only because the dead man was her brother and that she would not have done so otherwise. This does not contradict a belief that the gods want all bodies buried, since it addresses not the principle, but only the individual's obligation to carry it out. Even if it were still Antigone's obligation to bury a dead relative, she would have been constrained by the city, but that in the case of an orphan's brother, the fact that the brother cannot be replaced makes the obligation exceptionally powerful: 'So that's the law – the law of nature. That's why I chose to honour you' (913–14). She tries to move as close as she can to the point of view of the elders without giving up the very core of her claim to be right because she needs to demonstrate her rationality. The elders, however, do not change their view of her:

> she's still
>   distressed
>   disturbed
>
> 929–30

The change between the Antigone of the earlier scenes and the Antigone of the last episode in which she appears is thus both a response to the changed situation and rhetorical. Because the Chorus will not support her and Creon gives her no opportunity to confront the Theban people, her posthumous fame is uncertain. This gives her a reason to lament, but lamenting also constitutes a more 'normal' self-presentation and an argument to both Chorus and gods that her death is unjust. Her final argument narrows her case in yet another attempt to demonstrate her rationality. Yet although the vengeance for which she asks the gods swiftly arrives, the characters on stage seem to forget her.

Notes

1 Neuberg (1990) has a good summary of this debate.
2 Winnington-Ingram (1980) 138–9, considers various possibilities and argues that it is burial alive that drives the change.
3 Gibert (1995) 28–31.
4 A general introduction to attribution theory is Försterling (2001).
5 This chart is a simplified adaptation of Malle (2004) 175.
6 Malle (2004) 175–83.
7 Knox (1964) 72–3.
8 Mastronarde (1979) 95–6.
9 Murnaghan (1986) argues that Antigone places low value on marriage as an impersonal institution.

7

Antigone and the Rights of the Earth

Rush Rehm

Like most theatre performed today, fifth-century Greek tragedy was an embodied form of storytelling, taking place before an audience present in more or less the same space as those enacting the story. In ancient Athens, that space was the outdoor theatre of Dionysus, under the sky, the sun, the clouds and the birds, with actors and Chorus performing on the unpaved, beaten-earth floor of the orchestra. For the performers and audience alike, the earth and the elements surrounded them. Those who came from afar often travelled by boat (the City Dionysia took place in the spring, at the start of the sailing season) and made their way on foot or by cart from Piraeus to Athens. Those from the city and rural Attica travelled overland to the south slope of the Acropolis; from there, everyone walked up through the sanctuary of Dionysus Eleuthereus and into the *theatron*. When they took their seats, or stood on the hillside above the seating area, with the Acropolis at their backs they looked down over the southern part of the city, lying beyond the orchestra and the wooden *skênê*-façade. Depending on their vantage, they could see the city walls and several of the gates; outside the walls, the Ilissos valley and the Callirrhoe spring, source for the nuptial baths in the Athenian wedding ritual; to the east the slopes of Mount Hymettos; closer in, the Ardettos hill; to the south in the distance, the island of Aegina, whose tallest peak housed the shrine of Zeus Panhellenios; towards the west the bay of Phaleron (hidden by the hill of the Nymphs and of the Muses) and the Saronic Gulf.

Members of an unmechanized farming and pastoral community, Athenians and their fellow Greeks lived close to the land, and the theatre and its festivals reflected this reality. Performances themselves were organized around the seasonal demands of the agricultural cycle: ploughing, planting, harvesting and storing. The City Dionysia was celebrated in early spring, following the olive harvest; the Lenaia took place in January; and local deme festivals happened the month before, 'down time' for agricultural fieldwork. Nicholas Jones argues that these local theatre festivals, traditionally called 'rural Dionysia', were more accurately 'agrarian Dionysia', translating *ta kat'agrous Dionysia* (Aristophanes,

Acharnians l. 202) as 'Dionysia linked to agrarian life and culture'.[1] Kollytus, one of the five demes within the city walls of Athens, celebrated its own Dionysia, as did the port of Piraeus, clearly non-rural affairs that reflected the presence of fields and agricultural plots within the city.

Time and again, Greek tragedy evokes the interdependence of human and civic wellbeing and the health of the grain-bearing soil. In Aeschylus' *Libation Bearers*, Electra prays to 'the Earth herself, who gives birth to all things, / and once she has nurtured them receives their increase in turn' (A. *Cho.* 127–8). Eteocles in *Seven Against Thebes* calls on his countryman to defend the city in similar terms:

> Protect your city and the altars of the gods of the land,
> . . . and your children and your mother earth,
> dearest of nurses. For as you crawled as babies
> on her friendly soil, she nurtured you, readily accepting
> the whole burden of your rearing . . .
>
> A. *Sept.* 14–18

Later the Chorus praise their city as that 'delightful plot of earth . . . deep soiled land and Dirce's waters' (A. *Sept.* 304–6). So too, the Chorus in Aeschylus' *Suppliant Women* sing of 'the ever-flowing rivers and the earth deep and rich . . . that teems with wheat' (A. *Su.* 551–5).

At the opening of Euripides' *Suppliant Women*, the Chorus of Argive mothers interrupt Aethra as she performs the Proerosia, the annual Attic ritual for the success of the autumn ploughing. Like Antigone with Polyneices in Sophocles' play, the Argive suppliants want the corpses of their sons in the soil, under ground. By setting the play in front of the temple of Demeter in Eleusis, Euripides invokes the myth of Persephone's abduction and marriage to Hades, her recovery by her mother and the concomitant restoration of the earth's fertility. The play interweaves this mythic paradigm with the Argive mothers' desire to recover their children, along with the opening ritual for the productivity of the Attic soil. Here, as in *Antigone*, the embedded nature of Greek religion makes it difficult to disentangle efforts to appease the gods, the prosperity of the city, effective ritual practice, the health of the earth, and the wellbeing of the family.

Turning from agricultural crops to animal husbandry, recall in *Oedipus Tyrannus* that transhumance – the seasonal change between lowland to upland pasture – brings the Theban shepherd of Laius and the Corinthian servant of Polybus into fateful contact on Mt. Kithairon. In fact, herdsmen appear throughout Greek tragedy: Apollo in *Alcestis*, who has tended Admetus' cattle as punishment for challenging Death; the two shepherds in

Bacchae who witness marvels on Mt. Kithairon; the old Tutor in Euripides' *Electra*, who brings sheep, wine and cheese to the cottage-farm of Electra's husband. The Danaids in Aeschylus' *Suppliants* compare themselves to heifers chased by mountain wolves, lowing to let the herdsman know their plight (A. *Su.* 348–53). The Herald in *Agamemnon* likens the god who unleashes the storm on the Greek fleet to 'a shepherd turned betrayer' (A. *Ag.* 657). As for the fields that feed the herds, Lycus in Sophocles' *Trachiniae* addresses a crowd 'in the meadow where the cows graze in summer' (S. *Trach.* 188–9). In Euripides' *Electra*, Orestes slaughters Aegisthus in the usurper's horse pastures (E. *El.* 623), and the Messenger in *Andromache* offers 'sheep raised in the grasslands of Mt. Parnassus' to Apollo at Delphi (E. *Andr.* 1100–3). Tragedy provides many an image of the plains, hills, rivers and mountain slopes as the source of food and nurture, producing crops and fattening animals in a pattern of fertility, growth and harvest.

It may seem obvious that tragedy acknowledges the earth and calls attention to its importance. But does this awareness translate into the idea that the earth possesses 'rights'? Using that word rather loosely, scholars of ancient Greece claim that Athenian male citizens had the right to attend and vote in the Assembly and respected the rights of suppliants. As far as I can tell however, no Athenian thought of his duty or privilege to attend, address, and vote on the Pnyx in those terms, or that the poor souls who abased themselves in supplication had to be honoured because of some entitlement they possessed. In Euripides' *Suppliant Women* for example, Aethra persuades Theseus to recover the bodies of Argive Seven *not* by appealing to the rights of the suppliant mothers. Rather, she urges her son not to tarnish Athens' self-image as a city that helps the downtrodden and defends traditional Greek values (E. *Su.* 334–46, 523–7). These principles include the belief that the dead – even of the enemy – deserve burial, an issue of cardinal importance to Sophocles' *Antigone*.

As Theseus argues, death ritual represents a time-honoured Hellenic custom, one that aligns with the workings of the natural world:

> and each part returns to the place
> it came from, the breath to the air,
> the body to the earth; for we have life
> only when we live it; then
> the earth that bore us must take it back again.
>
> E. *Su.* 532–7

An appeal to rights plays no part in his discussion of burial, but the recognition of the 'rightness' that bodies return to the earth does. That the earth 'must take life back again' also motivates the heroine of Sophocles' play. Antigone invokes the 'unwritten laws' of the city (S. *Ant.* 453–5) as evidence that these time-honoured customs transcend politics, decrees, edicts and statutes. Such laws are not passed by the Assembly or recognized by the city's courts, although their *a priori* nature brings them closer to our sense of an inherent obligation, unassailable by proclamations such as Creon's.

Scholars of ancient Greek legal practice consider law in classical Athens as broadly procedural (concerned with the administration of justice) rather than substantive (concerned with rights, obligations and offences). Typically written in the form 'if someone does A, then B is to result', Athenian laws focused on the legal actions that should be undertaken by the prosecutor, rather than on the definition of which acts are prosecutable. As Michael Gagarin concludes, the 'rhetorical and performative features' evident in surviving Athenian law court speeches indicate that the trials were 'essentially rhetorical struggles' which were 'generally unconcerned with the strict applicability of the law'.[2] Even if there were some unarticulated notion of rights in ancient Athens (which I doubt), they were not guaranteed by law in the way we understand it.

To speak of someone's 'natural rights' or 'the inalienable rights of the individual' (as in the US Declaration of Independence and the French revolution's Declaration of the Rights of Man and the Citizen) or the 'universal rights of man' (the UN Declaration on Human Rights), would have made no more sense to an ancient Athenian than an appeal to the proscriptions in Leviticus or Deuteronomy. The idea of the 'rights of the earth' would have appeared no less incomprehensible.[3] We will need to go beyond the European enlightenment's interest in inalienable rights, whether by divine or constitutional guarantee, to understand any 'rights' owed to the earth in *Antigone*.

In order to bridge the gap, let me invoke the English homonym 'rites' (*telê*), of which the ancient Greeks had many. Rituals represented a proper way to acknowledge, honour, worship, appease and appeal to powerful forces 'out there' (gods, *daimones*, heroes), and to do the same for the special places associated with those powers (mountains, caves, rivers, meadows, crossroads, groves, springs, peaks, precincts). Greek religious rites also celebrated signal accomplishments (opening a festival, launching a trireme, commemorating an athletic victory), and they marked key stages in biological and cultural development (birth, puberty, marriage, death). If we can find meaningful links between rites (as performed ritual) and rights (as an intrinsic endowment or entitlement), we might better understand the Greek sense of the prerogatives owed to the natural world, and even expand our own sense of what we mean when we speak of the rights of the earth.[4]

In the sixth century, the Athenian poet and statesmen Solon invoked 'the greatest mother of the Olympian gods, black Earth'.[5] Indeed, most polytheistic religions depend on a divine or sacred connection to aspects of what we think of as 'nature'. In his three-volume tome *Zeus*, Albert Cook pointed out a century ago that the Olympian patriarch had more than 40 cult titles, connected with civic and domestic order (justice, the hearth, the city, suppliants, guests, oaths, freedom, safety) but also with the natural world and the elements (sky, rain, clouds, lightning, mountain peaks, springs, the soil's fertility). Over half a century ago in *The Earth, the Temple, and the Gods*, Vincent Scully championed (sometimes fancifully) the interdependence of the Greek architectural response to the gods and to the visible topography and lay of the land.[6]

Although fifth-century Athenians did not conceive of the natural world *per se* as sacred, they did recognize that their lives depended on that world and worked towards placating and harnessing its power. At times, the natural environment seemed wild and threatening, at other times as capable of being tamed and controlled. We find this view powerfully expressed in the 'Ode to Man' in *Antigone* (332–75). A similar anthropology of human progress vis-à-vis nature characterizes Prometheus' account of his gifts to the benighted human race in *Prometheus Bound* (447–506), and in Theseus' celebration of human progress in Euripides' *Suppliant Women* (195–218). Among other things, these passages reflect a realistic response to the wildness of the ancient environment, the lack of Greek industrial capacity, the limitations of ancient technology and the relatively light footprint made by a small human population.[7]

However, this same society recognized aspects, elements and specific locations in the natural environment that demanded respect and that prohibited violation and exploitation. The intermingling of gods and place, of the natural world and the divine, meant that humans played an essential role in investing these places with a sense of the sacred. If some part of the earth deserved to be honoured (reflecting its purpose, location, and/or attendant deity), then that honour was manifest in the appropriate religious rituals that humans performed there. Respect for, and protection of, the natural world were inseparable from the sacralizing instincts manifested in religious rites performed by the human community.

Many gods possessed their own 'precinct' or *temenos*, land 'cut away' from normal human activity and dedicated to the divinity. In our contemporary (and far more profane) world, we might imagine these areas as the ancient equivalent of a park or wilderness area, but one preserved for the relevant god. In Euripides' *Hippolytus*, the title character describes such a place, the *temenos* of Artemis in Troezen:

a virgin meadow,
a place where the shepherd does not dare
to pasture his flocks, where the iron scythe
has never come; no, it is virginal,
this meadow, where the bees pass through in spring.
Reverence and respect [*Aidôs*] tend it, with cool river water.

E. *Hipp*. 74–8

Preserved for the goddess, the precinct lies outside the realm of human cultivation and exploitation. In its pristine state, it remains a place divine and inviolate.

A more ominous version of a grove dedicated to Artemis occurs in Sophocles' *Electra* (566–77). Agamemnon accidentally ventures into the goddess' domain in Aulis and kills a stag, leading Artemis to demand that he sacrifice his daughter Iphigenia if he wishes the Greek fleet to sail to Troy. In some versions of the myth in *Philoctetes*, the hero's suppurating wound comes from a snakebite he suffers when he transgressed the *temenos* of the nymph Chryse. Untainted by human beings (unless they come to offer sacrifice), such sacred places also can offer safety and respite, as Oedipus discovers in the 'inviolable grove of the Furies' (Sophocles' *Oedipus at Colonus*, 37, 39).

Lacking inhabitants and unsullied by human activity, such 'eremitic spaces' (from *erêmos*, 'without people, desolate') occur several times in Sophocles' tragedies, and they play an important role in *Antigone*.[8] Even when not associated with a specific god, these places tend to evoke the sacred. Sophocles' Ajax describes the desolate part of the beach where he intends to purify himself (via suicide, we later learn) as 'a place where no one has ever stepped' (*Ai*. 657). Its untrodden nature suggests a sacred *temenos* and points towards the future, when Ajax achieves his own hero-cult in Athens. We find similar cults that link the place with the ritual honours due the hero at the conclusion of Sophocles' *Trachiniae* (Heracles on Mt. Oeta) and *Oedipus at Colonus* (Oedipus and Colonus).

Sophocles offers a variation on the sacralizing of an ostensibly desolate place in *Philoctetes*. To emphasize his hero's loneliness, the playwright depopulates Lemnos, and 'the word *erêmos* tolls like a bell' in the play.[9] Marooned by the Greeks, Philoctetes lives nine miserable years bereft of human companionship, until the play eventually sweeps him off to Troy at the end. Judging from Philoctetes' descriptions of the hardships he has endured, his island-*erêmos* seems a far cry from a place of respite or sacred communion. By the end of the play, however, he delivers a farewell in which 'the land is addressed as a divine power':[10]

> As I depart, let me call upon the land.
> Farewell . . . home that shared my watches
> and water nymphs of the lush meadows,
> and the deep sound of the sea beating on the rocks
> where often my face was drenched
> inside my cave by the battering winds,
> and often Mount Hermaion sent back to me
> a groan echoing my own voice, as the storm raged.
> But now, Lycian fresh-water springs,
> we are leaving you, we are leaving now . . .
>
> S. *Phil.* 1452–62

No idealizer of nature, the suffering hero comes to recognize his dependence on the natural environment, and his deep connection with the landscape that has been his home and companion.

Having looked at tragic references to the earth as essential to human wellbeing, and at passages in Sophocles where undefiled places evoke divine presence and power, we now can turn to *Antigone*. Creon's decree outlawing funeral rites for Polyneices sparks the dramatic action: 'No one shall bury or lament this corpse, / but they will leave the body unburied, for birds / and dogs to devour and savage, / a shameful sight (*idein*) . . .' (204–7).[11] Creon has Polyneices' corpse exposed on a high plain in the city, so that the Thebans will contrast his treatment with the honours granted his brother Eteocles. As Griffith observes, 'it is not enough merely to deny burial: for the proper public example to be made, the corpse must be *seen* to suffer violence and humiliation . . .'[12] As far as we can tell, however, no Theban freely chooses to view this desecration. That dubious privilege is reserved for the guards or 'watchmen' whom Creon orders to enforce his decree – the terms *skopoi* (215), *episkopoi* (217), *hêmerskopos* (253) emphasize the act of 'spying on', 'looking at' or 'watching over' the corpse.

When the guard reluctantly brings the news of the first challenge to Creon's prohibition, he describes the corpse as 'sprinkled with thirsty / dust' (246–7). Dumbfounded that the body 'had vanished, not in a tomb, but under / a light covering of dust, as if someone wished to avoid pollution' (255–6), the Guard points out that 'no wild beast or dog / had [yet] come and ravaged the body' (257–8). Lacking any sign of a perpetrator, the event seems uncanny. These details lead the Chorus to wonder if 'what was done was compelled by the gods (*theêlaton*) (278–9). That the 'dust' is 'thirsty' (*dipsian / konin*, 246–7) suggests that the earth itself longs for the funeral offerings that Creon has outlawed.

When the Guard returns with Antigone as captive, he describes her appearance in no less numinous terms: 'Suddenly a dust storm / swept across the plain . . . / blotting out the sky. / We had to shut our eyes before this god-sent plague (*theian noson*)' (417–21). When the wind drops, Antigone appears out of nowhere, standing over the body like a mother bird at her nest, orphaned of her young (423–7). Given the mysterious conjunction of natural, supernatural and human elements, the earlier judgement of the Chorus seems incontrovertible – the gods are involved in this apparently natural phenomenon.

Creon does not exert the control he imagines over the physical world, in particular over the ground where he leaves Polyneices' corpse to decompose. The arrival of Teiresias makes this perfectly clear. In *Oedipus Tyrannus*, the blind prophet must be sent for, and he comes reluctantly and speaks against his will. In *Antigone*, however, Teiresias appears of his own choosing, and he speaks without mystification or irony. The body that Creon has exposed will not stay put, for dogs and birds have scattered it across the city (1081–3). The birds, whose cries the prophet used to interpret, now scream incoherently and tear at one another (1001–3). Prophetic rituals run amok (1005–13), and the city's altars, 'stuffed full of carrion . . . / brought by scavenging dogs and birds . . . / refuse to burn' (1016–18). Pollution from the corpse has angered the gods, and they refuse to honour the prayers of the city (1019–20).

Echoing the Guard's description of the dust storm as a 'god-sent plague' (*theian noson* 421), Teiresias states that Creon's decree 'has sent a plague (*nosei*) on the city' (1015). Exposing the body so that 'birds and dogs can devour it' (206), Creon inadvertently spreads miasma across Thebes. Again using *Oedipus Tyrannus* for comparison, note that the horrific plague in that play arises from an unpunished murder. In *Antigone*, however, the actual physical bits of Polyneices' corpse cause the pollution, noxious material that has been 'wrongly placed'. In her classic study *Purity and Danger*, Mary Douglas defines impurity ('dirt') as 'matter out of place'.[13] A dead body in a grave does not pollute, but exposing it on a high plain of the city allows the dogs and birds to scatter the carrion. In *Antigone*, Polyneices' body spreads pollution across Thebes because it has not found its proper place within the earth.

In spite of Teiresias' warning 'Yield to this dead man; / do not keep killing one who is dead and gone' (1029–30),[14] Creon fails to accept that Polyneices belongs under ground in the world of the dead. The prophet also denounces the tyrant's other 'wrongful placement', when he imprisons Antigone in a cavern-tomb and condemns her to a living death:

> You hurl down below one who belongs above (*tôn anô . . . katô*)
> wrongly making a tomb the home for a living soul,
> while to a corpse that belongs to the gods below (*tôn katôthen . . . theôn*)
> you deny burial, the rites of the dead, all that is holy.
>
> S. *Ant.* 106–71

Confusing the living with the dead, Creon disrupts the natural order, doing 'violence against the gods of the dead' who, as the prophet declares, 'lie in wait and will destroy you' (1073–5).

In Greek mythology, Hades (brother of Zeus and Poseidon) is both the god who rules the underworld – and therefore a symbol of death – and the place where the insubstantial dead wander before coming to rest. The finality of Hades' kingdom makes ritual intercession with the god pointless, as the Chorus indicate in the first stasimon (the 'Ode to Man'): humans are capable of practically anything, but 'from Hades alone / they can find no escape' (361–2). The name Hades occurs frequently in the play, along with the idea that the proper place for the dead is 'below', 'underground', 'concealed in the earth', as opposed to the arena of the living, who belong above ground and not, like Antigone, entombed in a subterranean prison.

Antigone contrasts Polyneices' exposure with the burial of Eteocles, 'hidden / beneath the earth (*kata chthonos ekrupse*), honoured among the dead' (24–5). Creon uses similar language for the funeral he prepares for the Theban hero: 'I will conceal (*krupsô*) Eteocles in a tomb with all the rites / due to the noblest of the dead below (*katô nekrois*)' (197–8). Ismene hopes that those 'under the earth' (*hupo chthonos* 65) will forgive her for not joining her sister in her dedication to 'those below' (*tois katô* 75). Antigone knows that 'Hades longs after the laws [or 'customs'] of burial' (519) for both her brothers; 'the dead below' (*katô* 521) feel the same. Condemning her to death, Creon vows that she will 'join the ones below' (*katô* 524), telling Ismene that 'Hades will prevent her marriage' to his son (575) when 'Hades approaches to end her life' (581). Trying to stave off disaster, Haemon offers his father good advice 'on your behalf and behalf of the gods below' (*theôn tôn nerterôn* 749). However, the tyrant remains adamant: Antigone 'will marry someone in Hades' (654).

Creon eventually chooses not to kill Antigone outright, but to send her still living to the underworld, a prisoner beneath the earth:

> I will conceal her (*krupsô*) still living in a rocky cavern . . . / . . . /
> There she can pray to Hades, the only god
> she honours, and perhaps be spared from death,
> or learn too late what wasted effort
> it is to honour the things of the underworld.
>
> 774–80

Making her way to her prison tomb, Antigone considers herself married to death: 'Hades leads me away, still living, / to the shores of Acheron . . . / . . . / I shall be the bride of the river of death' (810–16). She imagines her mother and father 'in Hades below' (911), and the Chorus address her as 'one still living who goes down to Hades' (822).

When Creon finally realizes his error, he races to the plain where Polyneices 'still lay, torn apart by dogs' and performs burial rites, praying that 'Pluto [another name for Hades] restrain his anger in mercy' (1197–1203). Creon then makes his way to 'the maiden's bridal chamber of Hades' (1204–5), only to find his son already in the tomb, embracing Antigone who has committed suicide. After vainly thrusting his sword at his father, Haemon turns the blade on himself, lying with 'his bride in the world below (*katô*) / ... on their wretched marriage bed' (1224–5). In so doing, 'he fulfilled / his marriage rites in the house of Hades' (1240–1). Confronted by the corpse of his son and niece, Creon acknowledges the power of the god whose rites he has failed to honour: 'Unappeasable Hades, you harbour all in the end!' (1284).

Similar to the plain where Polyneices' body lies exposed, the site of Antigone's entombment escapes the control that Creon imagines he has. The rocky cavern lies 'down a track un-walked by men' (*erêmos . . . brotôn stibos* 773). There, he vows, Antigone 'will remain alone and deserted' (*monên erêmon* 887), wasting away in a living death. As discussed above, the very absence of activity and human habitation can lend 'eremitic' space in Greek tragedy a sense of the sacred. Cut off from the mundane world, such a location takes on an aura that can reveal divine presence and power, both beneficent and destructive. So it proves for the underground cavern where Antigone kills herself and Haemon joins her in the 'bridal chamber where all come to rest' (804–5).

Haemon discovers his fiancée 'hanging in the woven noose of her veil (*sindonos*)' (1222). The garment has strong ritual associations with both marriage and death rituals, linking the covering of a corpse and the unveiling of a bride – particularly appropriate for a heroine who sings her funeral dirge as if a wedding hymn (806–16).[15] After cutting Antigone down, Haemon completes the transformation of the cave into the setting for a perverse wedding night:

> . . . He pressed himself hard
> against the sword, and drove it half-way into his side.
> Panting for breath, he hugged the maiden in his arms
> and shot forth a sharp jet of blood,
> staining her pale white cheek
> He lies with her, corpse against corpse . . .
>
> 1235–40

Haemon's final moments with Antigone suggest both *la petite mort* of sexual orgasm and the defloration of a virgin.

When he decides to imprison Antigone rather than kill her, Creon aims to avoid pollution: 'I will hide her, still living, in a rocky cavern, / leaving enough food to escape pollution. / In this way the whole city can avoid miasma' (774–6). He refers to the pollution that arises from shedding kindred blood – for example, when Oedipus unknowingly kills his own father in *Oedipus Tyrannus*. In *Antigone* Sophocles emphasizes blood ties by using words with the root *haim* (as in our 'haematology'), evoked by Haemon's name (literally, 'Blood-being'). Creon vows to punish Antigone or any kinsman who challenges his decree, 'whether she is my sister's child or closer in blood (*hom**aim**onestera*) / than all of ours tied to Zeus *herkeios*, / she and her sister (*xun**aim**os*) will not escape the most dreadful death' (486–9). These blood ties apply all the more to his son, powerfully captured in the Messenger's description of the suicide: 'Haemon (***Haim**ôn*) is dead; his hand shed his own blood (***haim**assetai*)' (1175). Given the dead bodies on the cavern floor, the pollution Creon has unleashed clearly extends beyond the defilement of Polyneices' corpse.

Sophocles drives this point home with Eurydice's suicide. Following the Messenger's report of the burial of Polyneices and the deaths in the cave, Creon's wife returns silently into the palace (1244–6). We next see her on the *ekkuklêma*, draped over the household altar of Zeus *herkeios* (Zeus 'of the courtyard'), her maternal blood staining the sacred centre of the royal family. Eurydice's dying words curse her husband as the killer of their son (1305), and her corpse confronts Creon on his return from the cave with Haemon's body. Polyneices' remains have polluted the public altars of Thebes; the suicides of Haemon and Antigone have violated the 'untrodden' cavern; now Eurydice's lifeblood corrupts the ritual heart of Creon's home.

When Teiresias accuses Creon of spreading a miasma that plagues the city, the tyrant blasphemously denies that humans can defile the gods:

> You will not hide him [Polyneices] in a grave,
> not even if the eagles of Zeus want to seize
> his body and bring the carrion up to the god's throne!
> Not even that would frighten me of pollution [*miasma*]
> to make me allow him to be buried. For I know full well
> that no human being has the strength to pollute [*miainein*] the gods.
> 1039–44

Creon's assertion flies in the face of his fears about the contamination that will result if he kills his own kin, noted above. More significantly, as Robert Parker states, 'we can only understand this [Creon's] rejection of plain fact as lunatic defiance. Through pollution, the universe has given an unambiguous verdict ...'[16] Martin Cropp goes further, arguing that 'nature itself rebels against the unnatural exposure of the corpse, polluting the city and disrupting its religious processes (998–1022)... Antigone's rebellion is virtually a part of the rebellion of nature, and part of the mechanism of retribution.'[17]

As the play makes tragically clear, Creon does not operate independently of the earth and its gods. He cannot deny these forces their due without facing the consequences, any more than he can control pollution by decree and assertion. But how do these transgressions relate to our earlier discussion of the earth's productivity, its sacred aspects, and its role in ancient Greek ritual? When Creon consigns Antigone to 'marry Hades' rather than Haemon, he boasts that 'there are other furrows [for my son] to plough' (569). His language echoes the protocols of fifth-century Athenian marriage, arranged for 'the sowing of legitimate children', a phrase that associates human procreation with the fertility of the earth.[18] Just as Creon believes he controls the plain where Polyneices lies exposed, so he assumes he holds sway over the 'fields' where Haemon might sow his seed. By the end of the play, however, Creon confronts his true impotence. Bereft of wife, sons and potential heirs, he sees himself as 'no more than nothing' (1325).

In *Antigone*, disaster moves from the world of the dead to that of the living, from the physical defilement of carrion to the subversion of rites that honour the gods, earth, marriage and death. The suicides of Antigone, Haemon and Eurydice mark the final catastrophe, the destruction of Creon's home, his *oikos* ('house', 'home', 'family'). Our modern term 'ecology' (*oikos* + *logos*, literally, 'words about our home') connects the wellbeing of our local habitation to that of the environment at large. The dramatic action of *Antigone* depends on this relationship, moving from Creon's decree denying his nephew burial out to the broader 'ecology' of Thebes, and then back to the *oikos* of Creon. Pollution spreads from the barren plain where Polyneices rots to the Theban altars stained with his flesh, from the isolated cave where Antigone and Haemon die to the altar of Zeus *herkeios* where Eurydice kills herself. In no small part these disasters arise from Creon's overestimation of his power over the natural world.

Such a conclusion might seem at odds with a play that features the 'Ode to Man', a hymn to human subjugation of the land, the sea, and the beasts of the wild. However, as noted above, the Chorus issue a caveat – humans do *not* exercise power over death, our ultimate vulnerability. The simple fact that death takes all living things suggests the ode is less a celebration of man's triumph over nature than a reminder of nature's ultimate power over us. In the play, we see that power most clearly in the earth, whose fertility mirrors our own, and whose domain absorbs us after we die. Convinced he has control over the living and the dead, Creon fails to honour this primal power and its gods, and the earth takes its revenge – not from wilfulness (a human trait) but from its own inescapable nature.

The Athenians did celebrate various cults connected directly to Gaia ('Earth'), some of which emphasized the earth's role in fertility and as a nurturer of children.[19] Sophocles makes no reference to these cults in *Antigone*, preferring to invoke a complex mixture of rituals and ritual violations connected to Creon's refusal to bury Polyneices and his 'burial' of the living Antigone. These dramatic givens explain why the rectifying forces at work in the play depend on the natural processes of pollution and the attendant anger of the gods. In other Greek tragedies, characters appeal to the power of a dead hero to help them in their struggle. Orestes, Electra and the Chorus in Aeschylus' *Choephori* (306–509, 583–4) call on the dead Agamemnon to help them from below, as they do in Sophocles' *Electra* (453–60, 1417–21). The Chorus and Queen in Aeschylus' *Persians* raise the ghost of Darius to help cope with their defeat by the Greeks (A. *Pers.* 633–842), and the spirit of the murdered Clytemnestra appears onstage to goad the Furies to revenge in *Eumenides* (94–139). Antigone, however, makes no such appeal to her dead brother to come to her aid, reflecting his liminal status as an unburied corpse and also his treacherous role in the Argive invasion. Instead, Antigone appeals to unwritten laws and customs, whose violation takes the form of physical pollution and the subversion of funeral, marriage and sacrificial ritual.

We may not find in Greek tragedy a full-fledged concern for 'the rights of the earth', but Sophocles' *Antigone* comes close. Sophocles forcefully dramatizes how much more powerful are the forces of nature than the decrees of Creon. By polluting the rites meant to placate the earth and the gods, he violates the very means by which ancient Greek society honoured and tried to influence the natural world. Most of us today have lost our ritual connection to the earth and the primary powers it represents. Nonetheless, the modern scientific knowledge that has replaced ancient ritual presents us with a similar scenario: our treatment of the environment threatens our survival. If we continue to use the earth as an arena to play out our dominance, we will discover, like Creon, how powerless we really are.

Notes

1 Jones (2004) 124–7.
2 Gagarin (2003) 198–9 and 206.
3 See, for example, Shapiro (1986); Talbott (2005); Stamos (2013).
4 On 22 April 2010, the World People's Conference on Climate Change and the Rights of Mother Earth issued a Universal Declaration of the Rights of

the Earth in Cochabamba, Bolivia, and Bolivia's Plurinational Legislative Assembly passed 'The Law of the Rights of Mother Earth' (Ley de Derechos de la Madre Tierra, Law 071) in December of the same year.

5 Solon, Fr. 36.4–5, in West (1992).

6 Cook (1914, 1925, 1940); Scully (1962).

7 Plato (*Critias* 111c) complains of the radical deforestation of Attica, but merges myth with fact. See Meiggs (1982) 188–212, who discusses pressure on Athenian timber supplies during the fifth century, due to public building programmes, maintaining the naval fleet and smelting at the Lavrium mines.

8 For further discussion, see Chapter 3 in Rehm (2002).

9 Jones (1961) 217. In reality, fifth-century Athens maintained a lively commercial relationship with Lemnos.

10 Jebb (1898), on l. 1452.

11 All translations from *Antigone* are my own.

12 Griffith (1999), on ll. 205–6.

13 Douglas (1978).

14 Note that Creon threatens the Guard with a similar fate: 'If you fail to find the hands that worked this burial [of Polyneices], / . . . / a single Hades will not suffice for you' (306–8). Recall the gods' reaction in the *Iliad* to Achilles' treatment of Hector's body, dragging the corpse around the walls of Troy, as if a single death for Hector will not suffice. Achilles' refusal to acknowledge the fact of death outrages the gods, who help bring about the funeral rites for Hector at the end of the poem.

15 Sophocles does something similar with the blinding of Oedipus over Jocasta's corpse in *Oedipus Tyrannus*. For a fuller account of this motif, see Rehm (1994) 62–5.

16 Parker (1983) 33, 44.

17 Cropp (1997) 152, 154.

18 Writing in the first century AD, Plutarch observes that 'the Athenians perform three sacred ploughings [referring to agricultural rituals like the Proerosia, discussed above], but the most sacred of all is sowing at marriage and ploughing for the procreation of children' [*Coniugalia Praecepta* 42, 144 a–b].

19 Parker (2005) 416; see also 426–43 on the team of divinities associated with procreation and child-rearing.

8

Revealing Divinity in Sophocles' *Antigone*

Stephen Esposito

This chapter will examine two remarkable 'triptych' scenes wherein Sophocles reveals, in quite unusual and unexpected ways, the invasion of divinity into *Antigone*'s stage action.[1] The first scene involves the threefold sequence of Polyneices' first burial, followed immediately by the second choral song (Ode to Man), followed immediately by Polyneices' second burial. The second scene involves the threefold sequence of Haemon's confrontation with his father, followed immediately by the fourth choral song (Ode to Eros), followed by Antigone's 'bride-of-Hades' lament about being denied the joys of marriage and raising children.

I will examine how these two scenes invest the action with a turbulent divine energy that is virtually invisible to the actors but palpably visible to the audience. The first triptych progresses from mystery (what *man* is the culprit?) to prodigy (Man is the measure of all things) to revelation (a young *girl* is the culprit). And in that sequence's revelation segment what is revealed is that the theme of the triptych's central panel (Ode to Man) is surreptitiously and ironically destabilized by the third panel (the dust-storm as revelatory of Antigone's daimonic power). The second triptych progresses from mystery (what will happen to Antigone?) to prodigy (Eros is the measure of all things) to revelation (the young *girl* will become Hades' bride, not Haemon's). And in this sequence's revelation segment what is revealed is that the theme of the triptych's central panel (Ode to Eros) is surreptitiously and ironically instantiated by the third panel (the 'wedding / no wedding' as revelatory of Eros's daimonic power). In each of the two triptychs the outcome of the third panel is the direct result of the action in the first panel.

Part I

Antigone opens at dawn after the defeat of the Seven against Thebes. Creon has issued a pre-dawn edict that Polyneices' corpse must be left unburied; any violator will be executed by public stoning (36). Antigone, about 14 years old, asks her sister to help bury their brother, whose body she doesn't want to lie 'unwept, unburied, a sweet treasure of meat for the gazing birds to feast on as they please' (28–30). As H.D.F. Kitto notes, the sheer physical horror and bestial mangling (*sparagmos*, 1081; cf. 1198) of Polyneices' corpse constitute a major theme (cf. 205–6, 409–12, 426, 697–8, 1017–18, 1080–3) and motivate Antigone's 'overwhelmingly personal and instinctive' reaction to Creon's edict.[2] But Ismene refuses to help her sister: 'I don't dishonour Polyneices; but it's impossible for me by nature to defy the citizens' (78–9). So Antigone alone must perform her 'crime of piety' (*hosia panourgēsasa*, 74) because she refuses 'to dishonour what is honoured by the gods' (78). 'Make your excuses,' she says to Ismene, but 'I shall heap up earth into a tomb to bury him, my dearest brother' (*phil-tatos*, 80–1). What makes Antigone dangerous is that, unbeknownst to Creon and the chorus, her burial of Polyneices is mysteriously connected by Sophocles to higher natural and cosmic powers. How the dramatist makes this connection is shown brilliantly in a sequence of three scenes.

Creon has stationed several watchmen (217, 413) around Polyneices' corpse to prevent any burial rites. Sometime just before daybreak, in the brief interval between Creon's battle-field edict and the beginning of the night-watch over the corpse, Antigone somehow ritually 'buries' her brother with a thin layer of dust. Then a watchman announces the following news to the king: 'The corpse has disappeared – not buried in a grave but covered with light dust as if to deflect a curse. No sign was visible that any dog or savage animal had been tearing at the corpse' (255–8). The Chorus-leader suggests to Creon the possibility that the deed was 'prompted by the gods' (*the-ēlaton*, 279). The king replies furiously: 'Do you think the gods might be concerned with this corpse! Do you see them bestowing honour on this man's evil' (282–8).

Three important points emerge here. First, Antigone 'buried' the corpse to deflect a curse (*agos*, 256), i.e. she considered it her religious duty to avoid the pollution incurred by neglecting to cover with dust the corpse. Second, the Chorus-leader suggests that the burial is miraculous, the result of some supernatural intervention (279). Third, Creon is outraged by the suggestion that the gods might want to 'honour' the corpse (284, 287). Rather he immediately develops a conspiracy theory, suspects that the guards were bribed and warns that he'll kill them if they don't find the culprit. And so, as suddenly as the messenger had entered the action, just as suddenly Sophocles stops the action. It's time to get the heated actors offstage, time to reflect – as is the chorus' custom – on the preceding episode, which means, in this case, the mysterious nature of Polyneices' burial. And so it's here that the Chorus sing the most famous ode in Greek tragedy.

This second choral song (332–75), in its stunning interpretation of human history as a progressive march from savagery to civilization, clearly reaches far beyond the immediate context of the mysterious burial of Polyneices and suggests crucial themes that will resonate throughout the play. Not least it celebrates 'ingenious man' (*peri-phradēs anēr*, 346), the victory of human skill (*technē*) and wisdom (*sophia*, 364–5) over the forces of nature in the fields, forests and oceans, and finally the gathering of all this glorious wisdom into a singular space, the city, man's greatest achievement. Only death stands beyond the reach of his inventive powers. The Chorus concludes by narrowing its focus to the dramatic issue at hand, namely the lawless daring of the man who has defied the king's edict.

This brings us to scene #3 of our sequence – the revelation of the culprit. Immediately after the Ode to Man, the watchman from scene #1 enters suddenly and unexpectedly, escorting a silent Antigone under armed guard. He reports that she is the culprit; he has captured her in the act of burying the corpse a second time. The guards had undone the first burial and so, from Antigone's perspective, added insult to injury. The chorus, in shock, wonders if this is not a 'divine apparition' or 'portent sent by the gods' (*daimonion teras*, 376). Creon asks for the details of the event and the watchman replies thus (415–31):

> The taunting of us guards lasted for the time it took the shining circle of the sun to reach the centre of the sky. The heat was burning. Suddenly a whirlwind raised a pillar of dust from the ground, a trouble high as heaven, which filled up the plain, defacing all the foliage of the trees, and choked the mighty sky. We shut our eyes and bore that sickness sent by the gods (*theia nosos*, 421). It took a long time for the storm to pass. And then we saw this girl here wailing bitterly aloud, in the piercing voice of a mother bird who sees her nest is empty and her bed bereft of baby chicks. Just so did she, on seeing the corpse was naked (*psilon*), in this manner she burst into wailing laments and called evil curses down upon the ones who had performed this deed. At once she gathered thirsty dust with her bare hands, and lifting high a bronze pitcher, finely-wrought, she crowned the corpse by pouring three libation-streams.

This is an extraordinary account, even more uncanny than the first burial. As F.W. Schneidewin observed long ago, 'The full description of the violent storm, which so terrified the band of watchmen, sets in a beautiful light the undaunted devotion of the heroine.'[3]

Six important points about the second burial emerge here. First, the dust storm occurs in the hottest part of the day, at high noon, the time 'when supernatural visitations are especially likely to take place.[4] Second, the watchman calls this sudden whirlwind 'a sickness sent by the gods' (*theia nosos*, 421); thus he corroborates the Chorus-leader's opinion about the first burial.[5] Third, after the storm has passed, the watchman, in a poignant two-line simile, compares Antigone's cries of grief to the shrill cry of a mother bird who sees her nest empty and bereft of her chicks (424–5). The simile's pathos evokes the deep familial love that Antigone has for her brother. Of course, she is not Polyneices' mother but his sister; yet making her a mother here not only heightens the sense of loss and grief but also looks forward in the story, reminding us that Antigone never will be a mother. This simile is the closest she will get to motherhood (although at 823–33 she compares herself to the *mater dolorosa* Niobe). Furthermore, as George Steiner notes, the simile raises another crucial issue:

> Antigone's shrill lament voices instincts and values, older, less rational than man and man's discourse. Can the *polis*, built as it is on essential delimitations between the human and the animal spheres, fundamentally committed as it is to articulate speech, contain, give adequate echo to, such cries? Both storm and bird-cry stand outside civic reason. But it is precisely the bounds of civic reason, of immanent logic, which delineate Creon's map of the permissible, intelligible world . . . The economy of the drama is such that the wind-storm and the cry of the mother bird over her vacant nest precisely intimate those opaque existential areas towards which the chorus in turn advances and from which it recoils.[6]

Fourth, when Antigone saw her brother's corpse stripped of the dust she had sprinkled on it, she wailed and in her anger repeatedly called down curses on those who did the deed (428). The first burial was partially motivated by her desire to avoid a curse; in the second burial she is herself cursing those who have unburied her brother. Finally she sprinkled dust on the corpse again and from a bronze jug she poured three libations on her dead brother (430–1), thus consummating the burial and bringing it to closure. To conclude this section I quote William Arrowsmith's incisive observation on the dust storm:

> It is because the Sophoclean hero is a natural force that his turbulence is irresistible. His whole function is to excite new chaos in which *nomos* [conventional law/custom] will be freshly and rightly related to *physis* [nature], and the unnatural cut away. Thus Antigone's burial of her brother is announced by, and explained by, a sudden and prodigious dust storm; her action is confirmed and sanctified by *physis*.[7]

So let us review briefly our sequence of three episodes: watchman scene #1, the Ode to Man, and watchman scene #2. In this tripartite progression Sophocles moves from a question ('What man is the transgressor who buried the traitor?') to a choral song that celebrates the towering genius of man and his technological mastery to an answer of the opening question, namely 'The culprit is a young girl and she has been caught burying the traitor a second time!' David Seale nicely summarizes the triptych thus: 'The great showpiece of the play, the lofty ode to man, is framed by the two watchman scenes. The sequence is mystery, prodigy, revelation.'[8] The heart of that revelation, as it stands thus far, is that man and his highest artifact, the city, possess a deeply agonistic quality. In other words there is an ongoing struggle between the natural and the man-made, between *physis* and *nomos*. On the one hand, man is 'all-resourceful and all-inventive' (*panto-poros*, 358) in his impulse to 'civic law' (*asty-nomos*, 354) and the future can, astonishingly, throw nothing at him which he is 'without resource' to meet (*a-poros*, 358). And yet for all his awesome technological mastery over nature, there abides somewhere in this human project a moral, spiritual, and ontological darkness that it will take the remainder of the play to unravel. The dramatist suggests this tension in a striking verbal juxtaposition at the end of his famous Ode where, at line 370, he juxtaposes two compound adjectives describing the city, namely *hypsi-polis* and *a-polis*, 'high in the city' and 'outcast from the city.' This sharp enjambment of *polis*-adjectives paints a multivalent picture. On the one hand, man, through his *technē*, can stand 'high in the city' (*hypsi-polis*), while through his daring he can make himself 'an outcast from the city' (*a-polis*). On the other hand, the city itself can, through man's *technē*, be 'high' (*hypsi-polis*), almost transcendent, while through man's daring and hybris the city can be reduced to nothing (*a-polis*). Already early in the play the Ode to Man, despite its overtly celebratory aspects, is clandestinely and ironically signalling a fragility both in the city and in man.

Part II

The confrontation between Creon and Haemon occurs near the play's midpoint. Haemon tries to mediate the conflict between his father and his 'bride-to-be' (*mello-nymphos*, 633). But Creon is intransigent and harsh: 'Spit that girl away just like an enemy, and let her marry someone else, in Hades' house' (653–4). Initially Haemon's reply is lovingly moderate (718): 'Come, father, yield from your rage (*thymos*); allow yourself to change.' But Creon refuses (734–8):

Creon And shall the city tell me what I should command?
Haemon You see how like a very young man that was said.
Creon Am I to rule this land at someone else's whim?
Haemon There's no true city that belongs to just one man.
Creon By law is not a city his who holds the power?

Halfway through the play political discourse has exhausted itself, similar to *Oedipus Tyrannus* when the king, at the conclusion of his dispute with Creon, cries out, 'Yet I must rule. Oh city, city' (629–30). All that remains, at this point in *Antigone*, are Creon's raging threats to destroy his son's marriage (760–1). As Haemon rushes offstage for the last time, Creon announces his revised sentence on Antigone: he won't stone her to death but rather conceal her alive in a rock-chamber grave (773–6); that death-trap will come to serve as 'an image of her halfway position, her rootless hovering'.[9]

The tension is thick. Relief is desperately needed at this, the play's midpoint. Creon, perhaps, remains on stage.[10] What will the chorus say about all this strife they've just witnessed?

Strophe (781–90)

Eros, invincible in combat!
Eros, you who pounce upon men's possessions,
you who keep your night-watch, lying in wait
on a youthful maiden's soft cheeks,
you who range over the open sea
and among shelters in the wilderness.
Neither do any immortal gods escape from you,
nor any mortals, ephemeral creatures of a day,
but whoever feels your (erotic) grip is driven to madness.

Antistrophe (791–800)

And you, Eros, wrest aside even the unjust minds
of the just – to their ruin and disgrace. And you have stirred up
this confusing strife between blood-bound kinsmen.
Victorious is the desire (*himeros*) clearly seen
emanating from the eyes of a bride
who graces the marriage bed –
desire, the assessor enthroned in power beside the mighty ordinances.

For (in all this) she mocks, plays her game,
invincible in battle, the goddess Aphrodite.

Using a traditional hymnic structure and style, the Theban elders sing and dance this short two-stanza song about the omnipotence of sexual passion. The big question about this song is this: what is it doing here? One critic argues that it 'has little to do with the main issue of the play' and 'does not comment on any problem essential to the play'.[11] Another speaks of it as making 'a sublimely irrelevant deduction about Haimon's motives'.[12] I don't agree and will explain why.

Eros is here, as often, personified *as a god* because of his uncanny, irrational power over human lives;[13] he is here 'the orderer of disorder in the universe'.[14] But why does Eros make his *personified* appearance here, at the play's crucial midpoint? The ode raises numerous questions in this regard. Eros is immediately and emphatically described as 'invincible in battle' and certainly we've just witnessed a fierce battle in the preceding scene (Haemon vs. Creon: 626–780). But what did that strife have to do with sexual desire? Clearly the Chorus is attempting to explain what they understand as the underlying cause of that strife, namely Haemon's eros for Antigone – although he himself, in his one appearance, doesn't refer overtly to such passion (cf. 570, 750–1, 762–5, 1237–40).[15]

But does the song serve some larger purpose beyond explaining that one tense episode? I suggest that it does. First I'll trace some of the ode's specific referents and then try to show how, in their aggregate, they impact the play's larger themes and foreshadow the coming violence of the three suicides that occur in the space of 185 verses. So here are some questions, and suggestions. The song moves from the general to the specific; i.e. the strophe (781–90) deals 'the universality of Love's dominion'[16] and the antistrophe (791–800) hones in on several particulars that prove the rule.[17] But I would suggest that even the strophe's seemingly generic and impersonal observations have immediate bearing. Eros, for example, keeps his 'night-watch' (*en-nyx-eueis*, 784) on a maiden's cheeks. Does this not recall Antigone's fiercely devoted 'night-watch' (253) over her brother's corpse? And Eros keeps that night-watch perched on 'a maiden's soft <u>cheeks</u>' (*pareiais*, 793–4). Does this not foreshadow the 'white <u>cheeks</u>' (*pareiai*, 1239) whereon the *blood* of Haemon's violent *Liebestod* will spurt (*Haimon* ... *haim-assetai*, 1175) and thereby consummate his 'marriage' to his 'bride'. At 795–6 Eros roams far and wide 'over the sea and the shelters of the wilderness' (*hyper-pontios* ... <u>*agro-nomois*</u> *aulais*; contrast man's '<u>city</u>-regulating impulses', <u>*asty-nomous*</u> *orgas* at 354–5).[18] This ubiquity of Eros, Seth Benardete notes, 'resembles man's own *deinotēs* [his uncanny and terrifying awesomeness, *deina* ... *deinoteron*: 332–3], which set aside the apparent limits imposed on him by sea and Earth, the highest of the gods. Eros seems to supply the missing cause of man's *deinotēs*.'[19]

The strophe ends with 'unexpectedly strong and sinister language'[20] – neither immortal nor mortal can escape Eros and whoever possesses eros becomes 'crazed / mad'. 'Madness' (*memēnen*, i.e. *mania*, 790) is the strophe's emphatic last word and it links the two stanzas thematically. Presumably the choristers are referring to Haemon whose immediately preceding 'rage' (*orge*, 766) and 'dangerous resentment' (*nous* ... *barus*, 767) – both grounded in his youthful eros for Antigone – have led to 'this strife between blood-bound kinsmen' (*tode neikos* ... *syn-haimon*, 793–4), a strife that linguistically and thematically repeats the dispute between Polyneices and Eteocles in the first choral song (*Poly-neikous* ... *neikeōn*, 'Mr. Much-Strife urged on by a contentious strife', 110–11). But this combination of eros, rage and frenzy reverberates throughout the play – no family member escapes *the maddening assaults of Eros in all his guises and disguises*.[21] To wit, Creon had earlier spoken of seeing Ismene indoors, 'in a raving frenzy (*lyssa*, 492) and not in possession of her senses.' And when Creon hears of Haemon's entrance, he imagines his son will be 'in a raving frenzy' (*lyssa*, 633). And Haemon's parting words to his father were furious and prophetic (763–5): 'You'll never see my face before your eyes again; so you may rave on madly (*mania*) with whatever friends still want to share your company!' Soon the messenger will report that 'Haimon killed himself, in wrath (*mēnis*) at blood his father shed' (1177). And that same messenger reports to Creon that Eurydice, 'raging in her heart' (*kardia thymoumenē*, 1254), killed herself at the palace altars with a knife but not before 'with her last breath she chanted evil actions (curses) upon you, (whom she called) the son-murderer' (*paido-ktonos*, 1304–5).

Although this song focuses on sexual eros, the play's four other uses of the noun or verb for eros create a wider context for understanding this stasimon's personified Eros. The only other choral reference to eros occurred in the preceding ode in the context of the inherited family curse on Labdacus' house, its dangerous transgressions and reckless infatuation, and 'the wide-wandering hope that brings benefit to many men but to many more is a deception consisting of thoughtless passions (*apata kouphonoōn erōtōn*, 617) – a deception that comes to one who knows nothing until he scorches his foot in the hot fire.' To whose 'thoughtless passions' (*erōtes*, 617) is the chorus referring? Evidently to Antigone and her burial of Polyneices (cf. 602–3, 852–6). The three other appearances of eros move in that same thematic orbit. Ismene describes Antigone's desire to bury her brother as 'lusting for the impossible' (*eraō*, 90). And the Chorus-leader tells Creon he won't disobey the king's warning about collaborating with the unknown culprit since 'noone is so foolish as to lust for death' (*eraō*, 220) – though we already know that

Antigone has that exact desire: 'To me it's a beautiful thing to die (*kalon . . . thanein*, 72) performing such a deed.' And at the play's very end the completely crushed Creon will have the same overwhelming desire: 'But that [i.e. death] which I desire passionately (*eraō*, 1336) I summed up in my prayer.'

In the antistrophe, in exact metrical responsion to the verses about 'Eros who keeps his night-watch on a young maiden's soft cheeks' (783–4), the Chorus sings of 'Eros who wrenches the minds of just men from justice, to their ruin, and has raised this turbulent strife between kinsmen of the same blood' (*tode neikos . . . syn-haimon*, 793–4). This passage presents the song's clearest touchstone to the preceding action and although the punning Greek text highlights Haemon's name (*syn-haimon*, 794) and his eros for Antigone, Creon is insinuated as well. This verse is immediately followed by an implied reference to Antigone (795–9): 'Victorious is the visible desire (*himeros*) beaming from the eyes of the bride who graces the marriage bed – desire, the assessor enthroned in power beside the mighty ordinances.' The use of the genitives in the sequence *blepharōn himeros nymphas* (795–7) is ambiguous and at least two possibilities are competing: 'the desire of the [lover's] eyes for the bride' (= a subjective genitive followed by an objective one); and 'the desire [i.e. love-glance] of the eyes of the bride' (= two possessive genitives). In other words, as Mark Griffith notes about this expression, 'the associations are multiple, suggesting the mutually irresistible radiance of *both* lovers (implicitly, Antigone and Haimon)'.[22] Otherwise put, if there is any one passage in the play that implicitly refers to Antigone's eros for Haemon, this is it.[23] The bride here is described as *eu-lektros* (917), 'well-bedded,' implying the promise of marital happiness. But later Antigone will describe herself as 'un-bedded' (*a-lektron*, 917).

In verses 797–9, if the transmitted text is correct, Eros is the 'assessor / partner in office (*par-edros*) enthroned in power beside the mighty ordinances (*megaloi thesmoi*)'. Regarding the powerful metaphor of this emphatic final appositional phrase R.W.B. Burton notes that it 'imparts a certain magisterial quality to *himeros* [desire] . . . and is found in exalted contexts to describe the mutual relationships of gods and abstract powers'.[24] These 'mighty ordinances' clearly recall 'the gods' unwritten and unshakable laws' which Antigone had invoked earlier against the king's edict (454–5). It would appear that Eros, whom none of the immortals themselves can flee (787), is the equal partner of Antigone's unwritten Olympian laws.[25] Finally we might ask why the song ends with Aphrodite 'playfully mocking' or 'frivolously wreaking her will' (*em-paizei*) on her victim. Who is she mocking? Haemon? Creon? Antigone?[26]

Let us now take stock. Why does the chorus sing about the power of sexual desire at this pivotal moment? Because, I would submit, it's precisely erotic energy – titanic, irrational, crazy-making and uncanny – that percolates from the outset just beneath the Sophoclean surface and begins to take over here.[27] Until now Creon has been in charge, but that dynamic has just begun to change. The play's first two thematic sections – Antigone's plan of action and her defence of that action – are complete. The third segment – the consequences of her action – now begins.[28] As Charles Segal notes, the ode to Eros 'marks the rising tide of emotional violence in the play'.[29] The song's formal ring composition, with its first emphatic word (Eros) and its emphatic last word (Aphrodite), works to surround and contain, within its lyric parameters, that volatile, seething, and 'embattled' energy. Eros, personified as a male god, looks back to Haemon's sudden exit, while the goddess Aphrodite looks forward to Antigone's entry. I speak of 'embattled' energy because the word 'battle' stands at the ode's beginning and end (*Eros a-nikate machan*, 'Eros unconquered in battle', 781; and *a-machos ... Aphrodita*, 'unconquered Aphrodite', 799–800). The exemplification of that 'embattled' energy can be found most conspicuously in the play's relentless sequence of agonistic combat-scenes, unparalleled in extant Sophocles – Antigone vs. Ismene, Creon vs. the watchman, Creon vs. Antigone, Creon vs. Haemon and Creon vs. Tiresias.

This third stasimon is situated at the play's structural centre for a compelling reason. Just as the central choral ode of *Oedipus Tyrannus* (863–910) marks that drama's thematic pivot from city to house and public to private, so too does this ode – moving away from the political issue of Creon's civic edict (i.e. the prohibition on burying a 'traitor') to the familial theme of marriage. Furthermore I would suggest this song marks the thematic transition from *philia* to *eros*.[30] In the action leading up to this third stasimon the *philia* theme is perhaps seen most clearly in line 572 when Ismene addresses Haemon *in absentia*: 'O most beloved (*phil-tate*) Haimon, how your father dishonours you!' If, as most scholars think, line 572 is indeed spoken by Ismene (and not Antigone), then Antigone herself never speaks to or about Haemon.[31] And that's a major reason for this fourth choral ode – it articulates an energy that Antigone doesn't and can't articulate. As Robert Goheen explains, Sophocles doesn't want to complicate 'the concentrated dramatic action with a developed erotic subplot'.[32] The psychological question of why Antigone suppresses her eros for Haemon has been much debated. The best interpretation I've seen is Lawrence Jost's:

> Her absolute singlemindedness before the dead was all but necessary for its success. If she had allowed herself to temporize, to dwell on what life had in store for her – marriage, children, the continuance of the Labdakid line – she might never have gone through it ... The suggestion here is that Antigone is victimized by a repressed realization that she is not fated to bear children, that she must – out of loyalty to, as well as identification

> with, her parents' miserable end – renounce her opportunity to marry Haimon.[33]

Immediately following the ode to Eros comes the *kommos* (lyric dialogue) between Antigone and the Chorus (801–82), which comprises 'the emotional and musical climax of the play'.[34] This is Antigone's last appearance; she is led from Creon's palace into the orchestra by the king's guards. The Chorus-leader, speaking in anapests, announces her entrance:

> But now I too [like Haemon], seeing this spectacle,
> I am carried off course, beyond the sovereignty of ordinances,
> no longer capable of restraining the streams of tears,
> when I see Antigone here making her way
> to the bridal chamber (*thalamos*) where all must sleep forever.

Antigone, probably wearing a veil (1222),[35] and perhaps even a wedding dress, is preparing for her marriage ceremony. As Mary Whitlock Blundell notes,

> The Chorus' ode to Eros evokes a wedding celebration, especially in its emphasis on the erotic attraction between bride and groom (795–7) ... In a way, then, this *stasimon* is a substitute for the marriage song and dance that would have been performed at the wedding of Haimon and Antigone. As such it introduces a symbolic 'marriage' procession ... Antigone's own song of lamentation develops this theme, making her passage to death into a kind of inverted marriage ritual, in which she sings her own 'wedding song' to accompany this 'marriage' procession.[36]

In Antigone's heart-breaking lyric dialogue with the Chorus she sings and they respond in anapests (806–82).[37] Space doesn't permit discussion but there's one final important point to note about this lyric exchange. It's only after the ode to Eros that the delayed *explicit* emergence of the marriage theme can safely surface. 'For by this point in the play Antigone has done all she can to honour her brother, and her trial and sentence at Kreon's hands has already been accomplished. The pressure, as it were, is off, and she herself can reflect on the nuptial loss, in the *kommos* and elsewhere at the end ...'[38] The 'girl interrupted', the *parthenos* ('virgin') whose marital rite of passage to *gyne* ('woman') has been blocked such that she now instantiates the etymological meaning of her name ('anti-generation'), now that girl is finally and tragically 'free' to lament her losses and sing her song of immense suffering and desolation.[39]

Let me summarize the main points of this chapter. The sequence of the three panels of the triptych discussed in this section is manifest: 'Haemon vs. Creon > Ode to Eros > Antigone's farewell'; otherwise stated, 'Bridegroom interrupted > Ode to Eros > Bride interrupted'. This parallels the thematic sequence of the first triptych discussed in section one: *mystery* (Who is the culprit?) > *prodigy* (Ode to Man) > *revelation* (Antigone is the culprit). In this chapter's second section the *mystery* is this: What will happen to the *ephebe* Haemon and the *parthenos* Antigone? The *prodigy* is the choral song about the terrifying power of Eros. And the *revelation* is the 'bride's' tragic lament of her marriage to Hades rather than to Haemon. Just as in the first triptych we saw the uncanny power of the gods of justice, especially as manifested in the dust storm, insinuating itself into the double burial of Polyneices, so in the second triptych we see the prodigious power of the gods of eros, 'enthroned in power beside the mighty ordinances,' overwhelming the human actors and mocking their best laid plans. So without bringing the gods on stage *in person*, like Athena in the prologue of *Ajax*, in these two triptychs Sophocles brings the uncanny and turbulent energy of the gods onto the stage *in a more disguised fashion*, making it harder for the actors to see clearly and thereby reminding us of the complex, ambiguous, and often unstated and misunderstood double motivations – human and divine – behind the stage action.

Notes

1 Translations are from Blundell (1998), except for the third stasimon in Part II, which is my own, using the Oxford Classical Text of Lloyd-Jones and Wilson (1990a). Occasionally I modify Blundell's translations.
2 Kitto (1956) 148–9.
3 Schneidewin (1853) at 417 ff.
4 Griffith (1999) at 415–22.
5 On the dust storm as 'proof for the presence of the gods' see Jordan (1979) 98–102.
6 Steiner (1984) 227. On the simile compare also Rothaus (1990).
7 Arrowsmith (1965) 122 [reprinted (1992–3) 200].
8 Seale (1982) 92.
9 Reinhardt (1979) 81.
10 Griffith (1999) at 780 argues that Creon *probably* does remain on stage; similarly Kitto (1956) 167–70; Brown (1987) at 760. *Contra* Jebb (1900); Burton (1980) 112; Seale (1982) 98 and 111 n. 27.
11 Burton (1980) 117; contrast Adams (1955) 57 [reprinted (1957) 53]. Though I disagree with Burton on this particular point he has many excellent observations in his discussion of the ode to Eros.

12 Vickers (1973) 537; strong critique in Goldhill (1990) 102–3.
13 Brown (1987) 186.
14 Kitzinger (2008) 45–6.
15 von Fritz (1934) argues unconvincingly that Haemon is motivated solely by concern for his father and not love of his promised bride. *Contra* von Fritz, see Lloyd-Jones (1962) 739–40; Kamerbeek (1978) 20–1; Erbse (1991).
16 Pearson (1928) 141; Griffith (1999) at 785–6.
17 Cf. Benardete (1975–6) 45 [reprinted (1999) 96]: 'The song is composed of eleven statements about love, the central one of which says that he whom Eros possesses is madness. Around this center the two sets of five statements each are balanced.'
18 Cf. Nethercut (1978) on how the ode to Eros, compared to the earlier songs, adds a kind of a 'vertical perspective' to our experience of the play.
19 Benardete (1975–6) 46 [reprinted (1999) 97].
20 Brown (1987).
21 Cf. Euripides' *Antigone*, fragment 161: 'I was (or 'they were' – Antigone and Haemon?) in love (*ērōn*); and that showed love (*erōs*) is madness (*to mainesthai*) for mortals.' See Collard and Cropp (2008) 162–3.
22 Griffith (1999) at 795–7; similarly, and very nicely, Ditmars (1992) 102.
23 On 795–7 compare Campbell (1871): 'the ancients rather spoke of an influence passing from the eye of the beloved (*to erotikon omma*, Plato, *Phaedrus* 253E) to the soul of the lover. Desire was viewed as an emanation from the object.' Bayfield (1935) 109: 'The *himeros* is as much Haimon's as Antigone's; the influence coming from her has awakened love in him.' Lattimore (1964) 75: '*Himeros* (Desire, 796) must refer to the bride as well as to her admirer or the passage is untranslatable.' Contrast Winnington-Ingram (1980) 95–6; Brown (1987).
24 Burton (1980) 115–16 has fine remarks on why the manuscript reading *paredros* at 798–9 should not be emended; similarly Brown (1987). However, Jebb (1900), Griffith (1999) and Willink (2001) 77–8 argue that emendation is needed. Lloyd-Jones and Wilson (1990b) 136 maintain that 'the text gives good sense, and one cannot be sure that it is wrong.' Similarly Kitzinger (2008) 46 n. 68.
25 Cf. Coleman (1972) 15–16; Else (1976) 54; Winnington-Ingram (1980) 95 and n. 13; Segal (1981) 198; Kitzinger (2008) 46. Musurillo (1967) 53 notes that the ode to Eros 'is insisting on the two springs of human action: reasonable obedience to the laws, and the force of love. In this tension it is Aphrodite . . . which seems to exercise the strongest power: she 'plays without struggle'.
26 Cf. Winnington-Ingram (1980) 97 who sees the ode to Eros as 'a vital foreshadowing of the scene at the cave . . . It is Creon who fights the power of Eros and Aphrodite; it is Creon who is mocked.'
27 Cf. Kitto (1956) 167: 'The love-interest [of Antigone and Haemon], then, is not merely the pivot on which the catastrophe turns; it is part of the whole foundation of the play.'

28 For a synoptic view of the Chorus' role in this tripartite thematic movement see Esposito (1996) 89–90.
29 Gibbons and Segal (2003) 145; cf. Segal (1981) 198–9.
30 On some of the crucial differences between *philia* and *eros* see Goldhill (1986) 102 and (1990) 102.
31 The speaker of verse 572 is a notorious crux. Jebb (1900), attributing it to Antigone, writes: 'This solitary reference to her love heightens in a wonderful degree our sense of her unselfish devotion to a sacred duty.' But as Winnington-Ingram (1980) 93 n. 7 notes, 'The weight of the argument inclines strongly towards Ismene.' Convincing arguments for Ismene are made by Schneidewin (1853); D'Ooge (1900); Hester (1971) 30–1 n. 1; Knox (1968) 755 [reprinted (1979) 174]; Fagles and Knox (1982) 398–9; Mastronarde (1979) 95–6; Winnington-Ingram (1980) 93 n. 7; Seale (1982) 94–5 and 111 n. 20; Davies (1986); Brown (1987); Rudnytsky (1987) 301–3; Lloyd-Jones and Wilson (1990b) and (1997); Kirkwood (1991) 29; Zimmermann (1993) 103; Griffith (1999); Segal and Gibbons (2003) 138. The strongest arguments for Antigone are made by Kitto (1956) 162–3; Kamerbeek (1978); Dawe (1978) 106–8; Lesky (1983) 441 n. 38; Günther (1998). Cf. Sommerstein (1990–93) [reprinted (2010)], seemingly agnostic.
32 Goheen (1951) 39; on 138 he notes that the suppression of a more developed erotic subplot 'is the more noteworthy because of its probable prominence in the lost Euripidean version.' Similarly Rudnytsky (1987) 304. Cf. Winnington-Ingram (1980) 92–3; and Hogan (1991) 155 at line 683: 'Had Sophocles made Haemon's love for Antigone more than an adventitious theme, it might have muddied, or at least diluted, the central issue of the play, for then Antigone must either be torn between love for brother and fiancé, or she must clearly prefer one to the other. As the action goes, Haemon takes the line of a devoted son rather than a passionate lover.'
33 Jost (1983) 135. For more heavily Oedipal/psychoanalytic perspectives see Rudnytsky (1987) 292–312 and Johnson (1997) 388–95.
34 Ditmars (1992) 88–90, 109–31. Cf. Brown (1987) 188–90; Griffith (1999) at 801–2.
35 Campbell (1879); Jebb (1900); Seaford (1987) 113; Tyrrell and Bennett (1998) 99–100; Griffith (1999).
36 Blundell (1998) 94–5; cf. Seaford (1987) 107–8 and (1990a) 76–9; Goldhill (1990) 103–4.
37 For analysis of the *kommos* see Burton (1980) 118–26; Gardiner (1987) 91–2; Ditmars (1992) 104–31; Scott (1996) 48–54; Kitzinger (2008) 48–57.
38 Jost (1983) 135.
39 Cf. Seale (1982) 100: 'In the larger design the ode to love, the entry of Antigone and the lyrical contemplation of her doom are all bound together by the strong impression of the heroine's visual presence, which brings all the preceding scenes to a final climax of isolation.'

9

Religion in *Antigone*

Robert Garland

Our play presents the audience with a classic, one might say, perennial dilemma. Has the state, any state, the right to pass a law that is in violation of a widely upheld and cherished religious belief? We do not need to look far to find a contemporary parallel. In June 2015 the Supreme Court ruled that same-sex marriage was permissible nationwide. Three months later Kim Davis, the county clerk in Rowan, Kentucky, refused to issue marriage licences to same-sex couples on the grounds that her belief as an Apostolic Christian prevented her. Her defiant attitude led to her incarceration, during which she was accorded a private audience with Pope Francis, before being released and permitted to return to work. In essence, a compromise had been reached. In a more charged religious or political climate, the situation might well have escalated, had both the state and the individual implacably dug in their heels.

And that is precisely what happens in *Antigone*, at the heart of which lies a similar conflict between religious belief and secular law. The point is established in the Prologue, which takes place between Antigone and her sister Ismene, when Antigone first declares her intention to bury her brother Polyneices in violation of Creon's decree (76–9):

Antigone Dishonour the laws that the gods honour if you wish.
Ismene I do not dishonour them but I am powerless to resist the state edicts.[1]

Of course, there are significant differences between the example I just gave and the situation in Thebes. One is that leaving a body unburied is a much more sensitive issue for most people than same-sex marriage. The second is that the stakes are much higher in Thebes. The city has recently emerged from a period of bloody civil war, which quite literally divided brother from brother. Creon, who has only recently assumed the kingship, is understandably fearful of any action that challenges his authority. Determined to restore order at all cost, he passes an edict denying burial to his nephew Polyneices, who sought to wrest the throne from his brother Eteocles. Eteocles, who died 'fighting for the city' – or who more accurately died trying to retain the throne – is by contrast to be buried 'with rites that befit those who are the noblest among the dead' (194–7; cf. 23).

Following her arrest for conducting abbreviated burial rites on behalf of Polyneices, Antigone is apprehended and brought before Creon. She defends her action by demanding, 'Who knows whether this is pious in Hades?' (521). From her perspective the denial of burial, even to an adjudged traitor, is a violation of *eusebeia*. *Eusebeia*, conventionally translated as 'piety', more broadly categorizes correct behaviour in regard to the gods and the dead and is a key concept in Greek religion. As in the case of most religious concepts, however, there is no definition of it in either Greek literature or Greek law. In fact it defies even Socrates' attempt to define it in Plato's *Euthyphro*. Its opposite, viz. *asebeia* or *dussebeia*, covers a broad range of meanings, including insulting, disrespectful, and injurious behaviour either to the gods or to the dead.

It is the divergent and conflicting interpretations of piety and impiety that lie at the heart of Sophocles' play. From Antigone's perspective, 'There is nothing shameful in demonstrating piety to someone who shared the same womb' (511). What she means by this is that her kinship obliges her to honour her brother by burying him. In Creon's eyes, however, granting burial to a traitor constitutes impiety from the perspective of the loyal Eteocles (514–16). In other words, both Antigone and Creon see each other as dishonouring the dead.

So who is right? Well, certainly Creon has precedent on his side. We have evidence from Athens dating to the turn of the fourth century BCE that denial of burial was an established punishment for traitors, and there is no reason to doubt that such a law would have been in force long beforehand. Xenophon (*Hellenika* 1.7.22) tells us that the Athenians denied burial to traitors and tomb-robbers, whose bodies they deposited in the *barathron* (or pit), perhaps to be identified with a long depression near the Hill of the Nymphs. Likewise in Sparta the bodies of condemned criminals were tossed into a place called the Kaiades, which may have served a similar function to the *barathron*. Plato, who was writing with full awareness of Greek, especially Athenian practice, recommended in the *Laws* that murderers should be executed and their bodies cast out of the country unburied (9.874b). Those found guilty of patricide, matricide, fratricide or infanticide 'should be put to death and their bodies dumped naked outside the city at an appointed place where three roads meet ... Their corpses shall then be carried to the border and thrown out by legal sentence without burial' (9.873b). Even Antigone indicates that she would not have done what she did, were it a slave whose body was lying unburied (517). So it is highly likely that an Athenian audience would have been initially somewhat sympathetic to Creon's viewpoint, particularly given the circumstances in which his edict was passed.

Antigone performs two rites of burial on behalf of her brother. On her first visit she scatters a handful of earth on his corpse and does 'whatever else is necessary' to expiate the *agos* or curse, which she believes she would have incurred from the gods, had she omitted this rite (245–7). On her second visit she not only scatters earth over the body but also pours *trispondai choai*, 'thrice-poured libations'. *Choai* were the principal offering to the dead in the Classical period and regarded as more important than food. The liquid itself could be either unmixed or mixed, but the ingredients were always the same: honey, milk, water and wine. Prayers on behalf of the dead no doubt accompanied this observance but there is no record of what they consisted. 'Thrice-poured' presumably means that Antigone poured three separate libations. The number three and its multiples were especially potent in matters having to do with death ritual. For instance, rites were performed on the third, the ninth and the thirtieth day after burial. Incidentally, why Antigone performs the ritual twice is unclear. Conceivably she wished to be apprehended in order to force a confrontation with her uncle.

Though Antigone's observance is minimal, it is evidently deemed sufficient to satisfy the needs to the dead and to secure his welfare in Hades. It thus amounts to a serious violation of Creon's edict, though the Guard who apprehends her on her second visit overstates the case when he claims that he caught her 'burying' Polyneices (402).

In the encounter that now takes place between herself and Creon, Antigone comes closest to explaining her religious belief (450–7):

Creon Did you dare to break the law?

Antigone Yes, because it wasn't Zeus who passed this edict, nor did Justice, who dwells with the gods below, establish laws of this kind among men. Nor did I think that your edicts had such authority that a mere mortal could override the unwritten and eternal commandments of the gods. For these do not belong only to today or yesterday, but they exist for all time, and no one knows when they first appeared.

In somewhat similar fashion the Guard who reports the first burial suggests that the earth was strewn over the corpse 'as if by someone seeking to avoid *agos*'. He is evidently referring to the curse that would alight upon someone for dishonouring a corpse (256).

Instead of engaging in a theological battle of wits, Creon now charges his niece with *hubris*, not only because she has disobeyed his edict but also because she 'is exulting in and laughing at the deed' (480–3). Often translated as 'insolent pride', *hubris* is more accurately rendered a state of mind that induces an individual to commit impious acts. A classic example of *hubris* occurs in Aeschylus' *Agamemnon*, when Agamemnon steps onto the purple tapestries strewn by his wife Clytemnestra, knowing full well that he is likely to arouse the envy of the gods (763–71). *Hubris* was regarded as a crime punishable by law. In Athens a person could be charged with *hubris* for behaviour that involved physical, verbal, or sexual abuse. In the present instance the crime is made more heinous in Creon's eyes because the perpetrator is a woman.

It is important to note that Antigone is not motivated wholly by her desire to act in conformity with divine law. She claims she also wishes 'to assist the dead' (560), apparently because denying her brother the right of burial would arouse his enmity (94). She also says, 'I have an obligation to give pleasure to those who lie below the earth longer than I do to the living, for I shall abide below for ever' (74–6; cf. 46), though exactly what kind of 'pleasure' the dead are expected to receive from her action is unclear. Perhaps we are to suppose that Polyneices is comforted by the attention he receives from the living. Alternatively he may be gratified by the respect that Antigone's action awards him among the dead, as is hinted at the beginning of the play when Antigone declares that Eteocles' burial 'brings him honour among the dead below' (24–5).

Antigone also sees benefit accruing to herself from tending the dead. She asserts that her arrival in Hades will be pleasing to her father and mother because she washed and clothed their bodies and poured libations over their graves, and pleasing to her brother because she performed a perfunctory burial for him (897–903). To omit such observance would make her 'hateful to the dead' (94). The belief that family members encounter one another in Hades seems to have been widely upheld in Classical Athens, as indicated by the fact that scenes of reunion between the departed and the recently deceased are frequently depicted on funerary reliefs in the form of a handshake between both parties.[2]

We may easily forgive Antigone for her desire to be graciously received by the dead in Hades, but there is another side to her behaviour that makes her much less attractive, namely her audacious claim that by burying her brother she is winning *kleos* (glory). In the Prologue she merely states that her action will enable her 'to die well' (97). In her encounter with Creon, however, she demands, 'By what means could I have won a more glorious glory than by burying my brother?' (502–4).

Antigone's preoccupation with her own reputation is made more unpalatable by her determination to ensure that she alone is the recipient of *kleos*. This induces her callously to reject Ismene's well-meaning attempt to bear joint responsibility for her deed. Her self-absorption is all the more striking in view of the fact that Ismene's motive is of the purest. She wishes to die beside her sister and show honour to the dead (544–5). And when, rebuffed, she demands, 'What kind of life is dear to me, if I am bereft of you?', Antigone replies contemptuously, 'Ask Creon. He's the one you care about' (549).

The desire for *kleos* is what motivates Homeric heroes to risk their lives in battle. It is what Creon himself should be seeking, as his son Haemon points out, when he urges him to take decisions that will redound to his credit (703–4). Instead Creon's actions result in shame, as we will discover when the tragedy unfolds. *Kleos* is not, however, a quality to which an Athenian woman was expected to aspire. Pericles' famous statement that concludes his Funeral Speech, to the effect that women should be remembered neither for good nor for evil, is more to the point, however distasteful it may be to our modern sensibility. By seeking *kleos* Antigone is thus acting in a manner that would have offended Athenian mores, let alone the mores of the sexist Creon.

It is noteworthy that no one in the play, Antigone included, suggests that the soul of the unburied dead will not be able to find peace in Hades. This is in contrast to the *Iliad* where Achilles's refusal to bury Patroclus provokes his *psuchê* or spirit to appear in a dream, urging Achilles to bury him 'so that I can enter the gates of Hades as quickly as possible' (23.71ff.), and there is plentiful evidence from later times to indicate that the dead required burial to gain access to Hades. Instead, Sophocles directs all our thoughts to envisaging the horrific consequences of treating a human body like a carcass. Polyneices' corpse will become 'a sweet treasure trove for birds as they look down on it from above and anticipate their pleasure at consuming it', in Antigone's words (29–30); 'a body for birds and dogs to feast upon, disgusting to behold', as Creon proclaims when he issues his edict (205–6); 'devoured by carrion dogs and by birds', as Haemon warns his father (697–8); and 'mangled by carrion dogs', as it later became, as we learn from the Messenger (1198). Nor is there any reference either to the malignant influence of the unburied dead or to the necessity for burial on hygienic grounds. The refusal to bury Polyneices' constitutes an offence against both the gods and the dead in Antigone's view, and that is the sole basis upon which her justification for defying Creon's edict rests.

Antigone's death is all the more tragic because she dies affianced to Creon's son Haemon. In Classical Athens the graves of those who died before experiencing the pleasures of marriage were sometimes marked with a stone grave-marker in the shape of a *loutrophoros*, a vase containing purified water to be used in the ceremonial bridal-bath that preceded a wedding. The function of the marker was presumably to symbolize the poignancy of the untimely death.

Though Creon dismissively tells Haemon that he should let Antigone go 'so that she can marry in Hades', it is highly unlikely that the Greeks would have believed that any such happy outcome awaited the dead in the gloomy afterlife (653–4). Both the Chorus and Antigone describe her tomb as a 'bridal chamber', but there is no suggestion that this is other than ironic (804, 890). Hades was not a place where marriage could be consummated, any more than it was a place where children could be born. So Creon's remark should be seen as a cruel jibe, expressive of his contempt for Haemon's choice of bride and of his indifference for his son's feelings. Likewise there is merely pathos in the Messenger's description of Antigone's place of interment as 'a bridal chamber made of stone' (1204–5), and in his claim that Haemon, by taking his own life, 'now lies as a corpse beside a corpse, having fulfilled his marriage rites in the house of Hades' (1240–1). Unambiguous, however, is Antigone's assertion that she will have 'no share of the marriage bed, no wedding hymns sung on my behalf, no part in marriage, no nurturing of children' (917–18).

It was a strongly held belief that the shedding of blood was a cause of *miasma* or pollution. The pollution manifested itself in a contagiousness that affected humans, animals and crops alike. When Creon pronounces Antigone's doom, he declares that she is to be entombed alive with as much food as is necessary, expressly, as he says, to avoid causing pollution (773–5). Later, when she is being led to her doom, he claims, 'My hands will be *hagnoi* (pure) regarding this maiden.' He does so because the choice will be hers as to whether she wishes to die by starving herself or to continue living, albeit entombed, as long as her food supply lasts. His point is that, since he has not shed her blood, he is not responsible for her death – a legal quibble, which nonetheless had some force according to the belief system of the time.

Despite what the Chorus might at times suggest, there is no evidence to indicate that the gods orchestrate the action or play any part in Creon's downfall. On his first entry the king deferentially credits the gods with having righted the state after a period of civil war, but this should surely be interpreted as a judicious utterance intended for public consumption, rather than as evidence of a deeply held personal belief (162–3). Creon is rightly dismissive of the pious but simple-minded suggestion of the Chorus that it was the gods who might have engineered the burial of Polyneices since no human agency was detected (278–9). His later assertion that '*daimones* (divine beings) have no concern for this corpse', which he bases on the fact that Polyneices was guilty of sacrilege by burning shrines and votive offerings, is certainly reckless, but there is nothing to indicate that they actually do manifest any concern (285–7). It is unclear how we are expected to respond to the Guard's claim that the dust storm that arises after Antigone has first covered the body is 'a sickness sent by the gods' (421). Certainly the dust storm has a dramatic function because it enables Antigone to escape detection the first time she sprinkles dust on the corpse, but Sophocles does not offer any guidance as to whether or not the gods were culpable.

The Chorus' claim that Antigone and Creon are merely the victims of the curse of the house of Labdacus – the same curse that had previously brought ruin upon Antigone's father Oedipus – can hardly be taken as an explanation for the tragedy (593–602). Primarily out of deference to his father, and in the hope that he will avoid angering him by urging caution, Haemon states that it is the gods who implant reason in men's minds. Besides which, it is never suggested that the gods are responsible for removing reason from Creon (683). When Creon condemns Antigone, the Chorus tells her, 'You rushed headlong to the edge of daring, and you have fallen heavily at the pedestal of Justice, child, and you are paying for some sin of your father.' However, the Chorus is merely being deferential to Creon at this point out of political expediency, and the outcome of the play does not justify this interpretation.

Likewise the chthonic gods, that is to say, the gods who inhabit the underworld, play no discernible part in the action (749). When Creon mocks Antigone for praying to Hades, 'the only god whom she worships', it is obvious that he does so in the knowledge that Hades is powerless to secure her release (777–8). In fact Hades both as god and as place is only a vague concept in the play, as invariably, too, in the Greek imagination. When Creon is interrogating Antigone after she has been apprehended by the Guard, she defends her action by declaring, 'Hades desires these rites' (519). The verb she uses for 'desire', *potheô*, expresses intense yearning or craving. It is a verb that a lover might use of her beloved. It almost seems as if Antigone is transferring her affection for her brother to the god, because in general Hades is passionless (1284). Indeed the epithets that most frequently describe him are *adamastos*, 'implacable', and *ameilichos*, 'relentless'. Similarly when Teiresias warns Creon, 'The ones bringing about destruction after the crime, the *Erinyes* (or Furies) of Hades and of the gods, are lying in wait for you so that you may be apprehended for these crimes' (1074–6), it is evident that the Furies will act on behalf of the chthonic and Olympian gods only *after* the condemned has entered Hades. The compound adjective *husterophoroi*, which I have translated as 'the ones bringing about destruction after', indicates that the Erinyes play no part in engineering Creon's doom. In sum, it is the inflexibility of both Creon and Antigone that is largely if not wholly responsible for the tragedy.

As she departs for her execution, Antigone ruefully observes that it is pointless to look to the gods any more, since her piety has merely earned her a reputation for impiety (922–4). There is perhaps just the hint of a suggestion that she was expecting the gods to intervene and avert her death. 'If', she says, 'what is happening to me is pleasing to the gods, I shall through suffering discover what it was I did wrong. But if he [i.e. Creon] is doing wrong, my wish is that he suffers exactly the same evil as he has wrongfully inflicted on me' (925–9). It is unclear, however, how the gods are expected to communicate their judgement to her down in Hades. The Olympians had no interaction with Hades and, moreover, Hades was not a place of punishment for the ordinary dead that resembled the Hell of Christian belief.

Divine intervention is certainly not needed to explain Creon's downfall. Since neither Creon nor Antigone is prepared to back down, a showdown between two headstrong individuals becomes inevitable. And this of course accords with our understanding of human nature. Creon is the kind of person who digs his heels in further the more he is urged to change his mind. His refusal to respond to the reasonable pleas of Haemon lead him further down the path of ruin, as do those of the seer Teiresias, who arrives after Antigone has been condemned and who in a striking phrase urges him 'to yield to the dead' (1029).

It is in fact Creon's encounter with the seer Teiresias that comes closest to suggesting that divine intervention might be at work, since his refusal to give burial to Polyneices' corpse has resulted in the befouling of offerings to the gods. In consequence the gods are refusing to accept any sacrifices or heed any prayers from the Thebans. In addition, because birds have now tasted human blood, they are no longer capable of sending signs for augurs to interpret. The relationship between the human and the divine is therefore out of joint. Even so, this does not amount to a divine judgement passed upon Creon. On the contrary, it is the inevitable consequence of his ill-judged action, since the unburied corpse has caused pollution. 'Think about it, son', Teiresias advises. 'Everyone is capable of making a mistake' (1023–4). All he needs to do is bury the dead and relations between gods and mortals will again be normalized (1023–32).

Creon might have averted tragedy even now, had he immediately heeded Teiresias' warning. But he doesn't. Instead he accuses the seer of using his office for personal gain – a common charge in this period and no doubt in others as well, whenever a seer was thought to be proffering a prophecy that was politically motivated. Teiresias, who is as hot-headed as Creon, reacts by intemperately hurling abuse at the king and prophesying the death of his son Haemon. Creon, he declares, has upset the natural order. He has left unburied one who should have been buried and buried one who is living.

And now we learn, rather belatedly, that, to make matters worse, Creon has also denied burial rites to the Argive warriors who fought alongside

Polyneices, thereby causing pollution and arousing outrage far beyond the borders of Thebes (1080–3). It was an almost invariably observed custom throughout the Greek world to return the bodies of one's fallen enemies on the battlefield. Only exceptionally do we hear that this right was denied, as for instance following the Battle of Delium in 424 BCE, when the Boeotians initially refused to return the Athenian dead on the grounds that they had defiled a Boeotian sanctuary (Thucydides 4.97).[3] The fact that the denial of burial to the Argives receives only passing reference suggests that Sophocles wishes the audience to focus almost exclusively on Polyneices.

Though he ultimately heeds the seer's warning, Creon is powerless to alter events, which now take their inevitable course. It is Haemon's love for his betrothed Antigone and in turn Eurydice's love for her son Haemon that unleash an unstoppable train of events with death consequent upon death. And though Haemon's death was predicted by Teiresias, it was hardly decreed by the gods. Rather it was motivated by his love for his bride. To conclude, although Creon recklessly makes a bad situation worse by rejecting his son's appeal, there is no evidence that his 'fate' is brought on by the gods.

Little can be inferred about Sophocles' religious viewpoint from the Chorus of fifteen Theban elders. In the Parodos (or entry code) the Chorus invokes the sun for having shed light on the day that brought victory to Thebes. It then alludes to Zeus' abhorrence of boastfulness and claims Ares, the god of war, as its ally. Zeus is credited with routing the enemy and at the conclusion Bacchus is invoked (100–54). In the first Stasimon (or choral interlude) the Chorus speaks of man's daring and inventiveness. This is perhaps a reference to the fact that some individual, unidentified at this point, has had the audacity to disobey Creon's edict by burying a traitor. The Stasimon ends with the observation that ruin awaits the man who violates both human and divine law (332–75). In the second Stasimon the Chorus speaks of a curse inflicted by the gods that passes down from one generation to the next, citing the curse on the house of Labdacus, to which Antigone belongs. After celebrating the power of Zeus, which is ageless, the Chorus concludes by asserting ominously, 'Nothing that is great enters the lives of mortals without *atê*, viz. a curse' (613–14). In the third Stasimon, which follows Haemon's pleas on behalf of Antigone, the Chorus sings of the unconquerable power of Aphrodite (781–99). In the fourth Stasimon it recalls other royal personages who, like Antigone, were immured alive (944–87). 'Terrible is the power of fate', it declares. 'Neither wealth nor war nor fortification nor dark, sea-struck ships can escape it.' The Chorus cites the example of Lycurgus, the Edonian king who opposed the entry of Dionysus and who 'learned to know the god, whom he had profaned by slander.' This, however, has no bearing on Antigone's fate, other than the fact that she has 'learned' what happens when you offend someone more powerful than yourself. In her case, however, it is a fellow human, not a god, whom she has offended (960–1). Instead of a fifth Stasimon, the Chorus delivers a *huporchêma* or 'dance song' to Bacchus in the forlorn hope that as the protective god of Thebes he will be able to avert the ensuing tragedy (1115–54). Manifestly her appeal falls on deaf ears.

So is Sophocles' *Antigone* a play about religion? It depends what we mean by 'about'. It is certainly about religion in the sense that the theme of the play focuses on religious obligations and the interpretation of religious law. It is much less clear whether there is any specifically religious lesson to be drawn from it. As we have seen, the gods are invoked but they never appear and there is no evidence either that they are working behind the scenes. Bad decisions that are compounded by inflexibility, and then have their consequences, seems to be the play's essential message, such as it is. When Creon makes his final entry bearing the body of Haemon, the Chorus declares, 'This is *atê* (ruin) not brought on by anyone else but by his own mistake.' Conventionally *atê* is a ruinous and destructive state of mind caused by impious action towards the gods, which the gods then inflict on the guilty party, but there is no suggestion that this is the case here. And Creon accepts full responsibility for his fate in the next line when he exclaims, 'Alas for the stubborn mistakes of my evil-plotting soul that have brought on death!' (1259–62).

The word *hamartêma*, which I have translated as 'mistake', is notoriously difficult to convey in English. It is a lexical variant on *hamartia*, the word that Aristotle uses in the *Art of Poetry* in his celebrated definition of the tragic hero, viz. a man who is neither pre-eminently virtuous nor villainous, whose misfortune is brought about 'not by vice and depravity but by some kind of *hamartia*' (1453a9–10, 15–16). We might debate at length, as scholars have done, the precise meaning of the word. The literal translation is 'missing the mark', rather like an arrow which misses its target, but what is clear is that both Creon and the Chorus regard human error as the paramount cause of the tragedy.[4]

The Chorus' final words are the following (1348–53):

> Good sense is by far the most important element in happiness. One should never act impiously towards the gods. The boastful words of proud men receive their just deserts and teach them good sense in old age.

Pious words indeed, though how far this sententious observation serves as a useful guide for the challenges that life throws at us remains, as we head for the exit, debatable.

Notes

1 All translations are my own.
2 There follows a passage that many scholars consider to be spurious, in which Antigone asserts that she would not have taken it upon herself to break the law either if she had been a mother or if her husband had died, but since her parents were dead, she could never replace her brother and for that reason he deserves her act of sacrifice (904–20). The argument is thoroughly unconvincing, not least because it contravenes the divine law that she cited earlier (450–60).
3 See Garland (2001) 101–3.
4 See Lanzillotta (2014) 662–4.

10

Euripides' Reception of Sophocles' *Antigone*

Ioanna Karamanou

This chapter sets out to explore the reception of Sophocles' *Antigone* by Euripides in *Phoenissae* and in his own, fragmentarily preserved, *Antigone*. It seeks to investigate those aspects of the Sophoclean plot and characterization which were transformed by Euripides in his own plays, and which he imbued with further dramatic meaning and ideological nuances.

Sophocles' *Antigone* (plausibly dated to 442/441 BC) antedates Euripides' *Phoenissae* (dated between 411–409 BC) and *Antigone* (probably dated between 412–406 on the basis of metrical criteria), both of which belong to the last decade of Euripides' dramatic career.[1] Both Euripidean plays reiterate the key theme of the Sophoclean play, that is, Antigone's decision to bury Polyneices, within different types of plot-structure.

To explore Euripides' reception of the Sophoclean *Antigone*, I shall focus on two pivotal notions which the younger dramatist evidently derives from the Sophoclean play and refigures in both of his tragedies: Antigone's gender role, which, as I shall argue, Euripides associates with the choice that she has to make between her natal and her (future) conjugal household, and the manner in which her female role seems to be associated with Dionysiac power in each play.

In *Phoenissae* the authenticity of most of the scenes in which Antigone participates was challenged by earlier scholars: these include the scene known as the *teichoskopia* ('observation from the city-walls': *Ph.* 88–201), in which Antigone watches the gathering of the Argive army from the Theban walls, her subsequent lament over the body of her mother and two brothers (1480–1581) and the *exodus* (1582–1709) involving her expressed will to bury Polyneices and, after not being allowed to do that, her firm resolve to accompany her blind and aged father Oedipus to exile. Recent criticism, nonetheless, generally tends to accept that these scenes are genuine and essential for dramatic action and characterization, except for certain corrupt lines.[2]

On the basis of the available evidence, the plot elements that seem to have been introduced by Euripides in the action of *Phoenissae* are the *teichoskopia*, then the scene in which Antigone is summoned by her mother Jocasta to enter the battlefield and avert the duel between her two brothers (1264–83) and the maiden's decision to forsake her future marriage to Haemon, with the purpose of supporting her helpless, exiled father (1672–82).

In the scene of Antigone's observation of the Argive troops from the city-walls (*teichoskopia*), the very first lines addressed to the maiden by the old servant, who has been assigned with the task of accompanying her, draw a sharp distinction between male and female dramatic space and sphere of action (89–91). Antigone is kept sheltered in the female quarters of the house, whose border is the façade of the stage-building dividing the private, female domain of the household from the public, masculine sphere of action. She has been granted permission by her mother to observe the Argive army from the Theban walls being accompanied by the elderly slave, so as to avoid censure, in case any citizen appears on the path. The servant's words allude to the fifth-century Athenian practice of sexual segregation, according to which unmarried women should be kept within domestic space, so as to ensure the dignity of the *oikos* ('household'). The integrity of the household relied to a great extent on the dignity of its female members ensuring the production of legitimate offspring, which concerned the *polis* as a whole, since the latter aimed at maintaining the legitimacy and stability of the Athenian citizen body.[3] At the end of this scene the old servant urges Antigone to return to the women's apartments, thus resuming his earlier admonition to her to avoid arousing disapproval by being seen in public space (193–201). These opening and closing remarks construct an effective ring-composition focusing on the spatial boundaries of female activity, which are going to be transgressed by Antigone in the course of the play.

At the same time, the *teichoskopia* aims to display right from the outset Antigone's attachment to her natal family. The servant's initial address to Antigone reveals the strong bonds between father and daughter through an emotional metaphor (88: 'fine flower to your father'),[4] thus foreshadowing her determination to support him at the *exodus* of the play. Moreover, it is only after her persistent entreaty to see even from a distance her brother Polyneices, who has joined the Argive army, that Jocasta allows her to leave the women's quarters for a while, under the surveillance of the old servant (89–91). Antigone's affection for Polyneices emerges from her yearning to discern him amidst the Argive troops and throw her arms around his neck, which adds to the poignancy of her long separation from him (156–71).

The key idea of Antigone's secluded maidenhood is first challenged when Jocasta later summons her daughter to rush with her onto the battlefield, in order to prevent her brothers from dying at each other's hands (1264–83). Jocasta appeals to her to leave the female quarters, by drawing an eloquent contrast between her normal maidenly habits and the urgency of the imminent misfortune. This critical situation forces Antigone to abandon her maidenly modesty and shame and to cross gender boundaries, by moving from the sheltered domestic sphere towards the uncontrolled male crowd (1275–6).[5] The abandonment of normal female behaviour in this episode thus involves an inversion of the earlier *teichoskopia* scene, which focused on the norms defining Antigone's gender role.

This inversion becomes even more acute in her subsequent threnetic monody (lament) over the bodies of her two brothers and of her mother, who took her own life upon witnessing the death of her sons (1485–1538). Antigone no longer appears as a sheltered maiden; she has removed her veil and unfastened her robe, like a maenad, describing herself as a 'bacchant of the dead' (1489–90).[6] As I shall argue, this self-definition is multi-layered and bears special dramatic significance. Firstly, it serves to illustrate Antigone's powerful attachment to her natal family; she is a 'bacchant of the dead', that is, she is possessed by her beloved dead, as bacchants are possessed by Dionysus. This idea recurs a few lines later in v. 1492, where she also describes herself as 'leader of a much lamenting procession for the dead'. Bacchic metaphors are similarly employed elsewhere in contexts of death: Evadne describes herself as a bacchant while rushing to join her husband Capaneus in his funeral pyre (E. *Supp.* 1000–1), whereas the captive women attacking Polymestor and his children are likened to 'bacchants possessed by Hades' (*Hec.* 1077).[7] At the same time, the Dionysiac dimension brought forward in Antigone's lament suits the funerary context of this scene, in that the cult of Dionysus Iacchus in Eleusinian ritual was regarded as leading to the salvation of the dead.[8]

The infiltration of Dionysiac elements into the Antigone myth evidently goes back to Sophocles' *Antigone*. The *parodos* of the Sophoclean play includes an honorific reference to Dionysus, the patron-god of Thebes, as leader of the vigorous dances for the Theban victory over the invading army (153–4). Moreover, the famous hymn to Dionysus in the fifth *stasimon* of *Antigone* (1115–54) is an 'ironic illusion of hope',[9] expressing a misguided optimism for Antigone's return from the grave, where she has been enclosed alive. This song brings forward the polarity between life and death, between hope and calamity and between ritual, as represented by Bacchus, and the rationalism of Creon's rule. Above all, however, it seems to be a cletic hymn (an invocation) to Dionysus as liberator of women from confinement. This Dionysiac quality also emerges from Euripides' *Bacchae* 447 referring to the miraculous release of the maenads from their bonds and from the mythical accounts of Antiope's escape from her chains through the god's intervention and her flight to Mount Cithaeron ([Apollod.] 3.5.5, Hyg. *fab.* 7).[10]

Accordingly, I shall argue that the notion of Dionysiac liberation pervading the fifth *stasimon* of the Sophoclean *Antigone* is refigured by Euripides in *Phoenissae* in a symbolic manner, in order to bring forward Antigone's 'new self'.[11] The maenadic imagery employed in Antigone's monody is not merely suggestive of her irrational state of mind, as in the description of the Homeric Andromache (*Il.* 22.460: she rushes forth like a maenad in fear for Hector's life), from which this simile is considered to derive.[12] It is probably more complex than that. The 'bacchic' status that Antigone assumes – both with regard to her physical appearance and in metaphorical terms – may well open the way to her inner liberation, which emerges from her defiance of Creon in the next scene. In turn, she seems to be 'liberated' by Dionysus in a symbolic sense, in that the maenadic 'emancipation' that she displays in her confrontation with Creon, which will be discussed below, sets her free to contest the propriety of his orders and make her own choices as against the power exerted upon her by the king.

The burial conflict at the *exodus* of *Phoenissae* (see esp. 1626–72) derives from the Sophoclean *Antigone*. Euripides' reception of the burial motif comprising Creon's decree to leave Polyneices' body unburied and Antigone's forceful reaction to it is both thematic and conceptual. I would observe that in ethical terms Euripides revisits the opposing definitions of prudence as obedience of divine sanctions in Antigone's eyes and as good sense imposing submission to the decrees of the *polis* according to Creon (S. *Ant.* 451, 459, 469–70, 538, 662, 667, 671, 728, 742–3 and E. *Ph.* 1647, 1680). He also reiterates the Sophoclean polarity between the idea of deified *Dikē* (Justice) represented by Antigone (*Ant.* 451, 538) and Creon's own definition of justice as righteous political conduct (*Ant.* 662, 667, 671); Euripides transfers Antigone's position to the human sphere, in that she asserts that leaving Polyneices unburied is against lawful justice (*Ph.* 1651). Moreover, he enters into a dialogue with Sophocles over the definition of *hybris* (*LSJ* – 9th edn): 'insolence', 'violation'). In S. *Ant.* 480–3 Creon defines *hybris* as the transgression of the laws of the *polis* authorizing the punishment of traitors – a punishment, which, as he has already asserted (280–8), is approved by the gods; conversely, Antigone's 'response' in E. *Ph.* 1663 is that *hybris* involves the violation of divine sanctions, which impose respect for the dead. Furthermore, the Euripidean treatment of the burial motif showcases the conflict between family obligations and the interests of the *polis*, which pervades the Sophoclean play (S. *Ant.* esp. 69–77, 502–25, E. *Ph.* 1657, 1668).[13]

Antigone's bacchic associations need to be further explored with regard to the burial conflict. Her choice to defend the unwritten laws of nature (*physis*) imposing Polyneices' burial over Creon's state decree (*nomos*) is in line with Dionysus' intrinsic relation to nature as against social conventions.[14]

Antigone's fervent challenge of the king's judgement also involves a role reversal between ruler and subject, which is a further maenadic feature.[15] It is noteworthy that, when Antigone vigorously opposes Creon's will by freely asserting her decision to bury Polyneices, the king threatens to impose spatial confinement upon her (*Ph.* 1660). In this manner, he tries to reassert his control over her by seclusion, as in several cases in tragedy concerning women who challenge male control, including maenads, which could be congruent with Antigone's 'bacchic' status. Sophocles' *Antigone*, on which Euripides draws for this matter, similarly focuses on the title-character's seclusion initially in the female sphere of the household (*Ant.* 577–81) and, subsequently, by immurement (773–6), which is a regular form of punishment of unmarried women. Her underground prison serves both as a tomb and as a bridal chamber, especially given that Antigone's untimely death as an unwed virgin corresponds to the widespread motif of the 'bride of Hades' (*Ant.* 773–80, 810–16, 885–8, 891, 1204–5).[16]

As observed above, Antigone's self-definition as 'bacchant' of her dead kin eloquently articulates her powerful ties with her natal family. I would note that, in order to underscore the poignancy of Antigone's loss of her beloved family in her lamentation, Euripides refigures the Sophoclean mother-bird metaphor grieving for being robbed of her nestlings (S. *Ant.* 423–5) and presents Antigone as seeking for 'a lamenting bird in lone motherhood to join in her bewailing' (E. *Ph.* 1515–18). In her altercation with Creon, she asserts her will to die by her brother's side (*Ph.* 1658–9), which seems to be a reworking of S. *Ant.* 73:[17] 'I'll lie with him, a loving sister with her loving brother' (trans. Stuttard). When she is forbidden by the king to bury Polyneices, she makes the realistic choice to accompany her feeble father, Oedipus, into exile (*Ph.* 1679–1709).[18] The heroism of the Sophoclean Antigone is thus imbued with realism in her portrayal by Euripides. Again she declares her intention to die beside a member of her natal family, this time beside her father (*Ph.* 1681).

To follow her father into exile, Antigone forsakes her marriage to Haemon (*Ph.* 1672–82). When Creon tries to impose this marriage upon her, she even goes as far as to proclaim that in her wedding night she will turn into a Danaid. Famously, the Danaids (daughters of the exiled King Danaus of Egypt), forced into marriage against their will, murdered their husbands on their wedding night. I would observe that the use of the Danaid metaphor is very powerful, not only because it points to the act of murdering the bridegroom, as Antigone threatens to do, but also because it is suggestive of the indissoluble attachment of the bride to her natal *oikos*, given that it is their father's orders that the Danaids execute to the detriment of their marital households.[19] This idea further showcases Antigone's liminal position between her family of origin and her future family by marriage. The tension emerging from the contradiction between the natal and the conjugal *oikos* is brought forward especially in Euripidean drama, as Richard Seaford has argued in an influential article.[20] The ambiguous position of women between two different households may well endanger the continuity of either one of them, and this matter seems to mirror fifth-century socio-political conditions, if we take into account the preoccupation of the Athenian city-state to ensure the preservation of the household as an essential unit of the *polis*.[21]

This theme also underlies the Sophoclean *Antigone*: on the one hand, the title-character herself admits that she would not have disobeyed the law of the state for a husband or child, as she did for her brother (904–12), underscoring her utter loyalty to her natal family; on the other hand, just a few lines later she laments for not having experienced the joys of marriage and motherhood (916–18), reflecting a concept deeply rooted in civic ideology and intrinsically interwoven with the perpetuation of the *oikos*. This ambivalence is thus conveyed by Sophocles in a balanced manner. Euripides, nonetheless, sharpens this tension by giving it a new twist, in that he makes Antigone decisively choose blood ties over conjugal ties, freeing herself from the marriage that Creon is trying to impose on her.

The closing tableau of *Phoenissae*, which displays Antigone supporting her aged and frail father, provides an inversion of her childlike portrayal in the *teichoskopia* scene, in which the once sheltered maiden was in need of the guidance of an old man. Conversely, in this final scene she has grown into maturity through loss and disaster, showing decisiveness and offering service to her feeble father.[22] This is an eloquent 'mirror scene' (i.e. a scene reflecting and recalling in a striking manner an earlier scene from the same play[23]), which serves to delineate Antigone's character development within the course of the play.

Antigone's liminal position between her natal and future marital family is similarly brought forward in Euripides' own *Antigone*, which has come down to us in fragments. The learned hypothesis to Sophocles' *Antigone* by the Alexandrian critic Aristophanes of Byzantium attests that Euripides treated the same phase of the myth as Sophocles concerning Antigone's reaction to Creon's edict against Polyneices' burial; nonetheless, as the Alexandrian scholar reports, in the Euripidean play Antigone is detected at the burial together with Haemon, is joined with him in marriage and gives birth to a son, Maeon (see also Sallust. Argum. S. *Ant.* II, p. 70 Dain). This is a radically different plot-resolution than that in Sophocles' *Antigone*. At the same time, the preserved fragments suggest that the Euripidean treatment is imbued with certain Sophoclean elements, which are worth pointing out.

Firstly, Antigone's resolve to bury Polyneices' body, as in Sophocles' version, emerges from the plot-outline provided in the Aristophanic hypothesis, which attests that she was caught in the act of burying him. A powerful argument in favour of her brother's burial is employed in fr. 176 Kannicht (henceforth abbreviated as K.) asserting the futility of punishing him *post mortem*, which, in my view, could be an echo of S. *Ant.* 1029–30: 'Accept that the man's dead. Don't niggle at his corpse. There's no glory to be gained in destroying someone who's already dead' (trans. Stuttard). Antigone's determination to perform burial rites for Polyneices showcases her potent ties with her natal family, thus recalling the key idea of the Sophoclean treatment, which Euripides also reworked in *Phoenissae*. Nevertheless, his startling innovation in the Antigone saga consists in Haemon's involvement in Polyneices' burial and the unexpectedly happy ending of the couple's romance. It is noteworthy that Euripides reiterates and refigures the love theme, which formed a secondary idea in the Sophoclean play (see esp. *Ant.* 781–800, 1220–41), bringing it into special prominence in his own dramatic treatment.

In more specific terms, a number of fragments coming from the Euripidean *Antigone* focus on the romance of Antigone and Haemon. Fr. 161 K. refers to love as madness, thus echoing S. *Ant.* 790–2, whereas fr. 162 K. alludes to young people's tendency to become overwhelmed by love. Fr. 162a K. is likely to have been delivered by Haemon asserting that he wishes to have a wife, i.e. Antigone, with whom he will grow old. Accordingly, fr. 160 K. referring to the solidarity of young people in what the speaker (perhaps Creon) regards as folly may well be suggestive of Haemon's agreement with Antigone's stance regarding Polyneices' burial.[24]

Euripides thus revisits and develops further the burial conflict and the love theme of the Sophoclean play, bringing them together, in that these two ideas are conjoined through the presentation of Haemon as an 'accomplice' in the burial. In turn, the tension between Antigone's obligations to her natal family and her role as Haemon's future wife is soothed in this play. Due to her attachment to her blood kin, her marriage to Haemon ends up in Hades in Sophocles (1240–1) and is resolutely rejected in *Phoenissae*. Conversely, in Euripides' *Antigone* her duties to her natal and her future conjugal *oikos* are reconciled, as the title-character performs the burial rites on her brother with the support of Haemon, whom she marries, thus ensuring the continuity of his household through Maeon's birth.

The significance of the continuity of the *oikos* emerges from its pivotal role as an essential component of the *polis*, as mentioned above. The interrelation of household and city-state is often represented in fifth-century drama, and these socio-political associations seem to have been brought forward in a particular group of later Euripidean plays ending up in good fortune, such as *Ion* and the fragmentary *Antiope, Hypsipyle* and *Captive Melanippe*, which were staged during the Athenian crisis caused by the Peloponnesian War especially from 413 BC onwards. In these tragedies the household is rescued in the nick of time after a major crisis; in turn, the safety and protection of the *oikos* as the backbone of the *polis* seem to contribute allusively to the restoration of social order in that troubled period.[25] Hence, unlike the much earlier Sophoclean *Antigone* presenting the collapse of Creon's household, which is also spatially suggested through Eurydice's suicide at the household altar (see S. *Ant.* 1301–5), Euripides in his own *Antigone* chooses to rescue Creon's *oikos*, as well as reconciling the tension deriving from the contradiction between Antigone's natal and future marital household. This tension also pervades the closing scene of *Phoenissae*, as observed above, and it is interesting that the dramatist experiments with two fundamentally different types of plot-structure within the same period of time, which may well be suggestive of the vitality and multiformity of his dramaturgy.

The iambic fr. 177 K. praising Dionysus' overwhelming power seems to suggest that the god emerged *ex machina*, presumably in order to ensure Antigone's rescue and her marriage to Haemon. The tone of this fragment revealing human submission to the divine will is a recurring feature in lines delivered by characters addressing a *deus ex machina* (see *Andr.* 1274–6, *Supp.* 1227, *IT* 1475–6, *Ion* 1606–8, *Hel.* 1680–3, *Or.* 1666–70), and this could further tell in favour of Dionysus' appearance at the *exodus* of the play. It is also noteworthy that in this fragment Dionysus is addressed as son of Dione, who was Aphrodite's mother, according to a branch of the mythical tradition going back to Homer (*Il.* 5.370–417, [Apollod.] 1.3.1). Euripides' choice to present the god as Aphrodite's brother seems further to relate him to the love theme of the play, that is, the romance of Antigone and Haemon, which he leads to a happy ending.[26] Maeon's birth, which is reported in the Aristophanic hypothesis, is likely to have been foretold in this divine speech, as it is very improbable that it could have occurred in the course of the play for obvious reasons of dramatic economy.

Once again Dionysus is employed in association with issues that define Antigone's gender role. In *Phoenissae*, as observed above, he seems to have liberated her in a symbolic manner, giving her the inner freedom to confront and defy Creon. But this time Euripides chooses a different plot-resolution, in that he seems to present Dionysus, if he indeed appeared *ex machina*, as an *actual* liberator of Antigone, who is thus rescued from punishment and integrates herself into her marital *oikos*. This Dionysiac quality is similarly exploited in later Euripidean plays, such as *Hypsipyle* and *Antiope*, leading to the rescue of a household after a serious crisis and to a happy ending.[27] Hence, the ironic idea of the ultimate futility of Dionysus' role as liberator, who does not respond to the cletic hymn addressed to him by the Chorus in the fifth *stasimon* of the Sophoclean play, seems to be overturned in Euripides' own *Antigone*, where the god's epiphany may have led to the play's denouement.

Further bacchic associations might emerge from a papyrus fragment (P.Oxy. 3317= fr. 175 K.) ascribed to the Euripidean *Antigone* and presenting a woman, dressed as a maenad, who is seized by her opponents. Considering, however, that the titles *Antigone* and *Antiope* are easily confused by ancient scribes, it is feasible that this fragment might belong to the latter play, in which Dirce is attested to have appeared as a maenad accompanied by a subsidiary chorus of bacchants and to have been captured and punished by Antiope's sons. At the same time, there is no evidence for a maenadic appearance of Antigone in the homonymous play,[28] though admittedly such a possibility may complement her aforementioned symbolically maenadic features in *Phoenissae*, thus enriching the reading of both plays.

Overall, both Euripidean tragedies revisit the pivotal theme of the Sophoclean *Antigone*, that is, the burial conflict and its gender implications, which is refigured within diverse types of plot-structure. Euripides chooses to delve into Antigone's gender role and her liminal position between her family by origin and her future marital household either by sharpening this tension, as in *Phoenissae*, or ultimately reconciling Antigone's duties to her natal family and to her conjugal household, as in his own *Antigone*. It is noteworthy that these contradictions are intertwined with the notion of Dionysus' liberating power, which goes back to the fifth *stasimon* of the Sophoclean play, leading to a different denouement in each case. The dramatic transformation and further development of these features could thus yield insight into the vitality of Euripides' metapoetic 'dialogue' with the Sophoclean *Antigone*.

Notes

1 On the date of the Sophoclean play, see e.g. Griffith (1999) 1–2; Brown (1987) 1–2; Kamerbeek (1978) 36; on that of *Phoenissae*, see Mastronarde (1994) 14; Papadopoulou (2008) 24; Zimmermann (1993) 139 and n. 164 with further bibliography; on the date of Euripides' *Antigone*, Cropp and Fick (1985) 70, 74, 76; Zimmermann (1993) 161.

2 See especially Mastronarde (1994) 168–73 (on *Ph.* 88–201), 554–5 (on *Ph.* 1480–1581) and 591–4 (on *Ph.* 1582–1709); Papadopoulou (2008) 24, 128 n. 31, 131 n. 52; Zimmermann (1993) 141–4, bringing together earlier views;

Cairns (2016) 116 and 184, nn. 6 and 7; Craik (1988) 245; cf. the scepticism of Diggle, who deletes the *exodus* (Diggle 1981–1994, Vol. III on *Ph.* 1582–1766), followed by Kovacs (2002) *ad loc.*

3 For the spatial division between the private/female and public/male sphere of activity, see e.g. Rehm (2002) 21–2, 54–7; Scolnicov (1994) 11–28; Lefebvre (1991) 247–8. On sexual segregation in Classical Athens, see esp. E. *Heracl.* 43–4, 476–7, *Or.* 108, Lys. 3.6, Men. *Dysc.* 222–4; cf. also Ogden (1997) 25–36; Cohen (1991) 140–1; Des Bouvrie (1990) 44–8, 51–2; Blundell (1995) 135–8.

4 See Mastronarde (1994) 180. The translation of *Phoenissae* relies on Craik (1988) with minor adjustments.

5 See Mastronarde (1994) 501–3; Cairns (2016) 116; Craik (1988) 241.

6 On the physical features of maenads, see e.g. Bremer (1984) esp. 277.

7 See Craik (1988) 210–12, 257; Collard (1991) 188; Schlesier (1993) 97–103; Seaford (1993) 125–6.

8 See Bierl (1991) 130–1; Griffith (1999) 312–13, 318–19; Henrichs (1990) 265–70.

9 See Brown (1987) 214. Cf. also Kamerbeek (1978) 25, 186–7; Cairns (2016) 24–5, 175 n. 75.

10 On this Dionysiac feature, see the discussion in Bierl (1991) 127–32; Oudemans and Lardinois (1987) 146–8, 154–9; Seaford (1990a) 84–5, 87–8; Segal (1981) esp. 202–3; Winnington-Ingram (1980) 102–16.

11 On the evolution of Antigone's character in the course of *Phoenissae*, see Mueller-Goldingen (1985) 221–5; Zimmermann (1993) 152–6; Mastronarde (1994) 180, 591; Papadopoulou (2008) 30–2, 70–1; Burian (2009) 27–32; Lamari (2010) 111, 134. I have chosen not to consider the Dionysiac associations of *Ph.* 1751–7, as vv. 1736–57 are generally regarded as interpolated (see e.g. Mastronarde 1994: 635–7).

12 For the possibly Homeric origins of this simile, see Seaford (1993) 119–21; Mastronarde (1994) 563; for a discussion of the Iliadic passage, see Seaford (1993) 115–19; Tsagalis (2007) 1–29.

13 On the treatment of these moral values in *Antigone*, see Griffith (1999) 38–43; earlier Goheen (1951) 82–100; Dalfen (1977) 5–20. On *hybris* in particular, see Fisher (1992) 308–12, 429–30; MacDowell (1976) 19. On the clash between kinship duties and city-state interests in the Sophoclean play, see e.g. Winnington-Ingram (1980) esp. 122–36; Segal (1981) 152–86; Blondell (1998) 76–104; Griffith (1999) 48–50 (with further bibliography) and his note on *Ant.* 508–25.

14 On Dionysus' association with *physis* in *Antigone*, see Segal (1981) esp. 155, 163–4; Bierl (1991) 64–5.

15 On the reversal of roles in Sophocles' *Antigone,* see Syropoulos (2003) 58, 60–1; Blundell (1995) 174.

16 See Seaford (1990a) 80–8, for a number of tragic parallels of confined women. On the 'bride of Hades' pattern, see Seaford (1987) esp. 107–8, with regard to Antigone, Tyrrell and Bennett (1998) 97–121; Rehm (1994) 128–35; much earlier Rose (1925) 238–42.

17 See also Mastronarde (1994) 616.

18 For this matter, cf. Mastronarde (1994) 591.

19 On this metaphor, see also Papadopoulou (2011) 104.

20 See Seaford (1990b) drawing a number of examples from tragedy, though only passingly referring to this contradiction in *Phoenissae*.

21 For the *oikos-polis* interrelation, see Hansen (2006) esp. 109–12; Nagle (2006); Patterson (1998) 85–91. For its representation in tragedy, see particularly Hall (1997) 104–10; Goldhill (1986) 114.

22 See also Lamari (2010) 111–12; Mastronarde (1994) 553; Papadopoulou (2008) 93.

23 On 'mirror scenes' in tragedy, see Halleran (1985) 86–7; Mastronarde (2010) 68–77; Taplin (1977) 100–3, 357–9.

24 On the reconstruction of this play, see Cairns (2016) 118–19; Collard and Cropp (2008) I 156–9; Jouan and van Looy (1998–2003) I 193–201; Kannicht (2004) I 261–73; Webster (1967) 181–4; Zimmermann (1993) 162–71.

25 For the date of these plays, see for instance Collard and Cropp (2008) I 175 (on *Antiope*), I 589 (on *Captive Melanippe*) and II 254 (on *Hypsipyle*). On their socio-political resonances, see Karamanou (2012).

26 Cf. also Weil (1889) 331. The possible emergence of Dionysus *ex machina* has been favoured by Collard and Cropp (2008) I 157; Jouan and van Looy (1998–2003) I 200–1; Webster (1967) 182.

27 On Dionysus' role in *Hypsipyle,* see Collard, Cropp and Gibert (2004) 173–6; for his involvement in *Antiope*, see Zeitlin (1993) 173–7; Jouan and van Looy (1998–2003) I 232.

28 Collard and Cropp (2008) I 157–8 regard this papyrus fragment as likelier to belong to *Antiope* than *Antigone* (this ascription was favoured as early as Luppe 1981). On the other hand, Scodel (1982) 39–42, Kannicht (1992) 252–5 and Zimmermann (1993) 168–70, all explore Antigone's possible presentation as a maenad in Euripides' homonymous tragedy.

11

The Voices of Antigone

Helene Foley

> Antigone to Creon: 'Nothing you say can convince me. Nothing you ever *could* say will. And nothing I say can convince you either.'
>
> Creon to Antigone: 'Are you not ashamed to think differently from these men [the Theban Chorus]?'

In her first scene with Creon, after she has been caught by the Guard burying her brother, Antigone points out in these lines a central problem in Sophocles' play. No character in it agrees with what others say, nor does any character, with the exception of the seer Teiresias and the Chorus of Theban elders towards the end, fully persuade another person to change his or her mind. Moreover, although this is hard to capture in translation, no character in the play shares the same style of speaking and reasoning, or even in some cases interprets key words such as 'friend' and 'enemy' in the same way. By the end of the play, there is an answer of sorts to the issues that divide the characters. We learn from Teiresias, who has access to divine truth, that Creon should not have left the body of Polyneices unburied even though he was a traitor, because his body is polluting the land. Creon finally admits his error and recognizes his mistaken judgement about the traditional or unwritten laws that Antigone defends: 'I fear it's true, that the best and safest course must be to follow the established laws until the day we die.' The *polis* (city state) cannot legislate over the dead who now belong to another world. Above all, however, it is the play's clashing voices that make it dramatically and tragically certain that the central issues will not be resolved in time to prevent every character from suffering the loss of loved ones. Moreover, the failure of *Antigone*'s multiple voices to communicate with each other even at the end invites the audience to wonder how their own democratic city of Athens will ever resolve through dialogue in any simple fashion fundamental differences in point of view.

This chapter will take a look at the nature of these different voices in *Antigone* in order to understand better why and how the characters fail to communicate with each other and what is at stake in their failure of communication. It will then turn to how these very issues have been interpreted in a number of performances, adaptations, or new versions of the play across the globe in the twentieth and twenty-first centuries. This will allow us to consider how the play's dramatic clashes continue to resonate in very different situations now. For most people in Britain and America, for example, state refusal to bury the bodies of those viewed as political resisters is not a central political and social issue, nor are most of us facing a recent civil war. But this is very much the case elsewhere, and the voices speaking in defence of the various positions taken in this play predictably become different in those locations as well.

How does the play define its different voices and why?[1] In many respects, the voices of Ismene and Creon are least surprising until they are tested in action. In the first scene with her sister, Ismene adopts what she views as a voice and position that fits her role in the world of the play. She is a woman and a citizen of Thebes. Even if she loves her sister, wants to protect her, and agrees that Polyneices should be buried, she does not think that as either women or citizens she and Antigone can or should disobey Creon's edict. So Antigone cannot persuade her to act. Even now we might think Ismene represents a predictable female point of view. Interestingly, however, she changes her mind to some degree in her second scene with Antigone, not because she has come to agree with Antigone's action, but because she recognizes, as Antigone urged in the first scene, that her life is no longer worth living without a family. So, like Antigone, she is willing to take a risk and face death by claiming that she shared in the burial. Antigone will not allow her to claim a role in the deed. Ismene escapes punishment and survives, but her life will be meaningless. Her partial change of perspective fails to reconcile the sisters or establish full communication.

Creon's style of speaking, thinking and reasoning reflects his role in the play. He has suddenly become ruler of his country after a wrenching and bloody civil war between Polyneices and Eteocles. His edict concerning burial of the brothers reflects a need to re-establish law and order, and to differentiate between behaviour appropriate to the stability of the state or disruptive to it by inflicting punishment on the dead traitor Polyneices. He believes in putting the interest of the state above the interest of the individual and the family if these interests clash. 'I've no time for anyone who puts his family or friends before his country', he insists.

When he defends his point of view, he tends to use a set of prescriptive generalizations that apply from his perspective to all situations he faces as ruler. Those who attack the state must be punished. Women should not resist or take precedence over men: 'As long as I'm alive, I'll have no woman tell me what to do.' Sons should obey fathers. If people resist the ruler's commands they must be motivated by power or money. Not surprisingly, the kind of imagery Creon uses tends to be borrowed from contexts in which the natural world is brought under human control: the taming of earth and domestic animals or metal working, for example: 'Yes, but the strongest willed can be the easiest to break. The strongest iron, forged hardest in the fire, can shatter soonest. You see it all the time – the most spirited of horses, mastered by the thinnest bit. I *know*. Slaves can't afford fine principles when their master's close at hand.'

Creon goes so far as to assert that one cannot know the soul, thought, or judgement of a man (specifically a man) unless he has publically demonstrated his practice of governing and making laws. In principle, Creon's first speech was so convincing as an example of leadership to the Greek statesman Demosthenes (19.247) that he quoted it as an example to be imitated by the Athenian democracy. Arguably, Creon's basic approach makes considerable sense for a political leader who needs to make and establish choices that will hold in a wide range of complex public contexts.

Sophocles' play, however, repeatedly raises doubts about the voice adopted by Creon from the beginning. First, despite his plausible first speech to the Chorus establishing and explaining his edict, the audience already knows that Antigone will disobey the edict and has what she views are good reasons for doing so. We also soon realize that Creon is going to punish a relative for whom he is the legal guardian and who is engaged to his son: 'No. I don't care that she's my sister's child. I don't care that she's my closest family. She and her sister will not escape ... the ultimate penalty. Oh, yes! I consider Ismene equally responsible in the conspiracy ... to bury him.' Here Creon is making several mistakes in judgement regardless of the principles involved. He fails to adhere to one of his central principles, that a man virtuous in his household will be virtuous in governing a state: 'If a man behaves fairly at home, he'll present himself in public as a just man, too.' Creon is responsible for making sure that the family of Oedipus has male heirs; that is why Haemon is engaged to Antigone. Moreover, although he crudely tells Haemon that there are other furrows he can plough and that he will punish Antigone in front of him, his son is in love with Antigone and will soon kill himself over her dead body. The Chorus has to persuade Creon not to punish the guiltless Ismene. Indeed, viewers might be surprised at how little he knows both his son and his niece. Creon is not facing the contradictory aspects of his situation. He does have a family that needs to be considered and he is punished by losing every one of them including his wife, Eurydice, who blames him for Haemon's suicide.

The same difficulty in establishing his public ethical voice and judgement occurs elsewhere in the play. First, he misjudges the Guard who comes to address the attempted burial of Polyneices' corpse. The Guard is not, as Creon believes, motivated by being bribed and he is telling the truth. Later Creon initially resists the words of Teiresias until he is persuaded by the Chorus to change his mind. Finally, he agrees that he has made a mistake, but, against the Chorus's advice, he goes to bury Polyneices before going to Antigone's cave. By the time he gets there it is too late.

Confronting Haemon, Creon insists that Haemon should simply obey his father and accept his judgement. Haemon adopts a mediating male voice in the play. He agrees that he has come to support the interests of his father and not because of his passion for Antigone. But he wants Creon to look carefully at the specifics of this particular situation in order to protect his father's interests. Haemon has heard that the common people think that Antigone made an honourable choice and should be celebrated for it: 'More than any woman in the world, they're saying, she does not deserve to die in such a squalid way for doing something which should earn the highest praise. When her own brother fell in battle, she didn't let him lie unburied or be torn apart – and eaten – by the dogs and birds. Doesn't she deserve the highest honour? And this … disaffection's spreading silently all through the city.'

He does not want his father's rule to be destabilized by opposition and tries to show him that he should bend and change his mind in this particular case: 'Allow yourself to change your mind. If a young man like me can express an opinion, I'd say it would be wonderful to know everything there is to know – but, if you can't, and this is often the reality, it's still good to learn from those who offer good advice.'

If Creon's edict lacks authority for the population, Haemon adds, he is no longer a ruler of Thebes, but the ruler of a desert:

Creon Everybody knows that a city belongs to its most powerful citizen!

Haemon You'd do a great job ruling on your own – in an empty land where no one goes!

Haemon tries to appeal to his father by using generalizations that reflect his father's style, but he draws on imagery from nature, not technology: 'You see how, when the storm-winds come, a tree that bends and gives can keep its branches, but a tree that tries to stand inflexible, unbending, is torn up by its roots.' Generalizations are valuable tools but they must be responsive to contexts. Creon's lack of sympathy for his son's arguments soon generates anger between them and Haemon leaves threatening to take action. His reasoned attempt at mediating between the positions of Antigone and his father has failed.

Haemon's voice is perhaps unexpectedly mature for a young man in love, but Antigone's voice in this play is unique. From the first we see that she is willing to resist a public edict (she thinks her crime is holy) and take what she views as an honourable, even glorious action not to be expected of a woman. Moreover, she is willing to take responsibility for burying her brother and accept the punishment of death, and to respect the unwritten laws supported by the gods because of her unique sufferings as a product of incest who has lost her whole family except her sister. She tries to persuade Ismene, who also loves her family and agrees in principle on the burial, by demonstrating their unique emotional and ethical situation. When Ismene refuses, she stubbornly persists in pursuing her plan. When she later addresses Creon, she asserts both of these principles for action and explains why she made the emotional choice that she did in this context. In a sense she feels already dead. She loves both brothers equally, and it is not in her nature to join in hate, but to join in love. Later she shows that she has realized what she has sacrificed, as she goes to her death lamenting her loss of marriage and children.

Unlike Creon, she rarely generalizes; she does not insist at any point in the play that she would have taken action in any context. She surprisingly asserts that she would not have acted for a husband or child because she could get another. Although Creon sees her as offering a general resistance to his rule, she sees herself as forced to act in this case only. And it appears that the populace agrees and that even the Chorus, who disagrees with her civic disobedience, views her choice as pious. Antigone is clearly difficult and stubborn, like her father Oedipus. Many have questioned her final rejection of Ismene's complicity in her act even though it saves her sister's life. Yet the play proves her right in principle, and her last wish, that those who punish her will meet the same suffering that she has experienced, is fulfilled in the case of Creon: 'Which of the gods' laws have I broken? Or should someone as ill-used as me look to the gods at all? Will no one come to my defence? I did the moral thing, but they're calling me immoral! Well, if that's what the gods think, too, I'll soon find out the error of my ways. But if the crime is Creon's, I hope the punishment he suffers will be no less than the one that he's imposed on me – unjustly.'

The play is clearly not validating civil disobedience in general, but making vivid an ethical choice generated by a unique situation. In his *Rhetoric* (1.15.1375a–b) the philosopher Aristotle affirms Antigone's choice to defend the unwritten laws: 'it is the part of a better man to make use of and abide by unwritten rather than written law' because such laws are based on nature whereas written law (comparable to Creon's edict) varies in different contexts and may fail to accord in certain cases with justice.

The voices in this play are also defined by whether and when characters speak or sing. Singing, as in modern opera, can be a more emotional and lyrical form of speech. In this play, Creon in the final scene sings for the first time as he laments the bodies of his wife and son and his failure as a leader. The Chorus refuses to share his lament and do not sing with him. Mature males sing in Sophocles only in desperate situations. Creon's emotional song isolates him even further from the Chorus, which is now turning to the need for order and leadership of the city in the future. Antigone sings with the Chorus as she comes out of the palace to go to her death. Tears come from the eyes of the Chorus as they look at her and she perhaps expects much more sympathy from these men who have always been close to and supportive of her family. Yet the Chorus continues to cement her sense of isolation by disapproving of her act, despite its piety and the honour she has earned in death. Antigone goes to her death thinking that no one agreed with her, and it is significant that when she tries to explain why she would only have acted in this one situation against the state she turns back from song to the poetic metre of ordinary tragic speech.

When Sophocles wrote this play, we think that he knew that many in Athens would not accept burying a traitor in Athenian territory and there may at some point have been a law passed to this effect. (It is not clear whether this law would have permitted burial outside Athens to avoid pollution.) If so, Sophocles needed to create an unusually persuasive as well as dangerous voice for Antigone, a voice far more individualized and unusual than those of other tragic characters. At least in extant tragedy, there is no voice in other Greek tragedies like hers, whereas we can find precedents for the voices of the other characters in other plays. Her atypical female identity, her attempt to adapt and make comprehensible her dissenting mode of ethical deliberation, and her terrible situation seem to be part of her attraction to later playwrights and composers and to philosophers and psychoanalytic thinkers like Georg Wilhelm Friedrich Hegel, Martin Heidegger, Søren Kierkegaard, Jacques Lacan, Judith Butler and others.

In later dramatic versions of *Antigone*, however, the heroine develops a wide range of powerful voices. If Sophocles' heroine establishes a unique voice, in contemporary South America she can represent a multitude of lamenting and resisting female voices who want to learn the truth about the thousands of disappeared and unburied victims of dictatorial regimes and to lament and memorialize those dead and tortured. In a play called *Antígona oriental* directed and composed by Marianella Morena with the German director Volker Lösch performed at the Teatro Solis in Montevideo, Uruguay in 2012, Antigone was played by one professional actress and nineteen female survivors of imprisonment and torture during Uruguay's 1973–75 dictatorship.[2] Even Ismene becomes Antigone in the course of the play. The victims wanted the current democratic left-wing government not to repress the ugly past, but to remember it and respond to its injustices, such as the amnesty granted to the military in 1986. The play interwove real-life testimonies from the survivors with Sophocles' text; but these individual testimonies became a shared story of all the Antigones. This play gives Antigone's courage to all of these women and makes heroines and agents out of victims. At the surprising conclusion of this new version, the play's Creons offer an offstage apology and the twenty women enter the stage dressed in festal red attire, dancing, and recording their desire for a space to move on and survive:

> Sophocles, I beg you
> Send me an ending
> In which someone is saved
> So that we can start again.

In South America, innumerable new versions of *Antigone* preceded this production. In Griselda Gambaro's seminal 1986 *Antigona furiosa* in Buenos Aires,[3] Antigone became the voice of all the sisters, mothers and daughters who suffered death, disappearance, or losses during the Argentinian dictatorship of 1976–83 that caused more than 30,000 people, including many young people, to disappear. In response to these disappearances, a group of mothers and grandmothers bravely began marching in protest in 1977 on the central public square of the Plaza de Mayo, a location linked with Argentine independence and public transparency, to demand news of their loved ones and the return of missing bodies for burial. Later they continued to object to insufficient response to the perpetrators of injustice and to the continued silence about and failure to adequately memorialize the many disappeared.

This play begins with the dead Antigona coming back to life still in prison. After furiously re-enacting the fratricidal battle between her siblings, marching like the mothers of the Plaza de Mayo, symbolically performing the burial of her brother, and, refusing the belated pardon of Creon until all the dead are buried, she commits suicide once again: 'I will always want to bury Polynices. Even if I am born 1,000 times, and he dies 1,000 times.' Two other characters, Corifeo (his name means Chorus-leader) and Antinoo (meaning anti-mind) play the denizens of a modern café who observe Antigona. They sometimes mock Antigona – 'You will descend free and alive to death. It is not so tragic!' – and sometimes adopt both the role of Creon, who is represented as an empty shell that they put on, or other characters, even the dead Polynices. Antigona herself briefly takes on the roles of Ismene and Haemon. In the end, Antinoo confirms that Antigona herself has become one of the disappeared who always reappears: 'She is here and she is not here, we killed her and we did not kill her ... What a bore! She never ends it! ... If we know she dies, why doesn't she die?'

Among many other South and Central American *Antigones*, the 2004 Mexican *Las voces que incendian el desierto* ('The Voices that Set the Desert on Fire') by Perla de la Rosa similarly addressed the 'femicide' of actual women in Ciudad Juárez.[4] In this play three pairs of women, including the sisters Antigone and Ismene, search for missing sisters or daughters. If in Latin America Antigone often becomes a collective figure that insists on burying and memorializing many historical dead, in other countries she can adopt a different pointedly individual voice. A 2004 Japanese production of a new version of *Antigone* by Miyagi Satoshi's Ku Na'uka Theatre Company in Tokyo deployed Antigone's intense individuality to encourage his audience to develop a non-conformist voice that could challenge a state authority still too devoted to aspects of pre-Second World War nationalism and outdated social mores.[5] In this play a Chorus of multiple timid and obedient Ismenes represented (especially female) citizens who prefer to compromise with the legacy of the past rather than directly confronting power embodied by multiple patriarchal Creons. Only Antigone and Haemon stood outside these groups.

Staging the play in front of the National Museum of Japan, built in 1930 as a monument to Japanese nationalism, allowed the production to address symbolically the entire country. Stage left served as the entrance for women and represented nature and blood bonds and the western world of the dead, stage right served as the entrance for men and presented political authority. Haemon, however, linked himself with democracy by entering from the audience itself; he avoided the gruff and threatening language and gestures of the Creons. Antigone refused to use feminine Japanese, performed the burial of Polynices on stage, and walked under her own volition into the structure at centre stage that represented the cave in which she removed her black kimono before committing suicide accompanied by drums and other musical instruments and then donned a white robe appropriate for a wedding or death. Miyagi's feminist version removed those parts of Sophocles' text that criticized the heroine and reduced Creon to a Kabuki-style villain. The play used multiple Choruses, including a Chorus of the dead, which Polynices, Haemon, and Antigone joined, and a Chorus of Teiresiases, both of which articulated the play's overall point of view. The Chorus of ghosts, for example, sang Sophocles' famous 'Ode on Man' to stress the human inability to control the threat of death. They took apart Antigone's cave to create a structure resembling a lotus flower from which she emerged to join the world of the dead at the western exit. Creon, in dialogue with the Chorus of Teiresiases, rejects their advice, fails to express remorse, and is left alone as the Chorus of the dead, wearing photos of themselves (as at Buddhist shrines to the dead in Japanese homes), moved towards a large pool in front of the museum. They floated illuminated lanterns representing the souls of the dead on the water as in the Japanese obon festival and then joined a procession into the audience.

A version of *Antigone* performed a number of times since 2006 in the Italian Apennines at a German World War II military cemetery holding 30,000 bodies at the Futa Pass by Gianluca Guidotti and Enrica Sangiovanni's Archivio Zeta theatre company also addressed the past, not only through the setting but through special voices developed by the actors to address both the living and the dead, whether enemies or friends.[6] This play's Antigone treated all the dead as deserving to be remembered and loved at a site where Italians fought their former German allies as well as other Italian citizens in a civil war. Many of the victims were never properly identified or buried. Antigone, and often the other actors, spoke many of their lines looking directly at the gravestones rather than at the audience and out to the valley beyond it that sometimes echoed their shouts. All the actors used harsh, loud, anti-naturalistic voices that created a sense of remoteness from the present and included the dead, but Antigone's voice was especially linked with this mode of performance.

This project, originally addressed to local audiences who also participated in the performance, expanded to include broad audiences over time. The audience entered the cemetery and, guided by Chorus and actors, moved slowly up a hill to a funerary monument on a high terrace with one room and a crypt below that served as Antigone's cave. Creon was confronted not by a live guard but by an anonymous dead World War II solider who seemed to speak to his fellow dead as he described Antigone's mourning over her brother's body, a mourning he had not received. Antigone's first address to Creon and the Chorus on the terrace was powerful from the start. She accused the Chorus of cowardice in not facing the king and provoked a dictatorial anger in Creon. Ismene joined her sister and Haemon emerged from the audience as the only witness to speak out among characters and audience. Antigone spoke her last words from the crypt below the terrace that gave a strange sound to her voice as she slowly receded into its darkness. The audience was then invited to watch the scene between Creon and Teiresias on the sunny side of the monument. Both actors shouted at each other from a distance and addressed the tombs of the soldiers. Teiresias went back down the hill, leaving Creon on his seat of power until he heard of the deaths of Antigone and his family. The audience left him silent and alone as they too descended the hill at the behest of the Chorus-leader and exited from the far side of the cemetery at sunset.

Sahika Tekhand's version of *Antigone* in Istanbul in 2006, *Eurydice's Cry*, addressed issues relating to freedom of expression and human rights in contemporary Turkey, represented the conflict of 'voices' in the play through the movement of the actors' bodies.[7] In this version a Chorus of eight men and women wearing black were divided into two units of four. Each performer had a spotlight directed at his or her feet. Actors could only be seen, talk or move when lit. The voice and movement of the actors was stylized and limited to a finite number of poses. Movements associated with Creon were restricted and constrained, sometimes suggesting exaggerated or distorted versions of a military pose. Poses associated with Antigone were stylized, but more fluid, vibrant and emotional, as well as different for each performer; their hands moved to express grief or panic. In the beginning of the play the Chorus's movements were associated with the play's repressive leader Creon; when he was present, all moved in unison. But Antigone's rebellious movements gradually infected Ismene, Haemon, then Chorus members, and Creon's wife Eurydice until Creon was left alone while the others moved each in their own way in solidarity with Antigone, although the Chorus continued to speak together. Emotive sounds emitted by the actors underlined their reactions as well. The words of the text were spoken faster and faster, but the direction of the action remained clear through movement. The play's four episodes were divided by choral odes and moved from suspicion to fear to pain to rebellion and change. Once the other actors were aligned with Antigone, Eurydice, who had observed the action from the beginning, cried out, and, as in Jean Anouilh's French version of the play, broke her Sophoclean silence to scream, speak and curse.

Femi Osofisan's Nigerian *Tegonni: An African Antigone* brings a nineteenth-century Yoruba princess into dialogue with Sophocles' heroine.[8] The play is set under British colonial rule. The first production was staged in Atlanta, Georgia, due to a period of military dictatorship and corruption in Nigeria. The all black cast staged a romance and disrupted marriage between Tegonni and a young white district officer named Captain Allan Jones. The extraordinarily talented Tegonni had received support from Allan in her quest to become an official bronze caster and member of the guild of carvers, which generally excluded women. Her wedding procession is interrupted by the appearance of the dead body of one of her two brothers, who had been left exposed as a message against rebellion by the Governor, Lt. General Carter-Ross, the adopted father of Allan, who also disapproves of Allan's marriage to a black, African woman. Allan fails to persuade the General to change his mind about the burial and Tegonni is arrested – for burying her brother – along with her devoted female friends, who also serve as a Chorus that frequently performs African song and dance.

Tegonni is offered the chance of release if she officially apologizes for her action. After a series of escapes and further resistance on the part of Tegonni and her friends, she and Allan are eventually shot, the Governor has a heart attack, and the dead Tegonni and her friends reappear on the sacred boat of her patron deity, the water goddess Yemoja. Antigone has come across time to help orchestrate this scenario, and she plays an active role in the plot. In a final dialogue, Antigone tests Tegonni's resolve. Tegonni refuses to apologize to save her life and thus to confirm the subservient status of her people. Antigone finally joins Tegonni on Yemoja's boat. In this play the bonds between the assertive Tegonni, her female friends and her community add a new dimension to the myth and the play underlines an uneasy correspondence between the story of the Greek Antigone and the African Tegonni.

Among the many versions of *Antigone* chronicled by George Steiner in his book *Antigones*,[9] Bertolt Brecht perhaps offers in his *Antigone* the most critical view of the play's characters.[10] First performed in Chur, Switzerland in 1948 shortly before Brecht's return to Germany from exile after World War II, the play refused to allow Antigone to represent religious tradition, humanity, the family, the individual in opposition to the state, or opposition to tyranny. For Brecht the play becomes a quarrel among members of a ruling class. The Chorus of Theban elders follows and supports Creon's aggressive imperial war against the Greek city of Argos in order to acquire metals. Polynices is killed for deserting Creon's army after Eteocles dies. The Chorus, thinking the army was victorious, celebrates until they discover that the Theban young men, including Creon's son Megareus, have lost to the Argives and died. Yet the Chorus closes the play still following and collaborating with the failed Creon.

In this version Antigone rebels, but only after Polynices is killed: 'But she who saw everything / could help nobody but the enemy who is now coming and will quickly wipe us out.' At the same time, tied to a board after her capture, Antigone is allowed to speak the play's central point: 'Anyone who uses violence against the enemy will turn and use violence against his own people.' She objects to sacrificing Thebes' young men against peaceful Argos. 'When we forget the past,' she insists to Ismene, 'the past returns.' And once condemned, she strides off to her punishment with a movement suggesting a new freedom. This stride, which was performed as if it made Antigone famous by Brecht's wife Helene Wiegel, nevertheless seems to restore a powerful if flawed voice to Antigone. Yet in Brecht's version of the famous 'Ode on Man,' 'Man counts what is human / as nothing at all. He has become / his own monster.' Human corruption and imperialism rather than fate governs the action of this version of Sophocles' play.

Antigone has become the most performed Western play in a global context, and important productions have appeared in most countries worldwide. The performance of an apolitical *Antigone* seems virtually impossible. As these examples have shown, contemporary relations between family and state, ruler and ruled, or male and female inevitably condition audience responses to performances of the play in translation or in new versions of it. In the USA some productions have tried to avoid suggesting any correspondence between the American President and Creon, and have turned to the more sympathetic portrait of Creon in Jean Anouilh's French version of the play (see Chapter 12 in this volume), which also makes Antigone confused and far less ethically authoritative than in Sophocles. In other countries, directors have tried to hide behind the canonical status of Sophocles' play in order to make a political statement through its performance in a context where freedom of speech is repressed. In a number of the cases discussed above, Creon has simply become a villain in contrast to an unambivalently heroic Antigone. In Sophocles' original, however, representation of each character's individual voice remains complex and continues to provoke both philosophical controversy and varied versions and performances.

Notes

1 This discussion draws on Foley (2001) 172–200. This chapter cites earlier bibliography.
2 See further Fradinger (2014) 761–72.
3 Gambaro (1992). For a discussion see Fradinger (2011) 67–89, with further bibliography.
4 de La Rosa ([2004] 2005).
5 See Smethurst (2011) 221–34.
6 See Treu (2011) 307–23.
7 Erincin (2011) 171–83.
8 Osofisan (1999).
9 Steiner ([1984], 1996).
10 Brecht (1984).

12

Antigone Enters the Modern World

Betine van Zyl Smit

The Archive of Performances of Greek and Roman Drama in Oxford has 142 performances of Sophocles' *Antigone* or new versions of it on record for the twenty-first century alone. This indicates the continued engagement of creative artists with the drama and makes it impossible to give an adequate overview in one chapter of the part this tragedy has played in modern cultural life. Fortunately scholars and reviewers have also been busy in recording their research on and criticism of *Antigone* and its multitude of descendants.[1]

The modern Antigone, fearless champion of traditional piety and family loyalty, a bold rebel, defying tyrannical rule, springs from the way Sophocles shaped the myth in his tragedy. This chapter examines the way in which *Antigone* was re-imagined over the centuries, but concentrates on two recent adaptations that give a good indication of the importance this play still has in modern culture. *The Island*, first created by Athol Fugard, John Kani and Winston Ntshona in apartheid South Africa in 1973, with its play-within-the-play *The Trial and Punishment of Antigone* has become a classic in the modern world to depict resistance to authoritarian rule. *Antigone in Molenbeek*, written by the Flemish author Stefan Hertmans and first performed in 2016, responds to the contemporary crisis of cultural and religious conflict in Europe and the modern world. Attention is also paid to the way different nuances were brought to the conflict between Creon and Antigone in early modern Europe, the stimulus of the pioneering production in 1841 in Prussian Potsdam, which was to find echoes in France, England, Ireland and the Czech lands. Another most influential adaptation was that of Jean Anouilh in occupied Paris in 1944. In spite of its ambivalent treatment of the two central characters, it in turn spawned new versions which established Antigone as a symbol of heroic resistance to tyranny, and also a feminist icon.

Early modern Antigones

The confrontation of Creon and Antigone in Sophocles' tragedy has been reinterpreted in different ways in later literature. Sometimes Creon is represented as a tyrant. Antigone is sometimes a loyal family supporter or a doomed romantic. Many early modern versions take Ismene's decision not to oppose Creon's decree as the right one.

Early modern playwrights and scholars were intrigued by the conflict between Creon and Antigone and its moral ambivalences and the complexity of the character of Antigone, who can be judged, in Sophocles' version, to be an uncompromising protagonist as well as an innocent victim, at moments fierce and then pathetic, defiant and sufficiently heroic to face death. Many of the early modern scholars and translators interpreted the play as a lesson about the abuse of power, and made Creon a tyrant, who suffers the punishment he deserves for his stubbornness and pride. During the early modern period, when Greek tragedy was rediscovered by the Humanists, few people could read Classical Greek, and the Greek dramas were often translated into Latin. Several such translations were made in the sixteenth century.[2] Robert Miola explains how some of the translators used words that altered the emphases of the Greek version and ended up offering a new interpretation. The word *tyrannus* for a ruler tended to be interpreted in the modern sense of tyrant, and Creon often became an evil ruler and the direct opposite of the just ruler, which was the ideal of many philosophical discourses of the time. The great Humanist Erasmus was one of the scholars who saw Creon in *Antigone* as the incarnation of a bad ruler: 'Creon . . . who preferred to obey his own mind rather than wise counsels and destroyed utterly his family and himself'.[3] He calls him a tyrant and not a prince. Erasmus read *Antigone* as a story of deserved punishment, an object lesson against tyranny, obstinacy and impiety.

Haemon was often re-imagined as a romantic lead who died for love. Sophocles' Antigone does not show a great deal of interest in love or her husband-to-be. Haemon's suicide is motivated not just by his love for Antigone, but also by rage at his father's stubborn inflexibility.

One of the earliest adaptations of Sophocles' *Antigone* was the 1580 version by the French playwright Robert Garnier with the title *Antigone ou la Pieté*.[4] Garnier, a precursor of the Classical French tragedians Corneille and Racine, combined elements of Seneca's *Phoenissae*, Statius' *Thebaid* and Sophocles' tragedy to create a very long play with resonances of contemporary French politics. The drama includes the part of the myth where Oedipus is still alive, covers the war between Eteocles and Polyneices and contains a version of Sophocles' *Antigone* as the last two acts, lines 1516–2741. Scholars have analysed the play as portraying contemporary dynastic and religious civil wars in France and the prospect of tyrannical rule. Garnier's Antigone is pious, as the title indicates, but she is an eloquent and powerful character. She instructs Creon on the limits of royal power and the subordination of human to divine law:

> Nulles loix de Tyrans ne doivent avoir lieu
> Que lon voit repugner aux preceptes de Dieu.
>
> 1814–5
>
> [No Tyrants' laws should contradict the teachings of God.]

There are echoes of the traditional Catholic teaching in the play. The conflicting claims of secular and religious authority in France at the time undoubtedly provide a large part of the context for Garnier's interpretation. It is clear that such versions, where Creon becomes an uncompromising tyrant, lose much of the subtle ambiguities of the interplay between ruler and subject about secular and religious duties, which are part of the Greek tragedy.

Such one-sided interpretations were, however, not the only way Sophocles' *Antigone* was viewed in later years.

Antigone in Potsdam (1841)

During the nineteenth century German scholars were hard at work researching Greek tragedy in all its aspects, from textual correctness to the way the plays were staged in the ancient world. When the relatively young Friedrich Wilhelm IV became King of Prussia in 1840, this academic work was rewarded by being given the opportunity to be translated into practice. The new ruler enjoyed the reputation of being a romantic aesthete and was expected to inaugurate a period of liberalism. As crown prince the King had already shown a fondness for the arts and sciences and he was in the forefront of those who subscribed to the spirit of philhellenism, which imagined the Germans as destined to re-embody classical Greece. It was the King himself, who shaped the plan to produce historically accurate performances of Greek tragedy. Sophocles' *Antigone* was chosen as the first play for this bold initiative.

The staging of *Antigone*, in Potsdam in 1841 became widely regarded as epoch-making. It was exported all over Europe and considered as the model for a revival and totally new reincarnation of Greek tragedy. This opened a new chapter in the discourse on theatre. A follower of the Romantic school, Ludwig Tieck, was chosen for the task. The project was to be based on the latest research. The text used was a new verse translation by Johann Jakob Christian Donner. A leading scholar of Greek who was an exponent of the historical critical approach, August Böckh, was appointed as philological adviser. The theatrical space inside the *Neue Palais* in Potsdam was adapted to conform to the archaeological knowledge of the time as displayed in the famous study *Das Theater von Athen* by Hans Christian Genelli (1818). This knowledge in fact soon became outdated as a result of the findings of the new excavations of the theatre of Dionysus in Athens that started at the time of the performance.

The classicistic conception entailed the division of the stage into three levels: a subterranean level for the musicians; a slightly higher orchestra level, where the Chorus of fifteen and their leader moved and which also housed the altar of Dionysus (in which the prompt was concealed), in the centre; the raised stage formed the third level, 1.5 metres above, and represented the palace. The young Felix Mendelssohn-Bartholdy was commissioned to provide the choral music. He chose a romantic oratorio and symphonic style to set Donner's verse with great virtuosity as well as accuracy regarding the metre, as advised by Böckh. Mendelssohn soon became the driving force of the production. This innovative theatrical project combined historicism, Romantic notions and an attempt to convey an aspect of antiquity adequately. This was important for a theatre that set itself the task to serve as a 'cultural memory'.

Tieck tended to Christian interpretations, in the case of Antigone portraying her as a martyr. Dionysus was readily identified as Christ by the Romantics. At the same time this staging acknowledged the implicit relationship between Antigone and Dionysus that was long ignored by researchers. In this romantic fashion the appeal to the god to appear, which in Sophocles' tragedy is only indicated symbolically, was acted out as an epiphany in the theatre:

> come to us
>   dionysus
> come with your
>   cleansing step
>
> trans. Stuttard

Mendelssohn had reworked the ecstatic fifth stasimon as a call for help addressed to the god of the theatre to appear. Anton Bierl has argued persuasively that the scene was 'patently tailored to refer to the new king himself who had been for some time representing an equally Romantic Dionysus cult infused with Christianity in the architectural symbolism of

Charlottenburg castle'.[5] Friedrich Wilhelm IV was thus represented as a moral force in that he and the god were associated in the quest for purification. Creon is portrayed as having to bear the guilt of Antigone's death.

Sophocles' *Antigone* had not been staged in Britain during the seventeenth and eighteenth centuries, except as adapted in the Italian opera of Francesco Bianchi in 1796.[6] One of the reasons for the absence of *Antigone* may have been that there was no example of a recent French version of the play. It is significant that an English translation of the tragedy *Antigone*, which was produced at Covent Garden in 1845, was largely derived from the famous production in Potsdam in 1841. The London *Antigone* made use of the music Mendelssohn had composed and was further indebted to the Prussian production in its use of the German translation of Donner, rendered into English by William Bartholomew. The choice of this production may in part have been a tribute to Queen Victoria's marriage in 1841 to Prince Albert, who was an admirer of the cultural renewal at the Prussian court. The turn to German rather than French examples of the staging of Greek plays signalled a new source of inspiration for the British stage. The London production also reflected the awakening interest in archaeological and antiquarian studies at the time. Both costumes and set were products of careful research. This is but one of many examples of how different performances and adaptations of Sophocles' tragedy in their turn provoked new versions.

Jean Anouilh *Antigone*, Paris, 1944

One of the most influential modern reworkings of Sophocles' tragedy is that of the French playwright, Jean Anouilh. It was staged for the first time during the German occupation of France, on 4 February 1944. While many saw it as expressing French defiance to the Germans, Antigone embodying the French resistance and saying 'no' to German rule, Anouilh actually managed to preserve much of the ambiguity of the Greek drama. Some French intellectuals attacked Anouilh's interpretation charging him with creating a Créon whose attitude was an insult to the many who had died in resisting the Germans.[7]

In spite of the ambivalence of critical and scholarly reception of Anouilh's intentions, many subsequent adaptors of the play continued to see his Antigone as a modern incarnation of defiance to tyrannical rule. One of the most famous instances of this reception is *The Island*, a play created by the South African trio of Athol Fugard, John Kani and Winston Ntshona.[8] Athol Fugard, particularly mentioned the parallel circumstances in which these two plays were first presented: Anouilh's version in Paris with German officers sitting in the theatre enjoying French culture, while in South Africa, when

The Island was first performed in Cape Town in 1973, there were three Special Branch officers present in the audience.[9] They were ready to arrest and prosecute the actors and director if the play was deemed to break the law as defined under the State of Emergency in South Africa at the time. This did not happen, and *The Island* went on to tour the stages of the world. It has become one of the adaptations of Sophocles' drama that best encapsulates fearless resistance to an oppressive state.

The Island by Athol Fugard, John Kani and Winston Ntshona

This play grew out of the work of a group of amateur Black actors who had come to the playwright and theatre director, Athol Fugard, for help at his home in Port Elizabeth in the 1960s. Previously, in the early twentieth century, Sophocles' *Antigone* had been performed in South Africa by White cultural organizations as an example of Western high culture. No fewer than three translations into Afrikaans of the tragedy had been published and performed. This was at least partly aimed at validating the language of the Afrikaners who were striving for self-realization in the face of English cultural hegemony after the defeat of their forebears in the Anglo-Boer War of 1899–1902.[10] Performances of these Afrikaans translations had eschewed any overt application of Antigone's act of defiance to the situation in South Africa. Gradually, however, from the early 1960s *Antigone* was to be given a new lease of life in the Black Theatre of the townships and was eventually to be one of the plays that brought Black protest theatre to the attention of White audiences too. The impact went beyond the decision to stage versions of *Antigone*, and led to a deeper examination of Antigone as a figure who resists authority. This examination in turn caused a shift in the moral balance between the characters, with sympathies moving clearly towards Antigone.

Various township theatre groups staged productions of *Antigone* in the 1960s. It was one of the plays Athol Fugard rehearsed with the Serpent Players, a group in New Brighton, outside Port Elizabeth.[11] They were constantly harassed by the police and often members were arrested. Fugard did eventually succeed in producing *Antigone* with the Serpent Players in 1965, but he was unable to attend the performance as he was refused the permit needed by a White person to attend a Non-white gathering.

A further development of this project of the Serpent Players was that one of the actors involved, Norman Ntshinga, who was to play Haemon, but was arrested before the performance, actually put on a two-man version of

Antigone with another Serpent player, Sipho 'Sharkey' Mguqulwa, in prison on Robben Island. They used workshop techniques and relied on their memory of the play they were rehearsing before their arrest.[12]

This was not the only time *Antigone* was performed in the maximum security jail for political prisoners on Robben Island. In his autobiography President Nelson Mandela deals briefly with what he refers to as his 'thespian career':

> Our amateur drama society made its yearly offering at Christmas. My thespian career ... had a modest revival on Robben Island. Our productions were what might now be called minimalist: no stage, no scenery, no costumes. All we had was the text of the play.
>
> I performed in only a few dramas, but I had one memorable role: that of Creon, the king of Thebes in Sophocles' *Antigone*. I had read some of the classic Greek plays in prison, and found them enormously elevating. What I took out of them was that character was measured by facing up to difficult situations and that a hero was a man who would not break down even under the most trying circumstances.
>
> When *Antigone* was chosen as the play, I volunteered my services, and was asked to play Creon, an elderly king fighting a civil war over the throne of his beloved city-state. At the outset, Creon is sincere and patriotic, and there is wisdom in his early speeches when he suggests that experience is the foundation of leadership and that obligation to the people takes precedence over loyalty to an individual ...
>
> But Creon deals with his enemies mercilessly. He has decreed that the body of Polyneices, Antigone's brother, who had rebelled against the city, does not deserve a proper burial. Antigone rebels, on the grounds that there is a higher law than that of the state. Creon will not listen to Antigone, neither does he listen to anyone but his own inner demons. His inflexibility and blindness ill become a leader, for a leader must temper justice with mercy. It was Antigone who symbolized our struggle; she was, in her own way, a freedom fighter, for she defied the law on the ground that it was unjust.[13]

President Mandela's criticism of Creon's fatal flaw, his inflexibility, and his judgement that a leader should temper justice with mercy, were to be put into practice when he, as President of South Africa after the first fully democratic elections in the country in 1994, followed a policy of reconciliation. This was a decisive rejection of Creon's approach to governing his state. President Mandela's view of Antigone as a heroine in the struggle for justice encapsulates the interpretation of this role by Black South African theatre activists from the 1960s onwards. There is no trace of the ambivalence in scholarly debate about the roles of Creon and Antigone; for Black theatre in South Africa, she was constantly presented as a martyr and a heroine.

The appeal that Antigone's defiance had for the Black majority in South Africa, who were oppressed by laws that ran contrary to the spirit of justice and humanity, found its finest expression in a play devised by two new members of the Serpent players, again in collaboration with Athol Fugard.[14] This play was first staged in Cape Town under the title *Die Hodoshe Span*[15] at a multi-racial private theatre called The Space, on 2 July 1973. The play was directed by Athol Fugard and his two collaborators, John Kani and Winston Ntshona, formed the cast, John and Winston. Under its final title, *The Island*, the term used colloquially to refer to the jail on Robben Island, the play was destined to take around the world the identification of the South African struggle with Antigone's refusal to bow to tyranny.

The play is set in a prison cell on Robben Island. The two inmates, John and Winston are rehearsing for the annual prison concert, a two-man version of *Antigone*. John is the director. He produces the dialogue from memory as they have no script. Their props are homemade and rudimentary. They have been disempowered by a ruthless regime, and just like Antigone, a defenceless woman, they have only words to defend their cause. The plot is couched in terms familiar to convicts: it is the trial of Antigone, the accused is Antigone, the state, king Creon, and the charge is that Antigone buried Polyneices. Significantly he is referred to by John as 'the traitor, the one who I said was on our side' (p. 201).

They also reminisce about the production of *Antigone* by the Serpent players in Port Elizabeth in 1965. Thus they incorporate the lived experience of their theatre group into the play. John presents stage one of the trial thus: 'The State lays charges against the Accused . . . and lists counts . . . you know the way they do it. Stage two is Pleading. What does Antigone plead? Guilty or Not Guilty?' Winston instinctively replies: 'Not Guilty.' John reacts with: 'Now look, Winston, we're not going to argue. Between me and you, in this cell, we know she's Not Guilty. But in the play she pleads Guilty.' (p. 201). Winston maintains that Antigone is not guilty because she had every right to bury her brother. Winston reluctantly bows to John's insistence that he has to accept the wording of the play, but later Winston wants to say that Antigone lays charges against the state. This underlines his passionate conviction of the rightness of her cause.

They summarize the rest of the play as:

John Stage three: Pleading in Mitigation of Sentence. Stage four.
Winston State summary, Sentence and Farewell Words.

p. 203

When they have their 'dress rehearsal' and Winston has to try on the improvised wig and false breasts, John's laughter incenses Winston. He vows that he will not play 'a bloody woman' and expose himself to the ridicule of his fellow prisoners:

> 'Go to hell man. Only last night you tell me that this Antigone is a bloody ... what you call it ... legend! A Greek one at that. Bloody thing never even happened. Not even history! Look brother, I got no time for bullshit. Fuck legends. Me ... I live my life here! I know why I'm here, and it's history, not legends. I had my chat with a magistrate in Cradock and now I'm here. Your Antigone is child's play, man.'
>
> p. 210

The coarse, everyday language of *The Island*, often mixed with Xhosa and Afrikaans words, is in contrast with the elevated style of Greek tragedy and the way it was usually presented in South Africa, whether in English or Afrikaans translation. This language of ordinary people made the play accessible to everybody.

When the play within the play is staged, when John and Winston put on *The Trial and Punishment of Antigone*, Winston's gradual identification with Antigone and her conviction highlights the theme of the play so that every member of the audience understands it. The final scene of *The Island* is the prison concert. *The Island*'s audience becomes the prison audience when John addresses them: 'Captain Prinsloo, Hodoshe, warders ... and Gentlemen!' (p. 223). The last term is reserved for his fellow prisoners and accords them the dignity and respect they do not get in prison. John gives a brief synopsis of the background of *Antigone*. He then changes into his Creon costume and in that role makes a speech. The adoption of the fictive character gives him licence to send up the rhetoric of the South African regime with sly references to 'constant troubles on our borders', 'subversive elements' (p. 224) and so forth.

Winston then appears, dressed as Antigone, and is charged with having buried Polyneices. He pleads guilty. Given the opportunity to plead in mitigation Winston, like Antigone, asserts that there is a higher law than that of the state. This law comes from God. The dialogue in the play carries a triple layer of meaning: it represents Winston and John acting the words of Antigone and Creon in the Greek drama, but the ideas expressed apply equally to the position of Winston and John in *The Island* as well as to the conviction of Fugard, Ntshona and Kani in the reality of South Africa in the 1970s. This becomes explicit when John as Creon pronounces sentence: 'Take her from where she stands, straight to the Island.' This identification of

Winston with Antigone and consequently of *The Island* with *Antigone* is underscored in Winston's last words:

> Brothers and Sisters of the Land! I go now on my last journey. I must leave the light of day forever, for the Island, strange and cold, to be lost between life and death. So to my grave, my everlasting prison, condemned alive to solitary death.
>
> p. 227

But then Winston goes beyond the role of Antigone. He strips of his wig and confronts the audience as Winston:

> Nyana we Sizwe! [Son of the Land]
> Gods of our Fathers! My Land! My home!
> Time waits no longer. I go now to my living death, because I honoured those things to which honour belongs.

Thus he movingly declares his own renewed defiance before he is returned to his existence of serving punishment for daring to resist laws that are manifestly unjust. The impact of Winston's words is enhanced by the reversal of his earlier vehement refusal to play Antigone, a Greek legend, a bloody woman, child's play. His realization of the deeper meaning of her defiance thus underlines the convergence of the ideals that Antigone represents and those of the protesters against the unjust laws of the apartheid state.

While *Antigone* has a beginning, a middle and an end, *The Island*, has a ring composition. The play opens with the two prisoners caught in a Sisyphean task of endlessly filling a wheelbarrow with sand, wheeling it to a different spot, emptying it, filling it up again and wheeling it back. The convicts are shackled together and beaten. This brutal action to which they return after their performance puts into sharp relief the human dignity expressed in Antigone's last words with which they are completely identified at the end of the play. Outwardly the position of John and Winston are the same at the end of *The Island* as at the beginning, but change has been brought about in the audience's perception of them. Anonymous prisoners at the outset, the audience now knows them intimately. In the course of staging *The Trial and Punishment of Antigone* they have revealed themselves as human beings, who are undergoing a living death because of their beliefs in a higher justice. Their cause is the same as that of Antigone. The words spoken by the actors, by the prisoners, assert their humanity and transport them and their fictive audience, their fellow Robben Island convicts, beyond the reach of a repressive regime. *The Island* is a brilliant celebration of the power of Greek tragedy and the theatre to transcend obstacles and to give voice to the voiceless.

Another recent adaptation of *Antigone* has attempted to focus attention on the plight of families who are similarly marginalized and have become the collateral damage in terrorist attacks in Europe.

Stefan Hertmans *Antigone in Molenbeek*, 2016

After the terrorist attacks in Paris in November 2015 and in Brussels in March 2016, attention was focused on Molenbeek, a suburb of Brussels with which many of the *jihadists* associated with these attacks had a connection. Some had lived there for a number of years, or still lived there, and much of the planning for their attacks had probably been done there. In an attempt to find answers to the question of why such an area should have become a breeding ground for terror, a cultural event, 'Re:Creating Europe', was organized in Amsterdam in June 2016. Central questions to be considered were how authors or playwrights could react to the attacks, what could they say about them? And on whose behalf would they be speaking.[16] For this occasion the Flemish author, Stefan Hertmans, wrote a theatre monologue *Antigone in Molenbeek*. It was staged in the Bellevue Theatre in Amsterdam and the full text was published in a supplement to the Belgian newspaper, *De Standaard* on 3 June 2016. This play is a thought-provoking exploration of how the central conflict in *Antigone* can still shed light on some of the cardinal issues in contemporary multi-cultural societies.

The link to Sophocles' *Antigone* is in the title of the one-act play. The Antigone of this contemporary adaptation is a young Moroccan woman, Nouria. She goes to the police station to claim the body of her brother who has been killed. The dour policeman, to whom she addresses her request, is the representative of the state and thus has the Creon role. He is 'Meneer' (Mister) Crénom. Nouria is proud of her Belgian passport and is a law student in Brussels. She has become part of the contemporary world where she lives. Production photographs show her in modern Western dress, not in the garments prescribed by some Muslim communities.

The police officer's role is more limited than that of Creon. He has not made the law, but he has to enforce it. Nouria's mission, however is very close to that of Antigone. She wants to retrieve her brother's remains from the state so that they may be given proper religious burial. It becomes clear that her brother's body is no longer a body, but remains in the literal sense. Crénom even speaks of 'material'. This seems to point to the result of suicide bombing and is reminiscent of Anouilh's Créon's telling Antigone that the remains of Polynice and Etéocle were so intermingled that they could not be distinguished.[17]

In contrast to most Antigones, however, Nouria is timid and nervous. Nevertheless she insists on referring to her brother's remains as 'mijn broer', my brother, not 'Het Materiaal'. The insistence on his humanity is part of her resistance to the official approach. Crénom is drawn not without sympathy, as a bumbling official who has to toe the line. Only when he feels under pressure does he describe Nouria's brother as an enemy of the state and also a traitor to his own community. He also spells it out that her brother is practically now no more than a dossier, that there really is not a shred of his body that is whole. But Nouria insists. She is familiar with the view of body bags after a terrorist incident and persists that his remains must be somewhere, perhaps in a bag in a fridge.

There is a moment of metatheatre when Nouria speculates that her brother may be lying above ground somewhere, rotting and as prey to crows and worms. This immediately brings to mind Sophocles' opening scene where Antigone tells Ismene about the fate of the brothers, especially ll. 26–30 (But Polyneices . . . Polyneices' poor dead corpse . . . They say that Creon has had it broadcast publicly that no one is to bury him or mourn him. No! But they're to leave him there unwept, unburied, so much carrion for birds to glut on' (trans. Stuttard). Crénom's reaction, that this is no theatre, reinforces the link.

As Nouria becomes more emotional, the officer becomes more brutal. His initial restraint in referring to the young man is replaced by strong condemnation of him as an enemy of a tolerant society, a young man who embraced terror and random violence. Nouria's appeal that he was her beloved brother and that the officer should try to imagine losing his brother or sister is met with indignation and sarcasm – does Nouria perhaps want a state funeral for her brother? Nouria is sent away with the vague promise that if any news should become available she will be summoned.

More information about Nouria's family background is given. Her father has become blind and disappeared, thus assimilating him to Oedipus. Her brother used to be a keen football player, goalkeeper, but an accident in which he injured his head led to him abandoning the sport and eventually leaving for a foreign country, from where he sent a 'selfie' against a background of desert sand and black flags. These are the familiar marks of terrorist organizations. On his return to Belgium he was changed. This sketches the story familiar in contemporary media of young men of Muslim families who have grown up in European countries, but leave for terrorist training in camps in the Middle East. In this way the story of Nouria and her brother becomes the story of many other families in modern multi-cultural Europe. Nouria is not executed. That is not the way the modern state deals with family loyalty, but she is left bereft. The modern Creon, the state, is also left unpunished for its treatment of the family. This suggests the intractability of the problem of dealing with the clash between the two cultures. Both end up by losing.

This stripped down version of Sophocles nevertheless succeeds in deploying the conflict at the heart of the Greek tragedy to express one of the most pressing problems in the world today. It takes its place in the line of countless other transformations of *Antigone* to draw attention to contemporary issues.

Notes

1 Steiner (1984); Mee and Foley (2011); Willmer and Zukauskaite (2010). Cairns (2016) has an important chapter on 'Reception', 115–54. In all these works there are references to much more research on *Antigone* and its reception.
2 Miola (2014).
3 Miola (2014) 230.
4 Garnier (1997).
5 Bierl (2016) 263.
6 Hall and Macintosh (2005) 317.
7 Monférier (1968).
8 Fugard, Kani and Ntshona (1993).
9 Fugard (2002) 145–6.
10 See van Zyl Smit (2006).
11 Benson (1997); she wrote that Fugard had asked her to send him copies of the 'Penguin version of *Antigone*'. This was probably the volume, *Sophocles. The Theban Plays* with translations by E.F. Watling, first published in 1947.
12 Walder (1993), 'Introduction', xxviii.
13 Mandela (1994) 441–2.
14 For details about the way in which Fugard and the two actors created the play, see Vandenbroucke (1986) 171–8.
15 'Hodoshe' was the nickname of a notorious prison warder on Robben Island. It is a Xhosa word meaning 'green carrion fly'.
16 Discussed in *NRC Handelsblad* on 26 May 2016.
17 For Anouilh's Antigone it is not important that it may not be the body of Polynice she tried to bury. It is the gesture of defying Créon's unjust decree and honouring her brother that is important.

Sophocles' *Antigone*

Translated by David Stuttard

Dramatis Personae

In order of appearance

Antigone	daughter of Oedipus and Jocasta, sister of Eteocles and Polyneices, Theban princess
Ismene	sister of Antigone
Chorus	Theban elders
Creon	brother of Jocasta, general, recently elevated to Thebes' (autocratic) ruler
Guard	a member of the Theban army
Haemon	son of Creon and Eurydice
Teiresias	blind Theban prophet
Messenger	a member of Creon's entourage
Eurydice	wife of Creon

Various unnamed Attendants *of Creon*

Antigone was written for performance at the Theatre of Dionysus in Athens probably around the year 440 BC.

The action takes place outside the royal palace of Thebes on the morning after the battle between the Theban army led by Eteocles and an attacking army from Argos led by his brother, Polyneices.

No stage directions are given in the original text. All those contained in the translation are extrapolated from the context. Certain conventions are presupposed: the *skene* (stage building) represents the palace, with entrances and exits being made through its central door. There are two *eisodoi* (passageways) on either side of the *skene*. In *Antigone* one represents the road to the city, along which the Chorus enters, the other the road to the countryside, the location of Polyneices' unburied body, Teiresias' lair, and Antigone's rocky tomb. In the first production the *ekkuklema*, a low trolley wheeled into view from within the *skene*, was probably used to reveal a tableau showing Eurydice's corpse inside the palace.

Within the translation that follows, choral passages or passages that use verse forms other than iambic trimeter are usually identified by both a change of layout and the use of lowercase lettering, including for proper names. Line numbers correspond to those of the Greek text.

The half light before sunrise. Enter Antigone. *She is agitated, clearly waiting anxiously for someone. Enter* Ismene.

Antigone Ismene! Sister! Blood of my own blood! Has Zeus – wait! Tell me! Can you think of any punishment that Zeus is not inflicting on us two, the last survivors, for the sins of Oedipus? Pain, torment, shame, dishonour – we've experienced them all. And now? Now?

Have you heard of this new edict that they're saying the General's just broadcast to the city and the people? Do you know anything about it? . . .

Don't you know that sanctions more appropriate for enemies are being imposed on our own family?

Ismene Antigone, I've had no word about our family, no news good or bad, not since we lost our brothers. Not since they killed each other. Yesterday. I know the Argive army vanished in the night. But, since then? Nothing. I don't know if the situation's worsened or improved.

Antigone That's what I thought. That's why I asked you to come here, outside, where we can talk in private.

Ismene Why? What's happened? Something's obviously unnerved you. What?

Antigone Creon . . . He . . . His orders are that only one of our two brothers should be buried, while the other lies dishonoured. I've heard that he's already buried Eteocles with all due rites and ceremony, and so he now lies honoured with the dead beneath the earth. But Polyneices . . . Polyneices' poor dead corpse . . . They say that Creon's had it broadcast publicly that no one is to bury him or mourn him. No! But they're to leave him there unwept, unburied, so much carrion for birds to glut on. This is the edict that the 'good and noble' Creon has announced – for *you and me*, yes, yes, for *me*. And now – they say – he's coming here to make a speech, to issue his directives unambiguously to anyone who's not yet heard. He's seeing it as a matter of the utmost seriousness. And the penalty for disobedience? Execution in the city square by public stoning. So there you have it all. And in a moment you'll show me what you're made of – if you're worthy of your noble birth or if you're just the runt of a great family.

Ismene But what . . .? If that's the situation, what can *I* do disentangle it? More likely we'll just tie ourselves in knots!

Antigone Just tell me: are you with me? Will you do what must be done With me?

Ismene What? It's too dangerous! What do you mean?

Antigone Will you join with me and . . . lift his body?

Ismene You mean to bury him? But it's been publicly forbidden!

Antigone He's my *brother* – and yours, too – and with you or without you I *will* bury him. *I* shan't be seen to have betrayed him.

Ismene Don't be so headstrong! Creon's forbidden it!

Antigone Creon has no right to keep me from my family.

Ismene Antigone! Remember how our father died, hated, disgraced, when he found out what he'd done, when he gouged out his eyes with his own hands! Think, second, how his wife and mother – wife *and* mother, the same woman – knotted her own noose and hanged herself. And now think, third, of how in one day by some cruel twist of fate each of our brothers killed the other! At their own hands! Then think of us, and how we're all alone now, how *we'll* die in even greater torment, if we break this law, if we flout the edict, if we defy the power of these powerful men. We're women! Remember? Women. And we can't fight men. And the authorities are so much stronger than we are. All we can do is submit – in this and any other matter, even if it's worse than this. I have no choice, and so I ask the dead's forgiveness. I'll obey the government. There's no sense trying to do what is impossible.

Antigone Then I shan't ask you. Even if you wanted to, I wouldn't want your help. No. Do as you like. I'll bury him. For such a noble cause I'll die a noble death. I'll lie with him, a loving sister with her loving brother – a law-breaker perhaps, but one with principles. I must appease the dead for so much longer than the living. Death is for ever. But if you want to disrespect all that the gods hold dear, well . . . It's your decision.

Ismene I *do* respect them. But to go against the power of the state . . . I can't!

Antigone There's your defence, then. But I'm going to go and bury my dear brother.

Ismene I'm scared for you!

Antigone Don't worry about me. Stay safe!

Ismene At least don't tell anyone your plans! Keep them secret, and I will, too.

Antigone Oh, no – go, broadcast them! I'll hate you all the more if you stay silent, if you don't proclaim the news to everyone!

Ismene You're so hot-headed! What you're doing chills me to the bone.

Antigone I know I'm pleasing those I need to please the most.

Ismene If only you could! You've set your heart on the impossible.

Antigone I'll only stop when I have no strength left.

Ismene But there's no point even starting the impossible.

Antigone Don't say that. I'll only hate you. And you'll quite rightly earn the hatred of our dead brother, too. No! Leave me to my 'foolishness'. Leave me to do what I must do. I'd rather suffer anything than die in dishonour.

Ismene Go, if that's what you want. But know that even though I think you're wrong, I love you. And your family loves you too.

Exeunt Antigone *and* Ismene *in different directions. As the sun rises, enter* Chorus.

Chorus sunrise

bright shafts
of
sunrise

more beautiful
than any
which before
bathed
seven-gated thebes

gold daybreak
you blazed
rising high
above the dirke's streams
and watched
the men of argos
white shields

armour
bridles
glittering
as they ran
routed
home

yes
it was
polyneices
and his
bitter
family quarrelling
that brought them
here
to swoop down
screaming
shrilly

like an eagle
hovering

its snow white wings
outspread

his army
bristling
with weapons
horse hair
nodding
on their
helmet crests

he hovered there
above our houses
hunger
in his spears
such hunger
to devour
our city
of the seven gates

but then
he wheeled
and
he was gone
before
he
drenched
his beak
in our spilt
blood
before
the pitch fire flame
engulfed
our city
crowned
with towers

and
the bawl
of battle
boiled
behind him
thebes' dragon brood
too bold to be
subdued

zeus
hates
the boasts
of loud-mouthed men
and
when he saw them
pouring down
a raging torrent
gloating
in their clattering gold
zeus
struck one
with a ball of fire
because the man
was climbing up

the walls of thebes
all ready
to raise high
the shout
of victory

for a moment
the man
swayed
off-balance
then
he crashed
to earth
torch still
in hand
though
only just now
drunk
with the delirium
of battle
he had been
breathing fire
and storm wind
hot
against us

this was *his* fate

to others
other destinies
each given
by the war god
ares
god
who whips
his chariot team
to victory

their seven
generals
matched equal

one
for each gate
of thebes
one
against
each general
of thebes
left as his offering
his weapons
gifts of bronze
to zeus
who turns
our enemies
to flight

all but those
two
cursed
brothers

both levelled spears
which both
sank home
and so
shared birth
became
shared death

but now
since
famous victory
has smiled on thebes
and her war chariots
now
since
the war
is over
now
we should forget it all
and
visit

all the temples of the gods
with
singing
dancing
all night long
and
as he pounds
the theban soil
in his ecstatic dance
may
dionysus lead us

but

wait

here's creon
our king now

son of menoeceus

newly appointed

now that the gods
have sent
good fortune

he must have some new
policy
he wishes to
rush through

why else convene this meeting of the elders
now
at such
short notice
why else send such an urgent message
to us
all

Enter Creon.

Creon Gentlemen! It's been a stormy voyage, but the gods have set Thebes on an even keel again.

So. My reason for summoning you personally, for choosing you and no one else, is that I recognize your loyalty. You were always loyal to Laius' regime, and then to Oedipus, when he ruled Thebes, and when he died you remained loyal to his sons. Well. Now that they're both dead ... now that they've killed each other ... now that they've both died on the same day, fratricides, each ritually polluted as they *killed* ... as they *were* killed ... now I am king. Now I have ... total power. I was their closest relative. And they are dead.

One cannot be entirely certain of the character, the intellect, the judgement of any man until one's seen him tried and tested as a ruler, a law-giver. So, then. My principles? I think, and I have always thought that the worst leader's one who fails to follow the best policies through fear of being outspoken. And I've no time for anyone who puts his family or friends before his country. No! Let Zeus who sees all things be witness! If I had information that the security of our citizens was under threat, I'd not conceal it. I'd never have a friend who was my country's enemy. Because, I know that our security depends upon our country, and only when our country's on an even keel can we make firm alliances and friendships. This is the manifesto by which I mean to lead this city to prosperity.

So. Now. And closely related to all of which: I've had this edict broadcast to the citizens. About the sons of Oedipus. Eteocles – who fell fighting for his city, the bravest, most distinguished fighter in our army – Eteocles will be laid to rest with every honour given to the glorious dead below. But his brother – I refer to Polyneices, who returned from exile meaning to destroy the country of his fathers and his family's gods, to burn Thebes to the ground, to sate himself on the blood of his own family, to enslave any of his family who survived – I've had it broadcast to the city that no one is to bury him or mourn him. He is to lie unburied for the birds and dogs to feed on, a mutilated corpse for all to see.

This is my resolution. I shall always honour good men over criminals. And whoever serves his city well – in death as well as life I will respect him.

Chorus Creon, if this *is* how you wish to treat Thebes' enemy and Thebes' protector ... You have the power to decree whatever law you wish for the living and the dead alike.

Creon Then make sure my orders are obeyed.

Chorus Entrust this to a younger man!

Creon Don't worry! There are men in place already, guarding the corpse.

Chorus So what do you need us to do?

Creon I 'need you' to show no support for anyone who'd break my law.

Chorus No one's so foolish as to *want* to die.

Creon And death *is* the penalty – though it's not unknown for bribery and expectations of financial gain to trump even the fear of death.

Enter Guard.

Guard Sir! I shan't say I've come here hot foot . . . out of breath . . . at the double . . . on my toes! No. I kept on thinking, and I kept on stopping, and I kept on turning round in circles on the road and turning back. See, I kept hearing this voice in my head: 'Don't be silly! Don't go! You know he'll only make you pay for it!' 'What are stopping for, poor devil? Don't you think that you'll have hell to pay if Creon gets to know from someone else?'

I kept going over it. I dawdled on, reluctantly – at snail's pace – and so a short road turned into a long one! But in the end, well . . . here I am. And even if I've nothing concrete to report, I'll tell you anyway. You see, I've come here clinging on to one last hope – that nothing'll happen to me that's not already fated.

Creon What's the matter with you?

Guard First I want to tell you about *me*. Myself. I didn't do it. And I didn't see who did. And it wouldn't be fair for me to suffer for it.

Creon You're preparing your ground well. You're doing a good job covering yourself. You clearly have some curious news to report.

Guard It's daunting, sir. Yes! That's why I hesitate to speak, sir.

Creon Just tell me, won't you? Then you can go.

Guard I *am* telling you! The corpse. Someone buried it just now and went away. Someone sprinkled dust over the flesh. Someone performed the rites owed to the dead.

Creon What?! Who? What man has had the nerve to do this?

Guard I don't know. There was no mark of a pick, no sign of a shovel. The earth was rock-hard . . . bone dry . . . no tracks at all, no sign of wheels. Whoever did it left no evidence. When the men on first watch showed it us, we were all dumfounded, terrified. The corpse was covered, not like a proper burial, but with the thinnest film of dust – like it was someone trying to avert a curse. And no sign of a wild beast or a dog: nothing had clawed at him. That much was clear.

We started trading insults, guard accusing guard. It would have ended up in fisticuffs. There was no one there to stop us. Each man of us – we all accused each other; but no one to take the rap. We all spoke up in our defence. No one knew anything. We were prepared to hold hot metal in our hands, to walk through fire, to swear any oath you like before the gods that we'd not done it, and we'd had nothing to do with the planning of it or its execution.

And in the end, when we'd exhausted every avenue, someone spoke up and made us all hang our heads in fear. We couldn't contradict him. But equally, there was no way we go along with him and come out rosy. He said that . . . we should tell you what had happened. We shouldn't try to hide it. And everyone agreed. And me, I drew the short straw. Just my luck. I don't want to be here any more than you do. I know that. No one likes to break bad news.

Chorus Sir, I've been wondering for some time . . . Sir, I've been thinking: might this be the gods' work . . . sir?

Creon Enough! Stop! Now! Before you anger me, before your words show that you're not just old but senile! What you're suggesting . . . It's insupportable! That the gods should be concerned with this *corpse*?! Why would they bury *him*? Because they honour him? Because what he did was pious? He came here to burn their temples, immolate their statues, turn their country into ashes, scatter Thebes' laws to the four winds! Or perhaps you think gods *honour* criminals? Not possible.

No, from the start there have been men in Thebes who've taken issue with my edict, who've been shaking their heads and grumbling when they think that I can't see them, who've not knuckled under as by rights they should – as I expect them to. And they're the men who bribed these guards. I'm certain of it.

Money's the source of all corruption. Money turns cities into rubble, makes men refugees; it can indoctrinate, subvert, lead good men into crime; money sets them on a path to wickedness; money shows them how to sin. But they'll be punished. Sooner or later these mercenaries *will* be punished.

(*to* Guard) Well. Now. As surely as I worship Zeus – know this. I tell you on my oath, if you don't find whoever buried him, if you don't bring him here to me before my eyes, you won't enjoy an easy death! No, you'll be crucified, strung up alive to show your crimes to the whole world, so that in future you'll know the price you'll pay for swindling, and you'll be choosy where you get your money from! Chasing immoral profits sees more men ruined than set free!

Guard Can I say something, or should I just go?

Creon Don't you know how much it pains me to hear you?

Guard Is it in your ears, the pain – or in your heart?

Creon What's this? A diagnosis?!

Guard The guilty party pains your emotions. I just pain your ears.

Creon (*groaning in frustration*) What a windbag!

Guard Maybe. But I never did the burying.

Creon I think you did! And that you sold out your own 'heart' for money!

Guard (*sighs*) It's daunting when a man jumps to a conclusion – and it's wrong.

Creon Quibbling about conclusions now? Well, if you don't bring me the culprits, you'll reach your own conclusion – that the price of cowardice and insubordination is the severest punishment.

Exit Creon.

Guard I hope we find him! That'd be the best thing. But if he's caught or not – it's down to luck! Still, you won't see me back here again. I've got off now – I didn't hope to or expect to – so thanks be to the gods.

Exit Guard.

Chorus there is
much that is
miraculous and daunting
but
nothing
is more

daunting
or
miraculous
than man

man
has the power
to cross
the grey-wracked sea
when
southern storm winds
winter-laden
lash him
tacking
through the battering waves
surf
towering
thundering
above him

and
earth
most ancient of all gods
immortal
earth
unsleeping
earth
man wears
earth
down
ploughing the soil
turning the soil
trudging
year in
year out
behind his mule team

a flock
of careless birds
a pack
of wild beasts

or
a shoal
of fishes
in the ocean's deep
man
snares them all
man catches them
in his close-woven net
man
cleverest
most nimble
most adroit

with wit
and wiliness
man
subjugates
wild creatures
on the mountainside
tames
shaggy ponies
breaks them
to the yoke
tames
tireless
mountain bulls

speech

rapid
thought

how best
to keep
his city
safe

man
taught himself
all this

how
to build shelter
to escape
the frosts
that pour
from
icy
clear
night skies
the rains
torrential
drenching
rains

man
who invents all things

and so man
strides
into the
future

nothing
gives him pause

but though
he's found
a cure
for
the most puzzling
diseases

there's still
one thing
that he can't find
a cure
for

death

man's

ingenuity
man's
creativity
man's
innovation
goes beyond
the bounds
of hope

but it brings with it
the power
for bad
as well as
good

the man
who respects
the laws
of his country
and
the oaths
of his gods
deserves
the highest honour
in the city

there is no place
in any city
though
for anyone
who
arrogantly
recklessly
commits his life
to wickedness

a man like that's
not welcome in my house

and
i could never

sympathize
with him

Enter Guard *with* Antigone.

Chorus But here's a sign from the gods! There's no denying it! That girl . . . It's Antigone, poor Oedipus' child! (*sympathetically*) Oh, no! Antigone! What's happened now? Have you done something silly? Have they arrested you for disobeying Creon?

Guard This is the one that did it! We caught her burying him. Where's Creon?

Chorus He's coming now – just when he's needed!

Enter Creon.

Creon Why? What's happened? Why do you need me?

Guard Sir! Nothing's impossible! A bit of reflection, and you can change your mind. I could have sworn I'd not come back here in a hurry, not after all your threats! At the time I found them chilling! But now . . . When your dreams come true, it's the best thing in the world! So here I am! Though I'd sworn I'd not come back. And here she is! This girl. We caught her burying him. No need for drawing straws this time – no! What a godsend! Mine by rights and no one else's. So, take her, sir. Do what you want with her. Put her on trial, if that's what you want. But me – the only right thing is for you to clear me of all blame and let me go.

Creon Where was she? What was she doing when you arrested her?

Guard She was burying him. End of story.

Creon Do you understand the consequences . . .? Do you really *mean* what you're saying?

Guard I saw her burying the corpse which you'd forbidden to be buried. Can I be more clear than that?

Creon How did you see her? Did you actually *see* her burying him?

Guard It was like this. When we got there, we were all frightened by your threats, so we brushed off all the earth that was covering the corpse, and we made sure there was nothing on the body. It was clammy. And then we went and sat up on the rise, backs to the wind, making sure we sat where the smell wouldn't reach us, wide awake, bad-mouthing whoever happened to be nearest, threatening him, if it looked like he was slacking.

And time passed, till the sun hung huge and glaring in the middle of the sky, and scorching heat baked down. Then – suddenly – a whirlwind. Soil sucked from the earth. A dust-cloud, torment in the skies. It engulfed the plain. It stripped the trees of leaves. And all the air was choked with it. We kept our mouths tight shut – our eyes, too – and so we rode it out, this . . . plague from the gods.

At last – at long last – the storm passed, and we saw the girl. She was moaning – shrieking – like a bird shrieks when it finds its nest robbed and its chicks all gone. She was like that, sobbing, wailing, when she saw the body bare, uncovered – cursing the men who'd done it. Straight way she scooped dry earth and scattered it. Then she took up a bronze jar and poured the three libations due the dead. And so she honoured him.

Immediately we saw it, we rushed down and seized her – but she seemed . . . unconcerned. We charged her for her previous offence and this one, too, and she just stood there and made no denial. And that made me glad . . . but at the same time not glad at all. It's the best thing in the world to escape trouble. But to cause trouble to somebody you know, well . . . that's not so good. Still. What comes first is saving my own skin.

Creon (*to* Antigone) You! Hanging your head, eh? Do you admit it or deny it?

Antigone I admit it. I don't deny it.

Creon (*to* Guard). You. You can go now. Anywhere you want. You're cleared of any charge.

Exit Guard.

Creon (*to* Antigone) But you! Tell me. Briefly and to the point. Did you know that an edict had been broadcast, banning this burial?

Antigone Of course I knew! How could I not know? Everybody knew!

Creon But even so you presumed to break the law?

Antigone Yes! Certainly! It wasn't Zeus' law. Zeus didn't broadcast it! No! And *Justice* didn't lay down laws like this for mankind either – Justice who shares *her* kingdom with the gods beneath the earth. To my mind, 'edicts' that a mortal man like you imposes have no authority to supersede the gods' unwritten and established laws. No! They're eternal – not just for today or yesterday – and no one knows when they were first laid down. Me, I had no intention of failing in my obligations to the gods, just because I was afraid of some *man*'s whim! I knew I'd die. How not? We all must die some day – with or without your intervention. In fact, I count it as a benefit to die before my time. When you live like me, surrounded on all sides by suffering, how can death *not* be a benefit? For me, to face death is inconsequential. But if I'd left my brother's corpse to lie exposed, unburied, *that* would have troubled me so deeply. But all this? No! This doesn't trouble me at all! And if you think that what I did was stupid, well . . . Perhaps it's the one who thinks it's stupid that's stupid himself.

Chorus Her father was headstrong. The girl is headstrong, too. She's not learned how to knuckle under.

Creon Yes, but the strongest willed can be the easiest to break. The strongest iron, forged hardest in the fire, can shatter soonest. You see it all the time – the most spirited of horses, mastered by the thinnest bit. I *know*. Slaves can't afford fine principles when their master's close at hand.

This girl . . . Her first crime was to disobey my law; her second was to boast about it – laugh . . . at what she'd done. Now, I'd be the woman and she the man if she got away with this . . . if I *let* her get away with it. No. I don't care that she's my sister's child. I don't care that she's my closest family. She and her sister will not escape . . . the ultimate penalty. Oh, yes! I consider Ismene equally responsible in the conspiracy . . . to bury him.

(*to* Attendants) Bring her here, too! I saw her just now. Inside. Behaving like she was deranged. As if she'd lost her senses. This tends to happen – that when someone's plotting some clandestine act of treachery, their behaviour gives them away before they see it through. But a criminal who's caught red-handed, and then tries to make out he's a martyr . . . I find that quite intolerable.

Antigone And is it tolerable simply to kill me? Or do you want more?

Creon No. Killing you's enough.

Antigone Then what are you waiting for? Nothing you say can convince me. Nothing you ever *could* say will. And nothing I say can convince you either. But . . . What could I have done to win myself a better reputation than bury my own brother? Everyone here would agree with me, if they weren't so frightened. Being a tyrant has so many benefits, not least the power to say and do exactly what you want.

Creon *No one* in Thebes agrees with you.

Antigone Of course they do! They're just not speaking up because of *you*!

Creon Are you not ashamed to hold such views?

Antigone There's no shame in being loyal to my brothers!

Creon And Eteocles, the man that Polyneices killed – was he not your brother, too?

Antigone Yes he was! My full blood brother!

Creon So how can you humiliate Eteocles by honouring Polyneices?

Antigone Eteocles will not agree with you.

Creon He will if you give him equal honour as his enemy!

Antigone It wasn't some slave who died! It was a brother!

Creon Attacking his city. Eteocles defended it.

Antigone Death demands these rituals.

Creon And a good man demands not to share equal honour with a criminal!

Antigone Who knows what is considered sacred in the Underworld?

Creon An enemy can never be a friend, not even when he's dead.

Antigone I don't want to hate either of them! I want to love them both!

Creon In that case, you can love them in the Underworld. As long as I'm alive, I'll have no woman tell me what to do.

Enter Ismene.

Chorus look

by the gates

ismene

weeping

tears
for her
poor sister

brow
  clouded
cheeks
  flushed

  weeping

yet
  so beautiful

Creon (*to* Ismene) You, too! Coiling like a snake around my house! Going behind my back to try to undermine me! I didn't know that I was bringing up two demons, who would try to topple me from power! Come on then! Tell me! Are you going to admit you had a hand in burying him – or will you swear on oath that you knew nothing?

Ismene I did it. Yes! If she agrees! I share responsibility. I'll share the punishment.

Antigone No! Where's the justice in that? No! You didn't want any part of it! I did it on my own!

Ismene But the situation's changed! I'm not ashamed to stand beside you. I'm not ashamed to face whatever sentence he hands down.

Antigone Death and the dead know who's responsible. And this support of yours means nothing! It's all empty words.

Ismene But you're my *sister*! Don't push me away! Don't say I can't die with you! Don't say that I can't give the dead the honour that I owe them!

Antigone Don't share my death. Don't take responsibility for something that you didn't do. One death – *my* death's enough.

Ismene And what kind of life's ahead of me with you gone?

Antigone Ask Creon. He's the one you care about.

Ismene Why are you doing this? It won't do any good!

Antigone You think I'm mocking you? Well, maybe I am. But it breaks my heart.

Ismene Is there nothing I can do?

Antigone Yes. Save yourself. I won't be angry if *you* walk free.

Ismene Can't I share your fate?

Antigone You've chosen life. I've chosen death.

Ismene I warned you . . .

Antigone Some people would agree with your way of thinking – just as others would agree with mine.

Ismene But I agree with *you*! We're both equally accountable.

Antigone Don't worry. You're going to live. But me? I chose long ago to die, so I could *help* the dead.

Creon These girls! One's just shown herself to be irrational; the other's been irrational from birth.

Ismene Suffering causes even the most rational to lose their minds. They can't think straight.

Creon You lost *your* mind when you chose to practise crime with criminals.

Ismene What sort of life's ahead of me, alone, without her?

Creon Don't speak of her. She's dead already.

Ismene How can you kill her? She's engaged to marry your own son!

Creon There are other furrows he can plough.

Ismene But not such understanding as there is between them.

Creon I can't stand thinking of my sons with bad women.

Ismene Poor Haemon! Your father does you such discredit.

Creon You and your wedding have given me enough trouble already.

Ismene Are you really going to do that to your son?

Creon Not me. No. Death. Death will put an end to this marriage.

Ismene So that's your decision? She must die?

Creon That's the decision that I've made – on my behalf and yours. So. No more time-wasting. Take her inside. From now on they must behave like women and not be left unsupervised. Even the brave try to escape when they come face to face with death.

Chorus a life
without the taste of suffering

is
a blessèd life
indeed

yes

once a house is
thrown off balance
by the gods
it can't escape
from
ruin
coiling
from one generation
to
the next

it's just like when
the racing sea
the swollen sea
is lashed
headlong
by storm winds
as they batter south
from thrace
and it surges on
across
the black abyss
below

it sucks
and rolls
the black sand
from the ocean floor

and cliffs
gale-lashed
wave-battered
boom
and bellow back
the bawl of thunder

look
how the ancient sorrows
    of the house of labdacus
crash down
    on the sorrows
    of the dead

and generation
    can't stop
regeneration

no
but some god's
    coiling in
    new sorrows
and
    there's no escape

the last light
    dawning
on the last branch
    of the house of oedipus
is suffocated
by the blood-stained sand
    an offering
    to the gods of death
by thoughtless words
by minds
    possessed
    by madness

zeus
zeus
men may transgress
but they can never
thwart
your power

sleep
can entrap all things
but even sleep

cannot
bring down
your power

   no
nor the tireless cycle
   of the months
that gods
   command

   but
zeus
king
   nothing
neither age
nor time
   can wither you

you
   live for ever
   in the shining
   marble halls
   high on olympus

for times
   past
and times
   future
this ancient law
holds firm

for mankind
excess
   brings
disaster

hope
   wanders
   the wide earth
and while
to some

hope is
a blessing
to others
it is empty
a deceit
a worthless promise
of a worthless lust
fulfilled

too late
they realize
its emptiness

too late

already
they've been burnt
and blistered
in the fire

yes
the saying's
well-known
and
wise

that
the bad course
appears good
to those god
wishes to destroy

and only for the shortest time
they manage to escape
disaster

But here's Haemon – your last-surviving son, your youngest son. What is *he* feeling? Heartbreak for his bride Antigone? Heartbreak for a marriage that he'll never know?

Enter Haemon.

Creon We'll find out soon enough. No point trying to predict.

My son! You've heard about the vote condemning Antigone – your bride-to-be – to death? Are you angry with your father? Or are we still friends, whatever I do?

Haemon Father. I am *with* you. You're a wise man, and you've brought me up to follow your wise rules. You are my guide. I follow where you lead. If you forbid this marriage, who am I to disagree?

Creon Well said! Oh, my son, my son! That's how a man *should* think. Always obeying his father's wishes! This is why men *pray* for obedient sons: to repay their enemies, injury for injury, and to pay equal honour to their friends and family as their father does. If a man has uncooperative children, he only has himself to blame. And how his enemies gloat then!

My son! There's no point losing your mind over a women, whatever pleasures might be on offer. If you must know, it's a frigid enough embrace when you've got the wrong woman for your wife. And there's nothing more destructive than having someone in your house you don't get on with. Much better to get rid of her, decide she's bad news. Better to let the girl go find a husband from among the dead.

You see, I caught her disobeying me – flagrantly – a girl, the only person in all Thebes who disobeyed me, and I'm not about to let Thebes see me going against my word, oh no. I'll kill her. So she can pray to Zeus, the god of families, all she likes. Because . . . If I turned a blind eye when my own relatives broke my laws, I'd have to do the same for everyone else! If a man behaves fairly at home, he'll present himself in public as a just man, too. But if he's arrogant, or if he breaks the law, or if he sets his face against those in authority . . . well, I could never commend such a man.

No. When the state appoints a man to rule it, he must be obeyed at all times – whether it's some small matter, or to do with justice, or . . . or quite the opposite. In my opinion a man like that would rule well, and indeed would wish to be well counselled, a bulwark in the heat of battle, a good and just protector to his people.

There's nothing worse than anarchy. It can destroy cities, topple houses, cause the strongest shield-line to disintegrate. Whereas for most right-thinking people good governance and firm obedience of the law offer sure salvation. So it's our duty to protect all those who lead decent law-abiding lives . . . and never to let ourselves be weaker than a woman. It's better, if we must give in, at least to give in to a man, but to let it be said that we're weaker than a woman? No!

Chorus Unless I'm senile, what you've said seems to me to make good sense.

Haemon Father, the gods give men good sense, the highest of all our faculties. I couldn't for a moment suggest that you were wrong. In fact, I'd never dream of it. But maybe . . . it's just possible that there's another point of view.

I'm always watching out for you – to see what men are saying, what they're doing, where they're pointing blame. Because – the common citizens are frightened of you, especially if their opinions are not the sort you'd like to hear. But I *have* heard them, as they whisper in the shadows, and I've heard the city mourning for . . . this girl. More than any woman in the world, they're saying, she does not deserve to die in such a squalid way for doing something that should earn the highest praise. When her own brother fell in battle, she didn't let him lie unburied or be torn apart – and eaten – by the dogs and birds. Doesn't she deserve the highest honour? And this . . . disaffection's spreading silently all through the city.

Father, there's nothing more important for me than that you do well, that you enjoy good fortune. What greater benefit is there for his sons than the good reputation that their father wins through his success – or, indeed, what greater benefit for their father than his sons' good name?

Don't close your mind. Don't think that there's just one correct opinion – your own and no one else's. If someone thinks that only *his* opinions, that only what *he* says or feels is right, that no one else is – come the moment of truth and his inadequacies are exposed. But a clever man is not ashamed to keep on learning – or to change his mind. You see how, when the storm-winds come, a tree that bends and gives can keep its branches, but a tree that tries to stand inflexible, unbending, is torn up by its roots. Or a sailor, who keeps the canvas taut and never slackens off the ropes – he scuppers his boat, the rowing benches smack into the sea, and that's his voyage finished.

So now, then – stop being so angry. Allow yourself to change your mind. If a young man like me can express an opinion, I'd say it would be wonderful to know everything there is to know – but, if you can't, and this is often the reality, it's still good to learn from those who offer good advice.

Chorus Sir, if you agree, and if this is the time to say it, you should learn from one another. You've both spoken well.

Creon So you want men of our age and experience to learn lessons from a boy like him?

Haemon Only if they're good lessons. I know I'm young, but judge me on my merits, not my age!

Creon And it's a merit to champion an anarchist?

Haemon I'd never suggest championing anyone who did something wrong.

Creon And that diagnosis doesn't apply to her?

Haemon No one in the whole of Thebes thinks so.

Creon So Thebes wants to tell me what to do now, does it?

Haemon Who's speaking like child now?

Creon So, when it comes to governing, I ought to follow someone else's judgement, not my own?

Haemon A city doesn't belong to just one man!

Creon Everybody knows that a city belongs to its most powerful citizen!

Haemon You'd do a great job ruling on your own – in an empty land where no one goes!

Creon He's clearly taken the woman's side.

Haemon If you're the woman, yes! It's *you* I care about!

Creon You? You're beneath contempt! Questioning your father's authority?

Haemon Yes, because you're using that authority unjustly!

Creon So I'm doing wrong, am I, by having some regard for my own leadership?

Haemon But you're completely *dis*regarding it, when you show so much contempt towards the gods!

Creon You're a deviant! A degenerate! That's what you are! Letting a woman get the better of you.

Haemon Maybe. But I know what's right.

Creon Your argument is all on her behalf.

Haemon Hers, yes – and yours and mine. And the gods' beneath the earth.

Creon You'll never marry her. She won't live long enough.

Haemon Well, she won't die alone!

Creon You'd threaten me? You'd dare to threaten me?

Haemon Where's the threat in speaking out against such fatuous arguments as yours?

Creon It's your sophistry that's fatuous and you'll regret it.

Haemon If you weren't my father, I'd say you were half-witted.

Creon Don't blab at me, you woman's slave!

Haemon You want to talk and talk, and not to listen!

Creon Oh yes? Well, by all that's holy, listen to me now. This criticism and abuse won't do you any good. (*to* Attendants) Bring that loathsome girl out here, to die here, now, before his eyes, in front of him, her bridegroom!

Haemon No! No, not here! And not in front of me! Don't even think of it! I'm going. You won't see me again. No! I'll leave you to the company of those who can endure your madness.

Exit Haemon.

Chorus He's gone, sir. He was angry. He's run off. A young man can be most resentful when he's riled.

Creon Let him do what he wants. Let him think his superhuman thoughts, and go. But there's nothing he can do to save those girls.

Chorus So you intend to execute them both?

Creon No, not the one who's not involved. You're right.

Chorus And the means of execution? Have you decided that?

Creon I'll take her on a road where no one goes, an empty road, and I'll wall her up, alive, in a cave in the cliffs – with just enough food to be acceptable, so that the city can't be held responsible, can't be ritually polluted. And there she can pray to the one god that she worships – Death – to let her live, or realize at last what a grave responsibility it is to serve the dead.

Chorus love
          unconquered
                    on the battle-field

love
who ransacks
all we own

who watches
through the night time hours
a young girl's
soft
warm
cheeks
and

soars
across the ocean
to the homesteads
in the wilderness

no god can escape from you
or any man
whose life lasts for a day

but anyone whom you possess
loses his mind

you hold the reins
taut
force
good men
to do
bad things

you've whipped up
bloodfeud now
between
these men

the sparkling eyes
the gaze of longing
of a girl
in joy
and wonder

on her wedding night
conquers all things
enthroned in power
in the company
of the great laws

the goddess
aphrodite
dances on
and none
can fight her

Enter Antigone, *dressed as a bride.*

Chorus One look at her, and I would disobey his laws. I can't hold back my tears now that I see Antigone on her last journey – to her marriage bed of death.

Antigone look
on me
look

this was my fathers' country
you are my country's citizens

look
as i
go
on my last journey

look
as i
look
on my last sunlight

i shall never look on it again

but hades
where we all must lie
for all eternity in death
is drawing me

down
alive
to the shores
of the river acheron

no marriage songs
for me
no hymn sung
for my veiling
no
i'll be
the bride
of acheron
and death

Chorus but it's with
fame and
honour
that you leave us
on your journey
to the dead
untouched by wasting sickness
not falling to the sword
but
willingly
alive
alone of mortals
you go down
to hades

Antigone i've heard men talk
of niobe
a phrygian
the child of tantalus
a friend of thebes
and how
she died
in sorrow
on the mountain crags
at sipylus
and how
like clinging ivy

she was rooted fast
as the waves of petrifying rock
crept over her

i've heard men talk
of how the biting rains
and blizzards
lash her
eating at the rock
dissolving
in her tears
that brim beneath
her welling eyes
and soak her neck

death in the rocks
for niobe
death in the rocks
for me
some god is lulling me to sleep
just like her

Chorus but she was a god
and born of gods

we're mortals
mortal-born

and yet how wonderful
it is
for a woman
like you
for a woman
dead
like you
to be spoken of
as sharing in a fate
that's equal to a god's
not only when
she lived
but when

she died

Antigone you're mocking me

why

why are you mocking me
why by my father's gods
why are you mocking me
while i'm still alive

can you not wait
until i'm dead

thebes
and thebes' citizens
so wealthy and
so prosperous
waters of the river dirke
sacred groves of thebes
so rich in chariots
you are my witnesses

look on me
now
look
how I go
unmourned by friends
and family
the victim
of such laws
down to
my rock-cut cell
a strange tomb
for a stranger burial

not dead
but not alive
i have no home
and no belonging
not with the living

or the dead

Chorus you dared
to go
too far
child
and
you crashed against
the hard wall
of justice

you're paying
the blood-price
for some ancestral crime

Antigone you've found me out

my bitterest obsessions

grief for my father
a grief that never fades
grief for the heavy fate
that crushes
all my family

a father
sleeping with his mother
a mother
sleeping with her son
a union
whose result was me

and now
curs'd and
unmarried
i am going
back home
to them

and my brother too
you made a luckless marriage

and now you're reaching out
beyond the grave
to kill me too

Chorus honouring him
was honourable

but the powerful
won't let
power
be challenged

you were angry
and you knew
exactly
what you did
and that
was your undoing

Antigone no tears
no family
no marriage now

just sorrow

and the road
is ready

fate
won't let me see
the sacred circle
of the blazing sun
again

no friend
no family
to mourn me
as i go now
to my death

Creon You know, if a condemned man could prolong life by wailing and singing dirges, you'd never hear the end of them. (*to* Attendants) Take her away. At once! Wall her up in her rock-cut tomb as I commanded you, and leave her there alone, abandoned. We'll see what happens then: whether she dies or lives on, laid to rest in her new home. You see, as far as the girl's concerned, we're absolved of any guilt. But one thing's for certain: her life on earth is over.

Antigone My tomb. My marriage bed! My rock-cut home. My home for ever, reunited with my family – more of my family dead now than alive. And I'm the last. The greatest criminal! And now I'm going to join them before my life's been lived. But I have such hopes! My father hugging me so tenderly. My mother loving me. And you, too, Eteocles, blood-brother. When you died, I held you in my arms. I laid you out. I poured offerings at your grave. And Polyneices, too. Just now I honoured you as best I could. And now I face my punishment.

But I was right to honour you. Any fair-minded person would agree. Because – even if I'd been a mother and it was my *children*, or if it had been my *husband* who'd been killed, whose corpse was lying out there decaying, even then I'd *never* have done what I did. I'd never have gone against the power of the state. And why not? What law would I be following? I could marry again if my husband died. I could have a child by someone else. But my mother and father are both dead, and I can't get another *brother*! Ever. So that's the law – the law of nature. That's why I chose to honour you. And Creon thought it was a crime, an outrage, something terrible. My brother! My blood-brother!

And now he's tied my wrists. And now taking me away.

No wedding night for me. No bridal songs. No husband, no, no children growing up. Instead, abandoned now, no friends, no family, condemned, alive, I'm going to my tomb.

Which of the gods' laws have I broken? Or should someone as ill-used as me look to the gods at all? Will no one come to my defence? I did the moral thing, but they're calling me immoral! Well, if that's what the gods think, too, I'll soon find out the error of my ways. But if the crime is Creon's, I hope the punishment he suffers will be no less than the one that he's imposed on me – unjustly.

Chorus she's still
distressed
disturbed

Creon maybe

but her guards

will have cause for
lamentation
too
if there's any more
delay

Antigone that was
my death sentence

Creon i can't give you
any cause
for hope

there's no
reprieve

Antigone my country
thebes

city
of my fathers

gods
who gave us birth

they are taking me
away

i've no more time
to live

you
are the leading men in thebes
look on me now
the last of the royal family
suffering
at the hands of such as him
because
i held the sacred
in respect

The Attendants *lead* Antigone *away. The following Chorus is addressed as if to her.*

Chorus like danaë
the lovely
danaë

they forced her too
to leave the sunlight
for a bronze-walled cell

they shackled her
concealed her
in her marriage-tomb

although she too
was noble born

and pregnant
with the golden-flowing
seed of zeus

the force
of fate
is both
miraculous
and daunting

nothing can escape it
not wealth
not war
not strong defences
or black ships that cut across the sea
nothing escapes fate

take lycurgus
son of dryas
king of the edoni
quick to anger

dionysus
shackled him

for all his mockery
and walled him
in a rocky cell
and so his madness
so miraculous
and daunting
melted
and the bloom of his blasphemy
dissolved

in his madness
he'd abused
the god
with mocking words
but now
he recognized
the god's
divinity

he'd tried
to stop
the women
god-possessed
to quench
their fire
and so provoked
the anger
of the muses
who take pleasure
in the flute

and by the waves
that lap
the black rocks
by the bosphorus
between two seas
in thracian salmydessus
ares
the thracian
war god
watched

blood flow
watched
needles
rain down blows
watched
hands
that dripped blood
pummel eyes
gouge eyes
that burned for vengeance
as phineas' wife
hard
cruel
barbarous
blinded her step-sons
cleopatra's children
in an act
of cruel savagery

so they grew weak
in darkness
mourning their black fate
the sons
of cleopatra
and her catastrophic marriage

she was descended
from erechtheus
the king of athens
an ancient family
but still she was
walled up
in a cave
so far away
fed only
by the storm winds
that her father
boreas
the north wind
rules
swift as a horse

that gallops
on the hillside

she was the daughter
of the gods
but even so
the fates
which live for ever
showed her
no mercy

Enter Teiresias, *led by a young* Boy.

Teiresias Rulers of Thebes! We've come, two people on one road, one pair of eyes for both. Blind men must always find a guide to help them on their path.

Creon Teiresias! Your honour! What news?

Teiresias I'll tell you. And you must listen to my prophecy.

Creon I've never ignored your advice before.

Teiresias As a result of which you governed well.

Creon Proof of the benefits of listening to you.

Teiresias So listen now. You're standing on the razor's edge of fate.

Creon What? What are you saying? I hear you. You . . . you're making my flesh crawl.

Teiresias Hear what my skills have shown me, and you'll learn.

I was sitting in my usual place – in my observatory, where I keep watch on the birds, where every bird of every kind flocks down and congregates. And I heard a cry I did not recognize, a horrid screeching, angry and cacophonous. I could tell that they were tearing at each other, ripping at each others' flesh with talons dripping blood. The beating of their wings and what it meant was clear.

I was terrified. Immediately I lit a fire and tried to make burnt sacrifice. But the offering would not catch light in the god's fire. Instead, from the embers, a sticky discharge oozed, dripping from the thigh-flesh folded round with fat, smouldering and spitting. The gall sack burst, exploded, shooting bile high in the air, and the liquefying thighs were left bare as the fat contracted.

The sacrifice was meant to show the future, but it all came to nothing. The boy here told me everything. He guides me just as I am guide to others.

The city's sick. And all because of your decision. The public altars and the private hearths are all polluted by the dogs and birds with bits of meat torn off the poor dead Polyneices' body. So the gods are not accepting any of our sacrifices. Or our prayers. Or our burnt offerings. And there's no bird call to bring good omen, since every bird has drunk deep of the dead man's blood.

Consider this, my child. All men can make mistakes. But when a wise man, favoured by the gods, makes a mistake, he rectifies the situation by not stubbornly maintaining the same course – indeed, be stubborn and you might well be accused of being incompetent.

No. Accept that the man's dead. Don't niggle at his corpse. There's no glory to be gained in destroying someone who's already dead.

I'm thinking of your good. I'm speaking for your good. The best thing is to learn from someone who gives good advice, especially if what he says is to your own advantage.

Creon You feeble old man! You've used up every weapon in your arsenal – even tried prophetic hocus-pocus to get the better of me! (*to* Chorus) He and his flock of priests have always tried to bribe and bargain with me! (*to* Teiresias) Well, you can go and play the eastern markets, trade in gold and silver to your heart's content – but you'll never bury him, not even if Zeus' eagles were to rip his flesh and carry pieces up to Zeus' throne, not even to remove my own fears of being ritually polluted! I will not allow his burial! You see, I *know* that nothing that a *man* can do can pollute the gods. But even the most respected men can fall into disgrace, when they make disgraceful arguments seem good advice, and all for profit.

Teiresias Does anybody really know . . . Does anybody really realize . . .

Creon What? What cliché are you going to give us now?

Teiresias . . . that good judgement is greatest gift of all?

Creon And bad judgement does most harm.

Teiresias And yet you're riddled with bad judgement.

Creon I'm not prepared to bandy insults with a prophet.

Teiresias But you just have. You accused me of delivering false prophecies.

Creon Yes! Because every single prophet in the world loves money!

Teiresias Just as every tyranny loves to profit from its power, no matter how unethically.

Creon Have you forgotten that you're speaking to your king?

Teiresias I've not forgotten. It was thanks to me you saved this city.

Creon You're a clever prophet, but you've no respect for justice.

Teiresias You're provoking me to tell you everything I know, even what should never be revealed.

Creon Tell me! Just don't expect to profit from it!

Teiresias As far as you're concerned, there's no profit to be had.

Creon As long as you know that my mind's made up and you can't buy me off.

Teiresias Then know this! And believe it. A few short days, a few brief circuits of the sun, and you'll exchange one of your own family, one born of your own blood, a dead man given as a payment for the dead. You're burying someone alive; with no qualms you've entombed a living soul. And at the same time you're preventing a dead body from being buried, even though it's claimed by the gods beneath the earth, giving it no rites of burial, giving it no gifts of burial, giving it no sacrament whatever.

You have no jurisdiction over such concerns – nor do the gods of life. No! You have committed a gross sacrilege. So the forces of revenge, the agents of destruction who await their time, the vengeful Furies sent by Hades and the gods, are lying in wait for *you*, to make you suffer the same pain that you've dealt out to others.

So think on that, and tell me now that I've been bribed. The time is near when your house will echo to the sound of lamentation not just for men but women, too. And every hostile city seethes with hatred for you, every one whose mutilated citizens you've left unburied for the dogs or beasts or for the birds to flap their wings and carry back the stench of their pollution to their cities and their altars.

You provoked me. You angered me. My arsenal is empty and my weapons are all lodged deep in your heart. And there is no escaping from their pain.

(*to the* Boy) Boy, take us home. Leave him to vent his wrath on younger men, and learn to keep his tongue in check, and show more sense than he shows now.

Exeunt Teiresias *and* Boy.

Chorus He's gone, sir! His prophecies were terrifying. In all my years I've never known him give any prophecy to Thebes, which did not come true.

Creon I know. I know that, too. My mind is racing. To give in is daunting. But to resist, to risk destruction for the sake of pride . . . that's daunting, too!

Chorus Creon – son of Menoeceus – you must allow yourself to take advice.

Creon What should I do? Tell me. I'll listen.

Chorus Go, free the girl from her prison in the rocks. And consign the body to the grave.

Creon That's your advice? You think I should give in?

Chorus Yes, sir. As quickly as you can. The gods are quick to punish bad judgement.

Creon (*groans*) It's so difficult! To give up everything you stand for! But I'll do it. No point in fighting the inevitable.

Chorus Then do it now! Go! Don't leave it to others!

Creon I'll go now. Just as I am. (*to* Attendants) Go! Go! Go, all of you! Go now! Take spades and crowbars. There – look! We can see the place from here! I've changed my mind! *I* walled her up so *I* must set her free! I fear it's true, that the best and safest course must be to follow the established laws until the day we die.

Exeunt Creon *and his* Attendants.

Chorus you
    god
    of many names
you
    dionysus
    shining son
    of semele
you
    son of zeus
    deep thunderer
you
    who watch over

famous italy
you
who protect
the sheltered plain
where men
from every city
come in pilgrimage
to demeter's
eleusis
you
bacchus
you
whose home
is here
in thebes
the mother-city
of your bacchae
here
beside the gentle waters
of ismenus
on the plain
where once
the savage dragon's
teeth
were sown

high
above the twin-peaked rocks
we've seen you
wreathed in smoky
torch-fire
at
delphi
where corycian nymphs
dance
to your rhythm
and at
castalia's stream

you come
in your procession

from the slopes
that cling with ivy
from the high massif
of nysa
and otherworldly chants
proclaim
your name
as you come
here
to the streets
of thebes

you honour
thebes
above all other
cities

and you honour
semele
your mother
killed by the lightning blast

so now since thebes
is overwhelmed
held in the grip
of plague
come to us
dionysus
come with your
cleansing step
over
the ridges
of parnassus
over
the sighing sea

you lead
the dances of the stars
whose breath is firelight

you watch

the whispered voices
of the night

come now
great son of zeus
come
lord

and crowds of thyades
attend you
dancing all night
intoxicated
lord
by you
iacchus
you
gift-giver

Enter Messenger.

Messenger Thebans! Gentlemen! Nothing lasts for ever – no part of human life – nothing that allows for unchanging praise or blame. Chance is always raising up the lucky, and destroying the unfortunate. And no prophet can predict how our lives will end.

We all envied Creon once – I did – because he'd rescued Thebes from enemy attack, because he achieved the sole command, because he set us on a stable course, because he prospered, because he had good sons . . . But now all that is over.

When a man has known great happiness and loses it, his life is over. He's a dead man walking. So, accumulate as much wealth as you can – if that's what drives you – live like a king, but if you lack true happiness . . . I don't think any of it's worth a wisp of smoke compared to happiness.

Chorus You've bad news for the royal family. What is it?

Messenger They're dead. And the living are guilty of their death.

Chorus Who's dead? Who's killed them? Tell me!

Messenger Haemon's dead. And no one else responsible . . .

Chorus What?! Did his father kill him? Did he kill himself?

Messenger He killed himself. He was angry at his father because he'd killed . . .

Chorus Teiresias was right. He saw it all.

Messenger What's done is done. And now you must consider how to deal with it.

Enter Eurydice.

Chorus Look! Here's Creon's wife, Eurydice. Poor woman! Coming outside. Can it just be a coincidence? Or has she heard about her son?

Eurydice Gentlemen! All of you! I heard the news as I was on my way to make sacrifice to Athene. To pray. I happened to be drawing back the bolts, unlocking the doors, when the news reached me. Of my family's tragedy. I fainted! I was terrified. I fell into my servants' arms. What *is* the news? Tell me again. I'm used to suffering. I need to hear it.

Messenger I'll tell you, madam. I was there. And I'll not pass over anything that happened. What's the point of trying to soften the blow now, when you'll find out the truth later anyway? Truth's always the best way.

I accompanied your husband as his guide. Well, we went right to the farthest limit of the plain, where the corpse was lying – Polyneices, cruelly torn apart by dogs. And we prayed to Hekatè, goddess of the dead who haunts the crossroads, and to Pluto, king over all the dead, that they might turn aside their anger and look on us with kindness. Then we washed the corpse in sacred oils. And we gathered twigs and cut down branches and we collected what was left of Polyneices and we cremated him. And then we built a huge grave mound with the earth of his own homeland, and when we'd done that we went on – to the cave . . . the marriage chamber . . . for the girl who'd married death.

When we were still some way away, one of us heard a noise, a human voice raised loud, the sound of lamentation echoing from that marriage chamber, where no marriage rites were paid. And he came and told our master – Creon.

And as Creon came nearer, slowly, hesitating, the sound, still indistinct, met us again. A haunting groan. And Creon cried aloud and wept and said: 'I think I know! I think that *I*'m a prophet! I think this is the most cursed road I've ever travelled! That's my *son*'s voice! Go, men! Quickly! Nearer! Squeeze through the gap! The stones that blocked the cave-mouth have been torn away! Squeeze through the narrow passage-way! See if it *was* Haemon's voice I heard, or if the gods have tricked me!'

We hurried to obey our master's orders – he was desperate! And there we saw her – in the farthest recess of the tomb – hanging by the neck, held in a noose, a thread of softest silk. We saw *him* there, too, on his knees beside her – Haemon – hugging her, his arms around her waist, weeping for his bride, and for her death, for all he did, and weeping for his own unhappy love.

Creon saw him too, and cried aloud in pain, and ran to him and shouted, wailing, moaning: 'What have you done? What were you thinking of? What madness made you do this? Come on out outside! My son! I'm begging you on my knees! Please! Come outside!'

The boy stared at his father with wild, blazing eyes. He didn't say a word – but spat in Creon's face and drew his knife. His father dodged and ran, and Haemon missed. And then . . . poor boy . . . furious with *himself* . . . he didn't hesitate . . . he strained his muscles hard and drove the knife to half its length into his own ribcage. And then, before his senses failed, he hugged her to him in a last embrace. He fought for breath. He gasped. He coughed a stream of blood which trickled black down her white cheek.

They're in each other's arms, both dead. The poor boy's married now in death – proof for all the world to see that a lack of judgement is the greatest cause of suffering for men.

Exit Eurydice *into the palace.*

Chorus What's happening? Our lady's gone! No word from her to tell how she's reacting.

Messenger I wonder, too. I hope it's only that she doesn't want to make a public show of grief. She's just heard of her son's death, and she'll want to lead the mourning for her family with her household staff inside. She has good breeding. She won't do anything amiss.

Chorus I don't know. To me a silence like that – so intense – is just as ominous as any histrionic show of grief.

Messenger I'll go inside. I'll see what's happening – if she was keeping her emotions hidden. Yes. You're right. Silences like that . . . they're too intense.

Exit Messenger *into the palace. Enter* Creon *carrying* Haemon *in his arms, along with his* Attendants.

Chorus and now
our king
himself
is coming

carrying
the body
in his arms

if it's not blasphemous
to say it
i think that it was
creon's fault
he died

haemon's death
came
from no one
else

Creon oh
my stupidity
stubborn
stupidity
and now
it ends
in death

look at us now
blood of one
blood
killer
and
killed

and all my
resolution
empty

my son
you've gone now
in the flower
of your youth

you've left me

and all
through my own
stupidity

Chorus you've found out
too late
the true meaning
of justice

Creon yes
i've learnt
through suffering

a god
came down
and
crushed me
shook me
shoved me
on the path
to cruelty
upsetting
toppling
trampling
my happiness

human suffering
is so
hard
to bear

Messenger Master, I think you're suffering enough already, but there's more to come: first Haemon, then the rest – inside . . . You'll see it all too soon.

Creon What more can there be?

Messenger Our lady's dead. Now son and mother both. She killed herself just now.

Creon hades
harbour
of the dead
insatiable
why
are you
doing this
why
are you
destroying me
(*to* Messenger)
you
with your news
of pain
and sorrow
what are you
saying to me

tell me
boy
tell me

another
death

more
killing

my wife
dead
too

Messenger look

here's
her body

brought out
for all to see

Creon more
tragedy

what life's
left
now

just now
i held
my son
dead
in my arms
and now
look
now
another corpse
another death

poor
poor
unhappy
mother

and
poor
son

Messenger at the altar
with a sharpened blade
she stabbed herself

and as
her eyes dimmed
to the darkness
she called aloud
in her despair
remembering
megareus
her elder son
who died
a hero's death
in battle

and
remembering too
haemon

and
last
of all
she prayed
for you
that you
might suffer
endless
grief
because
you killed
her sons

Creon fear
makes me
shudder

will no one
bring a knife
and
kill me too

i have
such regrets
i'm drowning
in such deep regrets

Messenger look at her
now

she died
blaming you
for haemon's death
and hers

Creon how
did she die
how

did she kill herself

Messenger she
stabbed herself

when she
learned of
haemon's death
the pain
she
plunged a knife
into her heart

Creon there's no one else
to blame
just me

i killed you
that's the truth
i've no life left now

(*to* Attendants)

take me
away
as quickly
as you can

Chorus good
counsel
if any good
can come
from suffering

best
to act
fast
in times
of trouble

Creon may it come
fast

may it dawn
soon

that best
of fates
that brightest
sunrise
of the day
that brings
my death

yes

may it
come
and may i
never
see
tomorrow

Chorus all this
is for the future

first
we must deal
with what's
at hand

the future's
for
the future
for
the gods

Creon that's
my prayer
too

that's all
i want
now

Chorus no more
prayers
now

we mortals
can't escape
the suffering
fate brings us

Creon take me away
an empty
foolish man

i didn't mean
to kill you
haemon
or you
eurydice
my wife

i don't know
where
to look

there's no one
left
to comfort me

whatever i touch
turns
to dust

the crushing weight
of destiny
has overwhelmed
me

Chorus good judgement
is the
greatest element
in happiness

and in our dealing
with the gods
there's no room
for impiety

man's proud words
  earn
proud punishments
  from gods

and in old age
  they teach us
  to judge
  soundly

Bibliography and Further Reading

Adams, S.M., 'The *Antigone* of Sophocles,' *Phoenix* 9, 1955, 47–62; repr. in *Sophocles the Playwright*, Toronto, 1957.

Agard, W.R., '*Antigone* 904–920', *Classical Philology* 32, 263–265, 1937.

Allen, D.M., 'Why Don't Child Sex Abuse Victims Tell?', *Psychology Today*, October, 2012 <https://www.psychologytoday.com/blog/matter-personality/201210/why-dont-child-sex-abuse-victims-tell>. Accessed 14 December 2016.

Anouilh, J., *Antigone*, (J. Monférier, ed.), Paris, 1968.

Arrowsmith, W., 'Turbulence in the Humanities', *Wayne State University Graduate Review* 8.3, Spring 1965, 119–27 [reprinted in *Arion*, Third Series, 2.2/3, 1992–1993, 194–208].

Bayfield, M.A., *The Antigone of Sophocles* (2nd edn), London, 1935.

Beer, J., *Sophocles and the Tragedy of Athenian Democracy*, Westport, CT, 2004.

Benardete, S., 'A Reading of Sophocles' *Antigone*', *Interpretation: A Journal of Political Philosophy*, 1975–1976, 4:148–196; 5:1–55; 5:148–184 [reprinted as *Sacred Transgressions: A Reading of Sophocles' Antigone*, South Bend, IN, 1999].

Benardete, S., *Sacred Transgressions. A Reading of Sophocles' Antigone*, South Bend, IN, 1999.

Bennett, L. and Tyrrell, W.B., 'What is Antigone Wearing?', *The Classical World* 85.2, 1991, 107–109.

Benson, M., *Athol Fugard and Barney Simon: Bare Stage, a Few Props, Great Theatre*, Randburg, 1997.

Bierl, A., 'Germany, Austria and Switzerland', in B. van Zyl Smit (ed.) *Handbook to the Reception of Greek Drama*, Malden/Oxford, 2016, 257–282.

Bierl, A.F.H., *Dionysos und die griechische Tragödie*, Tübingen, 1991.

Blondell, R., *Sophocles: Antigone*, Indianapolis, 1998.

Blundell, M. (trans.), *Sophocles' Antigone*, Newburyport, 1998.

Blundell, M.W., *Helping Friends and Harming Enemies: A Study in Sophocles and Greek Ethics*, Cambridge, 1989.

Blundell, S., *Women in Ancient Greece*, Cambridge, MA, 1995.

Bonnie, H., *Antigone, Interrupted*, Cambridge, 2013.

Bowra, C.M., *Sophoclean Tragedy*, Oxford, 1952.

Brecht, B., *Antigone: A Version by Bertolt Brecht* (trans. Judith Malina), New York, 1984.

Bremer, J.M., 'Greek Maenadism Reconsidered', *Zeitschrift für Papyrologie und Epigraphik* 55, 1984, 267–286.

Brown A., 'Foreign Bodies: Sophocles *Antigone* 1080–1083', *Mnemosyne* 68, 2015.

Brown, A., *Sophocles: Antigone*, Warminster, 1987.
Burian, P., 'City Farewell!: *Genos, Polis* and Gender in Aeschylus' *Seven against Thebes* and Euripides' *Phoenician Women*', in D.E. McCoskey and E. Zakin (eds.) *Bound by the City: Greek Tragedy, Sexual Difference and the Formation of the Polis*, New York, 2009, 15–46.
Burton, R.W.B., *The Chorus in Sophocles' Tragedies*, Oxford, 1980.
Cairns, D., *Sophocles: Antigone*, London, 2016.
Campbell, L. (ed.), *Sophocles: Volume 1: Oedipus Tyrannus, Oedipus Coloneus, Antigone* (1st edn), London, 1871.
Campbell, L. (ed.), *Sophocles: Volume 1: Oedipus Tyrannus, Oedipus Coloneus, Antigone* (2nd edn), London, 1879.
Cohen, D., 'Seclusion, Separation, and the Status of Women in Classical Athens', in I. McAuslan and P. Walcot (eds.) *Women in Antiquity*, Oxford, 1996, 134–145.
Cohen, D., *Law, Sexuality and Society: The Enforcement of Morals in Classical Athens*, Cambridge, 1991.
Coleman, R., 'The Role of the Chorus in Sophocles' *Antigone*', *Proceedings of the Cambridge Philological Society* n.s. 18, 1972, 4–27.
Collard, C. and Cropp, M. (eds. and trans.), *Euripides VII: Fragments: Aegeus-Meleager*, Boston, 2008.
Collard, C. and Cropp, M., *Euripides: Fragments*, Vols. I–II, Cambridge, MA, 2008.
Collard, C., Cropp, M. and Gibert, J., *Euripides: Selected Fragmentary Plays*, Vol. II, Oxford, 2004.
Collard, C., *Euripides: Hecuba*, Warminster, 1991.
Cook, A.B., *Zeus* [3 vols], Cambridge, 1914, 1925, 1940.
Cooper, I. and Cormier, B.M., 'Inter-generational Transmission of Incest', *Canadian Journal of Psychiatry* 27 (3), 231–235, 1982.
Courtois, C., *Healing the Incest Wound: Adult Survivors in Therapy*, New York, 2010.
Craik, E.M., *Euripides: Phoenician Women*, Warminster, 1988.
Cropp, M., 'Antigone's Final Speech (Sophocles, *Antigone* 891–928)', *Greece & Rome* 44, 1997, 137–160.
Cropp, M. and Fick, G., *Resolutions and Chronology in Euripides: The Fragmentary Tragedies*, London, 1985.
Dalfen, J., 'Gesetz ist nicht Gesetz und fromm ist nicht fromm: Die Sprache der Personen in der Sophokleischen *Antigone*', *Wiener Studien* 90, 1977, 5–20.
Davies, M., 'Who Speaks at Sophocles *Antigone* 572?', *Prometheus* 12, 1986, 19–24.
Dawe, R.D., 'The End of Seven against Thebes', *The Classical Quarterly* 17, 1967, 16–28.
Dawe, R.D., *Studies on the Text of Sophocles*, Vol. III, Leiden, 1978.
de La Rosa, P., *Antígona: Las Voces que incendian el desierto, Guadalupe De La Mora*, in *Cinco Dramaturgos Chihuahuenses*, Juárez, Mexico, [2004] 2005.
Des Bouvrie, S., *Women in Greek Tragedy: An Anthropological Approach*, Oslo, 1990.

Diggle, J., *Euripidis Fabulae*, Vols. I–III, Oxford, 1981–1994.
Ditmars, E. van N., *Sophocles' Antigone: Lyric Shape and Meaning*, Pisa, 1992.
D'Ooge, M. (ed.), *Sophocles: Antigone*, Boston, 1900.
Douglas, M., *Purity and Danger: An Analysis of Concepts of Pollution and Taboo*, London, 1978.
Easterling, P.E., 'Constructing the Heroic', in C. Pelling (ed.) *Greek Tragedy and the Historian*, Oxford, 1997.
Easterling, P.E., 'Women in Tragic Space', *Bulletin of the Institute of Classical Studies* 34, 1987.
Else, G., *The Madness of Antigone*, Heidelberg, 1976.
Erbse, H., 'Haimons Liebe zu Antigone', *Rheinisches Museum* 134, 1991, 253–261.
Erincin, S., 'Performing Rebellion: *Eurydice's Cry* in Turkey', in E.B. Mee and H.P. Foley (eds.) *Antigone on the Contemporary World Stage*, Oxford, 2011, 171–183.
Esposito, S., 'The Changing Roles of the Sophoclean Chorus', *Arion*, Third Series, 4.1, 1996, 85–114.
Fagles, R. (trans.) and Knox, B., *Sophocles: The Three Theban Plays*, New York, 1982.
Faupel, S., 'Etiology of Adult Sexual Offences', 2014, <https://www.smart.gov/SOMAPI/sec1/ch2_etiology.html.> Accessed 14 December 2016.
Finglass, P.J., *Sophocles: Ajax*, Cambridge, 2011.
Fisher, N.R.E., *Hybris: A Study in the Values of Honour and Shame in Ancient Greece*, Warminster, 1992.
Foley, H.P., 'Antigone as Moral Agent', in M.S. Silk (ed.) *Tragedy and the Tragic: Greek Theatre and Beyond*, Oxford, 1996.
Foley, H.P., 'Sacrificial Virgins: Antigone as Moral Agent', in *Female Acts in Greek Tragedy*, Princeton, NJ, 2001, 172–200.
Foley, H.P., 'Tragedy and Democratic Ideology: The Case of Sophocles' *Antigone*', in B. Goff (ed.) *History, Tragedy, Theory: Dialogues on Athenian Drama*, Austin, 1995.
Försterling, F., *Attribution: An Introduction to Theories, Research, and Applications*, Hove, 2001.
Fradinger, M., 'An Argentine Tradition,' in E.B. Mee and H.P. Foley (eds.) *Antigone on the Contemporary World Stage*, Oxford, 2011, 67–89.
Fradinger, M., 'Tragedy Shakes Hands With Testimony: Uruguay's Survivors Act in *Antígona Oriental*', *Proceedings of the Modern Language Association*, 129.4, 2014, 761–772.
Fugard, A., 'Antigone in Africa', in M. McDonald and J. M. Walton (eds.) *Amid our Troubles*, London, 2002, 128–147.
Fugard, A., Kani, J. and Ntshona, W., *The Island*, in D. Walder (ed.) *The Township Plays*, Cape Town, 1993, 193–227.
Gagarin, M., 'Telling Stories in Athenian Law,' *Transactions of the American Philological Association* 133, 2003, 197–207.
Gambaro, G., *Information for Foreigners: Three Plays by Griselda Gambaro* [trans. from the Spanish and ed. Marguerite Feitlowitz], Evanston, IL, 1992.

Gardiner, C., *The Sophoclean Chorus: A Study of Character and Function*, Iowa City, 1987.

Garland, R.S.J., *The Greek Way of Death* (2nd edn), London, 2001.

Garnier, R., *Antigone ou La Pieté* (ed. J-D. Beaudin), Paris, 1997.

Garvie, A.F., *Sophocles: Ajax*, Warminster, 1998.

Gelinas D., 'Persisting Negative Effects of Incest', *Psychiatry* 46(4), 312–332, 1983.

Gellie, G.H., *Sophocles: A Reading*, Carlton, Victoria, 1972.

Gibbons, R. and Segal, C. (trans.), *Sophocles: Antigone*, Oxford, 2003.

Gibert, J., *Change of Mind in Greek Tragedy*, *Hypomnemata* 108, Göttingen, 1995.

Goheen, R.F., *The Imagery of Sophocles' Antigone: A Study of Poetic Language and Structure*, Princeton, NJ, 1951.

Goldhill, S., 'Antigone and the Politics of Sisterhood', in V. Zajko and M. Leonard (eds.) *Laughing with Medusa: Classical Myth and Feminist Thought*, Oxford, 2006, 141–161.

Goldhill, S., 'Character and Action, Representation and Reading: Greek Tragedy and Its Critics', in C. Pelling (ed.) *Characterization and Individuality in Greek Literature*, Oxford, 1990, 100–127.

Goldhill, S., *Reading Greek Tragedy*, Cambridge, 1986.

Grene, D., *Antigone*, in D. Grene and R. Lattimore (eds.) *Greek Tragedies* (2nd edn), Vol. 2, Chicago and London, 1991.

Griffith, M., 'Antigone and her Sisters: Embodying Women in Greek Tragedy', in A. Lardinois and L. McClure (eds.) *Making Silence Speak: Women's Voices in Greek Literature and Society*, Princeton, NJ, 2001, 117–136.

Griffith, M. (ed. and comm.), *Sophocles Antigone*, Cambridge, 1999.

Günther, H.-C., Review of Lloyd-Jones/Wilson (1997), *Bryn Mawr Classical Review* 5.1, 1998.

Hall, E. and Macintosh, F., *Greek Tragedy and the British Theatre 1660–1914*, Oxford, 2005.

Hall, E., 'Antigone and the Internationalization of Theatre in Antiquity', in E.B. Mee and H.P Foley (eds.) *Antigone on the Contemporary World Stage*, Oxford, 2011, 51–66.

Hall, E., 'The Sociology of Athenian Tragedy', in P.E. Easterling (ed.) *The Cambridge Companion to Greek Tragedy*, Cambridge, 1997.

Hall, E., *Greek Tragedy: Suffering under the Sun*, Oxford, 2010.

Halleran, M., *Stagecraft in Euripides*, London, 1985.

Hame, K.J., 'Female Control of Funeral Rites in Greek Tragedy: Klytaimestra, Medea and Antigone', *Classical Antiquity* 103, 2008.

Hansen, M.H., *Polis: An Introduction to the Ancient Greek City-State*, Oxford, 2006.

Henrichs, A., 'Between City and Country: Cultic Dimensions of Dionysus in Athens and Attica', in M. Griffith and D.J. Mastronarde (eds.) *Cabinet of the Muses: Essays in Classical and Comparative Literature in Honor of T.G. Rosenmeyer*, Chico, CA, 1990, 257–277.

Hertmans, S., *Antigone in Molenbeek*, supplement to *De Standaard*, 3 June 2016.

Hester, D.A., 'Sophocles the Unphilosophical: A Study of *Antigone*', *Mnemosyne* 24, 1971, 11–59.

Hogan, J., *A Commentary on the Plays of Sophocles*, Carbondale and Edwardsville, IL, 1991.

Holt, P., 'Polis and Tragedy in the *Antigone*', *Mnemosyne* 52, 1999.

Jebb, R.C. (ed., comm. and trans.), *Sophocles, Antigone* (2nd edn), Cambridge, 1898 [reprinted 2004, Bristol Classical Press].

Jebb, R.C., *Sophocles: The Plays and Fragments, Part III. The Antigone* (3rd edn), Cambridge, 1900.

Johnson, P., 'Woman's Third Face: A Psycho/Social Reconsideration of Sophocles' *Antigone*', *Arethusa* 30.3, 1997, 369–398.

Jones, J., *On Aristotle and Greek Tragedy*, Oxford, 1961.

Jones, N.F., *Rural Athens Under the Democracy*, Philadelpia, 2004.

Jordan, B., 'Miracles in the *Antigone* of Sophokles' in his *Servants of the Gods: A Study of Religion, History and Literature of Fifth-Century Athens*, Göttingen, 1979, 85–102.

Jost, L., 'Antigone's Engagement: a Theme Delayed', *Liverpool Classical Monthly* 8.9, Nov., 1983, 134–136.

Jouan, F. and van Looy, H., *Euripide: Fragments*, Vols. I–IV, Paris, 1998–2003.

Kamerbeek, J.C., *The Plays of Sophocles, Commentaries, III, The Antigone*, Leiden, 1978.

Kannicht, R., 'Antigone Bacchans: Eine Problemanzeige zur *Antigone* des Euripides', in *Kotinos: Festschrift für E. Simon*, Mayence, 1992, 252–255.

Kannicht, R., *Tragicorum Graecorum Fragmenta*, Vol. V 1–2: *Euripides*, Göttingen, 2004.

Karamanou, I., 'Euripides' "Family Reunion" Plays and their Socio-political Resonances', in A. Markantonatos and B. Zimmermann (eds.) *Crisis on Stage: Tragedy and Comedy in Late Fifth-Century Athens*, Berlin and New York, 2012, 239–250.

Kirkwood, G.M., *A Study of Sophoclean Drama: With a New Preface and Enlarged Bibliographical Note*, Ithaca, 1994.

Kirkwood, G.M., Review of Lloyd-Jones and Wilson (1990a) and (1990b), *Bryn Mawr Classical Review* 2.1, 1991, 22–31.

Kitto, H.D.F., *Form and Meaning in Drama*, London, 1956.

Kitto, H.D.F., *Greek Tragedy: A Literary Study*, New York, 1954.

Kitzinger, R., *The Choruses of Sophokles' Antigone and Philoktetes: A Dance of Words*, Leiden and Boston, 2008.

Kluft, R., 'Ramifications of Incest', *Psychiatric Times*, January 2011 <http://www.psychiatrictimes.com/sexual-offenses/ramifications-incest.> Accessed 6 December 2016.

Knox, B.M.W., Review of Müller (1967), *Gnomon*, 40, 1968, 747–60, repr. in *Word and Action: Essays on the Ancient Theater*, Baltimore and London, 1979, 165–182.

Knox, B.M.W., *The Heroic Temper: Studies in Sophoclean Tragedy*, Berkeley, CA, 1964.

Kovacs, D., *Euripides: Helen, Phoenician Women, Orestes*, Cambridge, MA, 2002.

Lamari, A.A., *Narrative, Intertext and Space in Euripides' Phoenissae*, Berlin and New York, 2010.

Lanzillotta, L.R., 'Hamartia', in H.M. Roisman, *The Encyclopedia of Greek Tragedy*, Vol. II, Chichester, UK, 2014.

Lattimore, R., *Story Patterns in Greek Tragedy*, London, 1964.

Lefebvre, H., *The Production of Space* (trans. D. Nicholson-Smith), Oxford, 1991.

Lefkowitz, M.R. , *Heroines and Hysterics*, London, 1981.

Lesky, A., *Greek Tragic Poetry* (trans. M. Dillon), New Haven and London, 1983.

Lesky, A., *Greek Tragedy* (trans. H.A. Frankfort, with Foreword by E.G. Turner) (3rd edn), London and New York, 1979.

Liapis, V., 'Creon the Labdacid: Political Confrontation and the Doomed *Oikos* in Sophocles' *Antigone*, in D. Cairns (ed.) *Tragedy and Archaic Greek Thought*, Swansea, 2013.

Lloyd-Jones, H., Review of von Fritz, *Antike und Moderne Tragödie* (Berlin, 1962), *Gnomon* 34, 1962, 737–747.

Lloyd-Jones, H. *Sophocles*, Vol. II. Cambridge, MA, 1998.

Lloyd-Jones, H. and Wilson, N., *Sophocles: Second Thoughts*, Göttingen, 1997.

Lloyd-Jones, H. and Wilson, N., *Sophoclis Fabulae*, Oxford, 1990a.

Lloyd-Jones, H. and Wilson, N., *Sophoclea: Studies on the Text of Sophocles*, Oxford, 1990b.

Luppe, W., 'Das neue Euripides-Fragment: P.Oxy. 3317', *Zeitschrift für Papyrologie und Epigraphik* 42, 1981, 27–30.

MacDowell, D.M., '*Hybris* in Athens', *Greece & Rome* 23, 1976, 14–31.

MacLeod, L., *Dolos and Dike in Sophokles'* Elektra, Mnemosyne Supplementum 219, Leiden, 2001.

Malle, B., *How the Mind Explains Behavior: Folk Explanations, Meaning, and Social Interaction*, Cambridge, MA, 2004.

Mandela, N.R., *Long Walk to Freedom*, Randburg, 1994.

Mastronarde, D., *Contact and Discontinuity: Some Conventions of Speech and Action on the Greek Tragic Stage*, Berkeley, CA, 1979.

Mastronarde, D.J., *Euripides: Phoenissae*, Cambridge, 1994.

Mastronarde, D.J., *The Art of Euripides: Dramatic Technique and Social Context*, Cambridge, 2010.

Mee, E.B. and Foley H.P. (eds), *Antigone on the Contemporary World Stage*, Oxford, 2011.

Meiggs, R., *Trees and Timber in the Ancient Mediterranean World*, Oxford, 1982.

Minadeo, R.W., 'Characterization and Theme in the *Antigone*', *Arethusa* 18.2, 1985, 133–154.

Miola, Robert S., 'Early Modern Antigones: Receptions, Refractions, Replays', *Classical Receptions Journal* 6.2, 2014, 221–244.

Monférier, J., 'Introduction to *Jean Anouilh*', *Antigone*, Paris, 1968.

Morwood, A.C., *The Syntax of Sophocles*, Leiden, 1982.

Mueller-Goldingen, C., *Untersuchungen zu den Phönissen des Euripides*, Stuttgart, 1985.

Müller, G., *Sophokles. Antigone*, Heidelberg, 1967.

Murnaghan, S., '*Antigone* 904–920 and the Institution of Marriage', *American Journal of Philology* 1986, 192–207.

Musurillo, H., *The Light and the Darkness: Studies in the Dramatic Poetry of Sophocles*, Leiden, 1967.

Nagle, D.B., *The Household as the Foundation of Aristotle's Polis*, Cambridge, 2006.

Nethercut, W., 'Vertical Perspective in *Antigone* 781 ff.', *Classical Bulletin* 55, 1978, 61–63.

Neuburg, M., 'How Like A Woman: Antigone's "Inconsistency"', *The Classical Quarterly* 40, 1990, 54–76.

NRC Handelsblad http://www.nrc.nl/nieuws/2016/05/26 (accessed 20 February 2017).

Nussbaum, M., *The Fragility of Goodness: Luck and Ethics in Greek Tragedy and Philosophy* (Revised edn), Cambridge, 2001 [originally published 1986].

O'Brien, J.V., *Guide to Sophocles'* Antigone: *A Student Edition with Commentary, Grammatical Notes, & Vocabulary*, Carbondale, 1978.

Ober, J., *Mass and Elite in Democratic Athens: Rhetoric, Ideology and the Power of the People*, Princeton, NJ, 1989.

Ogden, D., 'Rape, Adultery and the Protection of Bloodlines in Classical Athens', in S. Deacy and K.F. Pierce (eds.) *Rape in Antiquity*, Swansea, 1997, 25–41.

Osofisan, *Tegonni: An African Antigone. Recent Outings*, Lagos, 1999.

Oudemans, T.C.W. and Lardinois, A.P.M.H., *Tragic Ambiguity: Anthropology, Philosophy and Sophocles' Antigone*, Leiden, 1987.

Papadopoulou, T., *Aeschylus: Suppliants*, London, 2011.

Papadopoulou, T., *Euripides: Phoenician Women*, London and New York, 2008.

Parker, R., *Polytheism and Society at Athens*, Oxford, 2005.

Parker, R.C.T., *Miasma: Pollution and Purification in Early Greek Religion*, Oxford, 1983.

Patterson, C.B., *The Family in Greek History*, Cambridge, MA, 1998.

Pearson, A.C., 'Sophocles' *Antigone*', *The Classical Quarterly* 22, 1928, 179–190.

Rehm, R., *Marriage to Death: The Conflation of Wedding and Funeral Ritual in Ancient Tragedy*, Princeton, NJ, 1994.

Rehm, R., *The Play of Space: Spatial Transformation in Greek Tragedy*, Princeton, NJ, 2002.

Reinhardt, K. *Sophocles* (trans. H. and D. Harvey), New York, 1979.

Robinson, M., 'Declaring and Rethinking Solidarity: *Antigone* in Cracow', in E.B. Mee and H.P. Foley (eds.), *Antigone on the Contemporary World Stage*, Oxford, 2011.

Rose, H.J., 'The Bride of Hades', *Classical Philology* 20, 1925, 238–242.

Roisman, H.M, *Sophocles. Electra. Translation with Notes, Introduction, Interpretative Essay and Afterlife.* Indianapolis, 2008.

Rothaus, R., 'The Single Burial of Polyneices', *Classical Journal* 85.3, 1990, 209–217.

Rudnytsky, P., *Freud and Oedipus*, New York, 1987.

Schlesier, R., 'Mixtures of Masks: Maenads as Tragic Models', in T.H. Carpenter and C.A. Faraone (eds.) *Masks of Dionysus*, Ithaca and London, 1993, 89–114.

Schneidewin, F.W., *Sophocles: Part V. The Antigone* (trans. H. Browne), London, 1853.

Scodel, R., 'P.Oxy. 3317: Euripides' *Antigone*', *Zeitschrift für Papyrologie und Epigraphik* 46, 1982, 37–42.

Scolnicov, H., *Women's Theatrical Space*, Cambridge, 1994.

Scott, W.C., *Musical Design in Sophoclean Theater*, Hanover, 1996.

Scully, V.J., *The Earth, The Temple, and the Gods: Greek Sacred Architecture*, New Haven, CT, 1962 [Trinity University Press issued a 2nd edn in 2013].

Seaford, R., 'Dionysus as Destroyer of the Household: Homer, Tragedy and the *Polis*', in T.H. Carpenter and C.H. Faraone (eds.) *Masks of Dionysus*, Ithaca and London, 1993, 115–146.

Seaford, R., 'The Imprisonment of Women in Greek Tragedy', *Journal of Hellenic Studies* 110, 1990a, 76–90.

Seaford, R., 'The Structural Problems of Marriage in Euripides', in A. Powell (ed.) *Euripides, Women and Sexuality*, London and New York, 1990b, 151–176.

Seaford, R., 'The Tragic Wedding', *Journal of Hellenic Studies* 107, 1987, 106–130.

Seale, D., *Vision and Stagecraft in Sophocles*, London, 1982.

Segal, C., *Tragedy and Civilization: An Interpretation of Sophocles*, Cambridge, MA, 1981.

Segal, C. and Gibbons, R. (trans.), *Sophocles' Antigone*, Oxford, 2003.

Shakespeare, W., *King Richard III* (ed. J. Lull), Cambridge, 1999.

Shapiro, I., *The Evolution of Rights in Liberal Theory*, Cambridge, 1986.

Siewert, P., 'The Ephebic Oath in Fifth Century Athens', *Journal of Hellenic Studies* 97, 1977, 102–111.

Smethurst, M.J., 'Are We All Creons and Ismenes?: *Antigone* in Japan', in E.B. Mee and H.P. Foley (eds.) *Antigone on the Contemporary World Stage*, Oxford, 2011, 221–234.

Sommerstein, A.H. (ed. and trans.), *Aeschylus*, Vol. I, Cambridge, MA, 2008.

Sommerstein, A.H., 'Soph. *Ant.* 572: Dearest Haimon', *Museum Criticum* 25–28, 1990–1993, 71–76; repr. in *The Tangled Ways of Zeus and other studies in and around Greek Tragedy*, Oxford, 2010, 202–208.

Sommerstein, A.H., *The Tangled Ways of Zeus*, Oxford, 2010 [first published 1993].

Sourvinou-Inwood, C., 'Assumptions and the Creation of Meaning: Reading Sophocles' Antigone', *Journal of Hellenic Studies* 109, 134–148, 1989.

Sourvinou-Inwood, C., 'Sophocles' Antigone as a "Bad Woman"', in F. Dieteren and E. Klock (eds.) *Writing Women into History*, Amsterdam, 1990.

Stamos, D.N., *The Myth of Universal Human Rights*, London, 2013.

Steiner, G., *Antigones*, New Haven, CT, [1984], 1996.

Stuttard, D.A., *A History of Ancient Greece in Fifty Lives*, London, 2014.

Stuttard, D.A., *Greek Mythology: A Traveler's Guide from Mount Olympus to Troy*, London, 2016.

Syropoulos, S., *Unlike a Woman: Gender and the Social Function of Athenian Tragedy*, [British Archaeological Reports International Series 1127], Oxford, 2003.

Talbott, W.J., *Rights Should Be Universal?* Oxford, 2005.

Taplin, O., *The Stagecraft of Aeschylus: The Dramatic Use of Exits and Entrances in Greek Tragedy*, Oxford, 1977.

Trapp, M., 'Tragedy and the Fragility of Moral Reasoning: Response to Foley', in M.S. Silk (ed.) *Tragedy and the Tragic: Greek Theatre and Beyond*, Oxford, 1996.

Treu, M., 'Never Too Late: *Antigone* in a German Second World War Cemetery in the Italian Apennines', in E.B. Mee and H.P. Foley (eds.) *Antigone on the Contemporary World Stage*, Oxford, 2011, 307–323.

Tsagalis, C.C., *The Oral Palimpsest: Exploring Intertextuality in the Homeric Epics*, Cambridge, MA, 2007.

Tyrrell, W.B. and Bennett, L.J., *Recapturing Sophocles' Antigone*, Lanham, MD, 1998.

Van Erp Taalman Kip, A.M., 'Truth in Tragedy: When Are We Entitled to Doubt a Character's Words?', *American Journal of Philology* 117, 1996.

van Zyl Smit, B., 'Antigone in South Africa', in J. Davidson, F. Muecke and P. Wilson (eds.) *Greek Drama III*, London, 2006, 281–298.

Vandenbroucke, R., *Truths the Hand Can Touch*, Craighall, 1986.

Vickers, B., *Towards Greek Tragedy: Drama, Myth, Society*, London, 1979.

von Fritz, K., 'Haimons Liebe zu Antigone', *Philologus* 89, 1934, 19–33 [reprinted in *Antike und Moderne Tragödie*, Berlin, 1962, 227–240].

Walder, D., 'Introduction', in D. Walder (ed.) *The Township Plays*, Cape Town, 1993.

Webster, T.B.L., *The Tragedies of Euripides*, London, 1967.

Weil, H., 'Observations sur les fragments d'Euripide à propos d'une nouvelle édition des fragments des Tragiques grecs', *Revue des Études Grecques* 2, 1889, 328–331.

West, M.L., *Iambi et Elegi Graeci ante Alexandrum cantati*, Vol. II (editio altera), Oxford, 1992.

Whiteley, R., 'Was Antigone Really A "Bad" Woman? Christiane Sourvinou-Inwood's Reading of Sophocles' *Antigone*'. Retrieved from http://www.moyak.com/papers/sophocles-antigone.html (accessed 29 December 2015), no date.

Willink, C.W., 'Critical Studies in the *Cantica* of Sophocles: I. *Antigone*', *The Classical Quarterly* 51, 2001, 65–89.

Willink, C.W., 'Sophocles, *Antigone* 23–5 and the Burial of Eteocles', *Mnemosyne* 60, 2007, 274–280.

Willmer, S. and Zukauskaite A., *Interrogating Antigone in Postmodern Philosophy and Criticism*, Oxford, 2010.

Winnington-Ingram, R.P., 'Sophocles and Women', in *Sophocle. Entretiens sur l' Antiquité Classique*, Vol. 29, Vandeouvre-Genève, 1982.

Winnington-Ingram, R.P., *Sophocles: An Interpretation*, Cambridge, 1980.

Young, S., 'The Use of Normalization as a Strategy in the Sexual Exploitation of Children by Adult Offenders', *Canadian Journal of Human Sexuality* 6.4, 1997, 285–295.

Zeitlin, F., 'Staging Dionysus between Thebes and Athens', in T.H. Carpenter and C.A. Faraone (eds.) *Masks of Dionysus*, Ithaca and London, 1993, 147–182.

Zeitlin, F.I., *Playing the Other: Gender and Society in Classical Greek Literature*, Chicago and London, 1996.

Zimmermann, C., *Der Antigone-Mythos in der antiken Literatur und Kunst*, Tübingen, 1993.

Index

Lightning Source UK Ltd.
Milton Keynes UK
UKHW012341100219
337089UK00005B/158/P

9 781350 112766